Asset Markets, Portfolio Choice and Macroeconomic Activity

A Keynesian Perspective

Toichiro Asada
Professor of Economics, Chuo University, Tokyo, Japan

Peter Flaschel
Professor Emeritus, Bielefeld University, Bielefeld, Germany

Tarik Mouakil
Research Associate, University of Cambridge, Cambridge, UK

and

Christian Proaño
Assistant Professor of Economics, The New School for Social Research, New York, USA

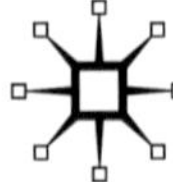

© Toichiro Asada, Peter Flaschel, Tarik Mouakil and Christian Proaño 2011

All rights reserved. No reproduction, copy or transmission of this publication may be made without written permission.

No portion of this publication may be reproduced, copied or transmitted save with written permission or in accordance with the provisions of the Copyright, Designs and Patents Act 1988, or under the terms of any licence permitting limited copying issued by the Copyright Licensing Agency, Saffron House, 6–10 Kirby Street, London EC1N 8TS.

Any person who does any unauthorized act in relation to this publication may be liable to criminal prosecution and civil claims for damages.

The authors have asserted their rights to be identified as the authors of this work in accordance with the Copyright, Designs and Patents Act 1988.

First published 2011 by
PALGRAVE MACMILLAN

Palgrave Macmillan in the UK is an imprint of Macmillan Publishers Limited, registered in England, company number 785998, of Houndmills, Basingstoke, Hampshire RG21 6XS.

Palgrave Macmillan in the US is a division of St Martin's Press LLC, 175 Fifth Avenue, New York, NY 10010.

Palgrave Macmillan is the global academic imprint of the above companies and has companies and representatives throughout the world.

Palgrave® and Macmillan® are registered trademarks in the United States, the United Kingdom, Europe and other countries.

ISBN 978–0–230–29017–4

This book is printed on paper suitable for recycling and made from fully managed and sustained forest sources. Logging, pulping and manufacturing processes are expected to conform to the environmental regulations of the country of origin.

A catalogue record for this book is available from the British Library.

A catalog record for this book is available from the Library of Congress.

10 9 8 7 6 5 4 3 2 1
20 19 18 17 16 15 14 13 12 11

Printed and bound in Great Britain by
CPI Antony Rowe, Chippenham and Eastbourne

Contents

List of Figures

List of Tables

List of Abbreviations

AS–AD	Aggregate Supply–Aggregate Demand
CB	Central Bank
CGE	Computable General Equilibrium
DAE	Department of Applied Economics
DAS–AD	Disequilibrium Aggregate Supply–Aggregate Demand
DSGD	Dynamic Stochastic General Disequilibrium
DSGE	Dynamic Stochastic General Equilibrium
EMS	European Monetary System
FCGE	Financial Computable General Equilibrium
FSAM	Financial Social Accounting Matrix
GBR	Government Borrowing Restriction
IMMPA	Integrated Macroeconomic Model for Poverty Analysis
IS–LM	Investment/Saving–Liquidity Preference/Money
IS–LM–BP	Investment/Saving–Liquidity Preference/Money plus BP-curve
KMG	Keynes–Metzler–Goodwin
KMGT	Keynes–Metzler–Goodwin–Taylor
LM	Liquidity Preference/Money
MFT	Mundell–Fleming–Tobin
NAIRU	Non-Accelerating Inflation Rate of Unemployment
PCs	Phillips curves
PPP	Purchasing Power Parity
SAM	Social Accounting Matrix
SFC	Stock Flow Consistent
UIP	Uncovered Interest Rate Parity

Preface

This book builds on what we have sketched as 'road ahead' in the final chapter of Asada, Chiarella, Flaschel and Franke (2010). It reflects and puts into perspective from a post-Keynesian angle the Keynes–Metzler–Goodwin (KMG) disequilibrium growth dynamics and also the various AS–AD approaches that surround this model of demand-driven distributive cycles. It does this in particular with respect to those studies which explicitly deal with stock-flow consistency and the stock-flow interactions they imply, i.e., the need for specifying all macro budget equations and the asset accumulation equations they give rise to.

We start from small models of the dynamics of aggregate demand and supply. Against this background we then reflect the KMG modelling framework in its methodological premises and its position concerning the modelling of Keynesian macrodynamics, which significantly distinguishes this approach from what is now called the new Keynesian D(ynamic) S(tochastic) G(eneral) E(equilibrium) paradigm. This paradigm insists on market clearing with respect to all real markets, makes use, in general, of a single representative household, in addition, makes use of perfect interest rate parity conditions in place of imperfect asset substitution and, above all, employs so-called rational expectations solutions in order to get by assumption a stable deterministic core dynamics around which the implications of stochastic shocks (ad shockeries) can then be considered. The resulting 'rocking horse methodology' is in striking contrast to what we will pursue in this book, where we focus on feedback-channel guided dynamic analyses of endogenously generated, demand-driven distributive cycles in the context of heterogeneous expectations formation and with a particular focus on a Tobin portfolio module in addition to the original primarily real KMG modelling framework.

The resulting model of KMG–Tobin type will be discussed and analysed in core chapters of the book, after its detailed motivation has been provided in the first two chapters. This portfolio approach to KMG growth is formulated in closed economies in terms of stocks of financial assets demanded and supplied. It needs reformulation for open economies, since capital accounts are to be represented in terms of flows. To achieve this we build on the Mundell–Fleming–Tobin (MFT) portfolio approach of Chiarella, Flaschel, Franke and Semmler (2009) which simplifies the real side of the KMGT macroeconomy considerably, in order to focus on the analysis of stock-flow interactions for small open economies as well as for interacting two-country macrodynamics.

The portfolio adjustment processes we introduce on the financial markets of these models of open economy macrodynamics are extended in the final chapter of the book to the treatment of more than one risky asset and the implied term structure of interest rates which was so far absent in the considered KMGT and MFT models where only equities and fix-price bonds were considered. We therefore sketch in this chapter again 'a road ahead' for future research which significantly enriches the structure of the financial side of the economy.

We hope that this book is capable of showing that there is a common core in the Keynesian literature (without any prefix), which in our case took its point of departure from Chiarella and Flaschel's (2000) critical overhaul of the achievements of the old neoclassical synthesis and which in other cases may be closer related to work of Kalecki in particular. We stress that their common view surely is that the new (Keynesian) neoclassical synthesis is devoid of issues that were of importance for both Keynes and Kalecki.

TOICHIRO ASADA
PETER FLASCHEL
TARIK MOUAKIL
CHRISTIAN PROAÑO

1
General Introduction

Methodological premises

The traditional view of business cycles is usually presented through Wicksell's famous 'rocking horse' metaphor. If a rocking horse is hit with a stick, the horse will move and its movement will be different from that of the stick. In other words, erratic *exogenous* 'shocks' are the cause of economic cycles (providing the necessary energy to keep the horse moving) and the fundamental law which determines the form of these cycles is given by the *equilibrium conditions* of the economic system.

The current book relies on a completely different conception of economic cycles. Our premises are, first, that business cycles are in essence *endogenously* generated and, second, that the form of business cycles stems from the interaction between *stocks* of assets and monetary *flows*. The first premise means that, in our view, business cycles cannot be explained only by hits on Wicksell's rocking horse. We do not deny the importance of exogenous shocks, such as economic, political, social or natural events, in explaining economic fluctuations but we do trust that a great part of these fluctuations can be explained by mechanisms which are endogenous to economic systems. In other words, unlike new classical macroeconomics, our approach does not explain business cycles by introducing stochastic exogenous disturbances in linear dynamical structures. In our work cycles arise instead from the 'natural' *nonlinearities* exhibited by high-dimensional dynamic models which seek to describe the complex structure of economic systems.[1]

Of course to study the properties of such models requires the use of rather elaborate mathematical tools such as the Routh–Hurwitz theorem and local Hopf bifurcation theory.[2] However, we trust that the reader will find the insights given by our dynamic models to be worth these complexities and to be far more convincing than those of their new classical counterparts. In particular those of our readers who feel uncomfortable with the paradigm of equilibrium economics will be pleased to find a representation of the economy in which well-known macroeconomic adjustment processes can generate complex self-sustaining business fluctuations.

One can describe our conception of economic cycles through a 'predator–prey' metaphor[3] based not on a rocking horse, but on a closed natural system with foxes (predators) and rabbits (prey). Fluctuations in both species' populations (though of course subject to exogenous shocks) are generated endogenously by the combination of reproduction and predation mechanisms. Moreover, an increase in the number of foxes will reduce the number of rabbits which in turn will have a negative impact on the future number of predators. The last statement corresponds to our second premise. It means that to represent properly the dynamic behaviour of a given economic system requires one to take account of the fundamental principle that current economic flows modify the levels of existing stocks of real and financial assets, which in turn have an impact on agents' economic behaviour and future economic flows. Therefore, in line with the textbooks of dynamic macroeconomics written in the 1970s by Thomas Sargent (1979) and Stephen Turnovsky (1977), the present book will give particular attention to stock-flow interactions:

> The main emphasis of our analysis is on what we shall refer to as the **intrinsic** dynamics of the system. By this we mean the dynamic behaviour stemming from certain logical relationships which constrain the system; specifically the relationships between stocks and flows. (Turnovsky, 1977, p.3)

Inspired by the portfolio model of Tobin (1969), both Sargent's and Turnovsky's textbooks show that, for the dynamics of a macroeconomic model to be consistent, the behavioural equations defining the interaction between stocks and flows have to be compatible with the budget constraints facing the decision makers in the economy.

In a consistent macro-model, the behaviour of every economic sector (both in regards to its assets and its assessment of realized results) must respect two kinds of budget constraints: 'one is a **stock** constraint, the other is a **flow** constraint' (Turnovsky, 1977, p.43). The flow constraint arises from the concept of *net savings* which are defined as the difference between a sector's flows of income and its expenditures. This constraint asserts that the net amount of assets accumulated (liabilities issued) by one sector must equal its net savings (expenditures). In the same way, the stock constraint arises from the concept of *net wealth* which consists of the sum of a sector's assets minus the sum of its liabilities. This constraint states that, when a sector is managing its balance sheet by reallocating its financial assets (liabilities), the sum of all the net claims (commitments) it wishes to hold (undertake) must equal its net wealth (debt). In our models, as in the models of Sargent and Turnovsky, the flow constraint applies to all the sectors of the considered economy while the stock constraint concerns only households, who are the only agents to manage their balance sheet through portfolio choices.

In an n-sectors economy, the expenditures (income flows) of an economic sector are simultaneously income flows (expenditures) of another sector. Therefore, a model which takes into account the budget constraints of $(n-1)$ sectors is necessarily consistent with the flow budget constraint of the nth sector. This principle, which may be referred to as Walras' law, also applies to stock constraints since financial assets (liabilities) of a sector are simultaneously liabilities (assets) of another. In the models of the present book households are the only agents to be really concerned by a stock budget constraint and therefore Walras' law for stocks simply means, as shown by Sargent (1979, p.67), that if $(n-1)$ financial markets are in equilibrium then the nth market is also in equilibrium.

The Keynes–Metzler–Goodwin framework

Accounting consistency is far from being the only feature that our dynamic models have inherited from the textbooks of Sargent and Turnovsky. Indeed the models presented in the present book are extensions of the Keynesian growth model of Chiarella and Flaschel (2000a, b), which was itself an extension of the growth models of the neoclassical synthesis as discussed in the textbooks of Sargent and

Turnovsky. Neoclassical growth models can be described as 'aggregate supply-aggregate demand (AS–AD) growth models'; they are based on IS–LM equilibrium, and the so-called AD curve that derives from it, as well as the AS schedule representing the situation where prices equal marginal wage costs. This AS–AD framework is then made dynamic through a Solow-type growth of the stock of capital and an expectations-augmented Phillips curve for wages.

Chiarella and Flaschel's main contribution to this body of literature was to introduce disequilibrium elements into the AS–AD framework in order to overcome its logical inconsistency. In an influential paper, Robert Barro (1994) showed that coupling together IS–LM equilibrium with the assumption that prices always equal marginal wage costs amounts to trying to combine two conflicting theories of production and pricing. On one hand, one assumes that firms produce to meet demand by making quantity adjustments while keeping the price fixed. On the other hand firms produce to maximize their profits and are price takers. Thus, for a given level of price, the AS–AD framework determines two different levels of output:[4]

> The AS-AD model is logically flawed as usually presented because its assumption that the price level clears the good market is inconsistent with the Keynesian underpinnings for the aggregate-demand curve. (Barro, 1994, p.5)

Barro showed that one way to make the AS–AD framework consistent is to assume that the AD curve applies only when the price level has adjusted to ensure market clearing; which is to say that price expectations are *rational* and enable the level of effective demand to become consistent with the profit-maximizing level of the output.[5] However, in this case, the AS–AD framework is no longer Keynesian and becomes equivalent to the rational expectations-based new classical models of Lucas (1972) and Sargent and Wallace (1973, 1975). In the same way, Flaschel *et al.* (1997) showed that when rational expectations are introduced into the AS–AD growth model of Sargent (1979, ch.5), it becomes a new classical model (with a vertical Phillips curve) where monetary shocks have nominal but no real effects.

In his paper, Barro advocates market-clearing closures but acknowledges that another way to achieve a consistent model is to build on the IS–LM framework by using gradually adjusting wages *and* prices. It is precisely in this way that Chiarella and Flaschel modified Sargent's model in order to achieve a consistent Keynesian growth model which was later labelled 'Keynes–Metzler–Goodwin' (KMG).[6] In the KMG model all real markets are demand-led and remain in disequilibrium. In particular there is nothing which leads towards an equality between supply and demand of labour; that is, to full employment. As for the product market, supply cannot adjust instantaneously to demand and firms are forced to hold inventories which are modelled along the lines of Lloyd A. Metzler's (1941) work. In the absence of market-clearing mechanisms, the model exhibits sluggish wages and prices the dynamics of which are defined through a pair of modified Phillips curves inspired by the models of Rose (1967, 1990). These two Phillips curves exhibit 'cost-push' components (represented through the weighted average of the actual inflation rate and the 'inflation climate')[7] and 'demand pressure' components (represented through the utilization rate of the two factors of production, labour and capital). Moreover, regarding consumption demand, the model differentiates between workers (who consume their total wages) and capitalists (who save a fraction of their rentier income) and therefore generates an interaction between income distribution and growth which is similar to the one achieved in Richard Goodwin's (1967) model. Another innovation of the model is the use of a Kaleckian investment function according to which the rate of accumulation of capital depends on the level of its utilization rate and the spread between the rate of return of capital and its opportunity cost (the real interest rate).

Instead of having introduced rational expectations in the AS–AD framework, Chiarella and Flaschel used the assumption of *adaptive* expectations according to which medium-term expectations (not short-term ones) are based on the observation of past data. Though this assumption has a bad reputation in some quarters, we believe that the representation of expectations found in the KMG model is more convincing than the new classical one for the following two reasons. First, there is widespread evidence from economics and behavioural sciences that adaptive expectations are used by real economic agents. Even supporters of rational expectations like Mankiw (2001, p.C59) recognize that 'the assumption of adaptive expectations is, in essence, what the data are crying out for'. Second, the KMG model adopts a pragmatic view which combines adaptive expectations with myopic perfect foresight on the real markets and with so-called *regressive* expectations in the financial part of the model. The latter are based on a general idea from the asset markets (that is, a *fundamentalist* view), according to which the variable is expected to return to its normal level after some time.

For the rest, the KMG model remains very close to AS–AD growth models developed in the 1970s and, in particular, it is written in *continuous* time. In his textbook, Turnovsky (1977, p.44) distinguishes four arguments in favour of analysing a growth model in continuous time instead of discrete time:

> First, there is the important reason ... of analytical tractability; differential equations are easier to study than difference equations. Secondly, discrete-time analysis suffers from the serious disadvantage of assuming that all decisions of a particular type are perfectly synchronized. Thirdly, a related difficulty with discrete time analysis is that in most economic contexts there is no obvious interval to serve as the natural unit. Fourthly, while discrete-time analysis is conceptually simpler, it does suffer from the danger that its underlying assumption of a fixed period length may unwittingly yield misleading conclusions. To test whether or not this is the case, it is desirable to allow the period length to vary and ultimately let it shrink to its limit.

The first advantage of working in continuous time is obvious in the case of the KMG model which, even in its intensive form, remains a system of differential equations of high dimension (6D). By applying the Routh–Hurwitz theorem to a sequence of subsystems of increasing dimensions, Chiarella *et al.* (2005) proved that variations in given parameters of the KMG model bring (in-)stability through a Hopf bifurcation. Working in continuous time facilitated the mathematical analysis of this model by saving them the difficulties attached to the use of lags. Studying a similar 6D non-linear system of *difference* equations would have been far harder, if not impossible. The use of continuous time not only simplifies the mathematical analysis of dynamic models, but is also the better choice to approach macroeconomic issues. In the case of discrete-time macroeconomic models it is very hard to give a theoretical interpretation of the use of a uniform period length which generates a synchronization of economic decision making across all sectors and activities. Moreover most empirical macroeconomic models in discrete time ignore the discrepancy between the frequencies of actual *data generating* and the corresponding *data-collection* processes of the great majority of macroeconomic variables. While the actual data-generating process at the macroeconomic level is by and large of a quasi-continuous-time nature (with a less than daily frequency), the corresponding frequency of data collection available nowadays, at least in the real market of the economy, is on a quarterly or even yearly basis. Ignoring this discrepancy can be misleading when the resulting dynamic properties of the calibrated theoretical model depend not on its intrinsic characteristics, but mainly on the length of the iteration intervals. This issue is particularly clear in discrete-time dynamic models of dimension one or two which exhibit chaotic properties (with annualized data), whereas in their analogous continuous time representations the occurrence of such chaotic properties is simply impossible from the mathematical point of view.

Two 'Old Keynesian' models

The aim of the present book is to propose 'old Keynesian' dynamic macroeconomic models which help to understand how the interaction between monetary flows and financial (as well as real) stocks can generate self-sustaining business cycles. The 'old' prefix refers to the theoretical framework developed by James Tobin. According to the Nobel-prize winner, the five features that differentiate his old Keynesianism from the neoclassical synthesis are the following:

(i) Precision regarding time
(ii) Tracking of stocks
(iii) Several assets and rates of return
(iv) Modeling of financial and monetary policy operations
(v) Walras' law and adding-up constraints. (Tobin, 1982, pp. 172–3)

The first feature, precision regarding time, corresponds to the idea that the short-run determination of macroeconomic variables is one among several steps of a dynamic sequence, not a repetitive equilibrium in which the economy settles. Therefore macroeconomic models have to be thought of as dynamics systems. The second and fifth features state the necessity of using a stock-flow modelling methodology: the dynamics of macro models must be determined by the relationships between stocks and flows and, for these dynamics to be consistent, stocks and flows have to be compatible with the budget constraints of all economic sectors. As already mentioned, these three features of Tobin's old Keynesianism all apply to the textbooks of Sargent and Turnovsky and to the subsequent KMG model.

The two remaining features refer to Tobin's (1969) theory of financial markets. Although some of the models presented in the textbooks of Sargent (1979, ch.1) and Turnovsky (1977, ch.7) make use of this theory, it does not play any role in their AS–AD growth models. Tobin's theory of financial markets does not appear either in the KMG model which still relies on the conventional LM representation of asset markets behaviour.

The first model presented in this book, labelled 'KMG–Tobin model', fills this gap by replacing the rudimentary functions of demand for assets arising from the LM block with Tobinian portfolio choices (in line with the third feature of old Keynesianism). In this new model, households decide to allocate their wealth between money, bonds and equities so that: (a) the demand for each asset varies positively with its own rate of return and negatively with the rates of other assets (that is, assets are imperfect gross substitutes); (b) the stock constraint requirements are fulfilled (any increase in wealth is allocated to some asset and any increase in the demand for a particular asset is met by a compensating reduction in demand for some other asset). Thus the KMG–Tobin model improves the representation of the interaction between real and financial markets provided in the KMG model; in particular it offers a comprehensive representation of the way monetary policy operations (corresponding in this case to the adoption of a money supply policy rule) are channelled through financial markets before they impact on the real part of the economy (feature iv).

In addition to the portfolio version of the KMG model, this book also presents a portfolio version of the Mundell–Fleming model which takes into account the open economy issues neglected by the former. We will analyse the MFT model in three versions corresponding to: (i) a small open economy with fixed exchange rate (for instance the situation of Germany within the European Monetary Union),

(ii) a small open economy with flexible exchange rates and Dornbusch (1976) type overshooting exchange rate dynamics (for instance Australia), (iii) two interacting open economies (for instance USA and the Eurozone).

The reader will inevitably wonder why we did not choose to study these issues through an open-economy version of the KMG–Tobin model. The answer has to do with practical issues. As shown in the *Open Economy Macrodynamics* textbook of Asada, Chiarella, Flaschel and Franke (2003), open-economy versions of the core KMG model are systems of differential equations of very high dimension (up to 14D for the complete two-countries KMG model) and it is extremely hard – though still possible – to study analytically their stability properties (Asada *et al.*, 2003). Therefore, given that the introduction of Tobin portfolio choices would increase even further the complexity of these models, we prefer to approach the issue of stock-flow interactions in dynamic open-economy systems through a slightly modified version of the Mundell–Fleming–Tobin (MFT) model proposed in the *Open Economy Macroeconomics* textbook of A. Rødseth (2000). This model is a combination of Tobin's portfolio equations and the well-known IS–LM–BP model of Mundell (1963) and Fleming (1962) which adds a balance of payments condition (and a BP curve) to the IS–LM framework. By presenting the MFT model we will therefore go back to the conventional IS device instead of continuing to use a Metzlerian adjustment process. For the purpose of simplicity we will also abandon Goodwinian wage–price dynamics and use instead a standard expectations-augmented open-economy Phillips curve. Despite these simplifications, which may be considered as limit cases of the KMG assumptions, the MFT model is not different in spirit from Chiarella and Flaschel's growth models and it should be considered as a first step towards a future open-economy KMG–Tobin model.

Outline of the book

In Chapter 2 we present two simple macroeconomic models that serve as an introduction to the KMG–Tobin model. The first model, labelled DAS–AD model (disequilibrium aggregate supply–aggregate demand), can be seen as the missing link between Sargent's AS–AD growth model and the KMG model. It is a first extension of Sargent's model that exhibits gradually adjusting wages and prices, through a pair of modified Phillips curves, where however the financial side of the economy is still modelled through a textbook-like LM equation. The second model helps illustrating Tobin's portfolio approach to macrodynamics by introducing Tobinian portfolio equations into a fixed-price multiplier model *à la* Blanchard (1981).

Chapter 3 introduces in detail the structure of the KMG–Tobin model, whose stability properties are studied analytically in Chapter 4. We present for this model type so-called social accounting matrices (SAM) in order to show in one table the interactions that are assumed to take place between the various sectors and markets.

Chapter 5 presents an advanced approach to small open economies: the Mundell–Fleming–Tobin model. Chapter 6 proposes two extensions of this model type. In the first extension, domestic bonds, that are non-tradables in the original MFT model, are now traded internationally. The second one is a two-country extension of the baseline MFT model with international trade of domestic as well as foreign bonds.

Chapter 7 serves as a foundation for further research into the macrodynamic modelling of financial markets. In this concluding chapter we model financial markets through a combination of Tobinian portfolio equations and disequilibrium adjustment processes, which open the road towards a future research programme: dynamic stochastic general *disequilibrium* modelling.

2

Advances in AS–AD Model Building: Real Disequilibria and Portfolio Choice

In this chapter we present two simple macroeconomic models that serve as an introduction to the KMG–Tobin model introduced in the next chapter. The first model, labelled DAS–AD, is a 'disequilibrium' extension of the AS–AD growth model of Sargent (1987, ch.5) that exhibits gradually adjusting wages and prices through a pair of modified Phillips curves. The second model introduces portfolio equations in a simple dynamic multiplier model inspired by Blanchard (1981).

Introducing disequilibrium elements into the AS–AD framework

Starting from Barro (1994) criticism of the growth models of the neoclassical synthesis, we introduce sluggish wages *and* prices within the AS–AD framework through a pair of modified Phillips curves. Moreover, we replace rational expectations with a combination of *adaptive* expectations (according to which medium-term expectations come from the observation of past data) and *regressive* expectations (according to which financial variables are expected to return to their *normal* level after some time).

Wage–price spiral and medium-run aspects

We consider two Phillips curves (PCs) instead of a unique one. They describe wage and price dynamics separately, and are based respectively on the measure of demand pressure in the market for labour $e - \bar{e}$ and in the goods market $u - \bar{u}$. We denote by e the rate of employment on the labour market and by $\bar{e}$ the NAIRU-level of this rate. In the same way u is the rate of capacity utilization of the capital stock and $\overline{u}$ the normal rate of capacity utilization of firms. These demand pressure influences on wage and price dynamics are augmented by a weighted average of cost-pressure terms (that is based on forward-looking perfectly foreseen price/wage inflation rates) and a backward looking measure of the prevailing inflationary climate, symbolized by π. Cost pressure perceived by workers is thus a weighted average of the price inflation rate $\hat{p}$ and some longer-run concept of price inflation, π, that is based on past observations. Similarly, cost pressure perceived by firms is given by a weighted average of the (perfectly foreseen) wage inflation rate $\hat{w}$ and the measure of the inflationary climate in which the economy is operating.

We obtain in this way the following two Phillips curves for wage and price inflation that are formulated in a similar fashion:

$$\hat{w} = \beta_w(e - \overline{e}) + \kappa_w\hat{p} + (1 - \kappa_w)\pi \tag{2.1}$$

$$\hat{p} = \beta_p(u - \overline{u}) + \kappa_p\hat{w} + (1 - \kappa_p)\pi \tag{2.2}$$

Inflationary expectations over the medium run, π, i.e., the *inflationary climate* in which current wage and price inflation is operating, could be (i) adaptively following the actual rate of inflation (by use of some exponential weighting scheme); (ii) based on a rolling sample (with hump-shaped weighting schemes); or (iii) based on other possibilities for updating expectations about the medium run. For simplicity of exposition we will use the conventional adaptive expectations mechanism. We thus use weighted averages of this economic climate and the (foreseen) relevant cost pressure term for wage setting and price setting. In this way we get two PCs that represent a significant improvement over single reduced-form price Phillips curves. Various studies have estimated these two PCs in the case of the US economy and found that wage flexibility was greater than price flexibility with respect to demand pressure in the market for goods and for labour.[1] Such a finding would not have been possible with the conventional framework of a single reduced-form Phillips curve.

Let us note that the inflationary climate variable does not matter for the *evolution of the real wage* $\omega = w/p$, whose law of motion is given by:

$$\hat{\omega} = \kappa[(1 - \kappa_p)\beta_w(e - \overline{e}) - (1 - \kappa_w)\beta_p(u - \overline{u})] \tag{2.3}$$

with $\kappa = 1/(1 - \kappa_w \kappa_p)$.

This can be shown easily from the equivalent representation of the two PCs:

$$\hat{w} - \pi = \beta_w(e - \bar{e}) + \kappa_w(\hat{p} - \pi) \tag{2.4}$$

$$\hat{p} - \pi = \beta_p(u - \bar{u}) + \kappa_p(\hat{w} - \pi) \tag{2.5}$$

It implies that the *reduced form* of the two PCs is given by:

$$\hat{p} = \kappa[\beta_p(u - \bar{u}) + \kappa_p \beta_w(e - \bar{e})] + \pi \tag{2.6}$$

$$\hat{w} = \kappa[\beta_w(e - \bar{e}) + \kappa_w \beta_p(u - \bar{u})] + \pi \tag{2.7}$$

which represent *a generalization of* the conventional view of a single-market price PC (whose only measure of demand pressure is the one in the labour market). The first reduced form $\hat{p}$-equation will look like a traditional expectations-augmented PC formally if Okun's Law holds in the sense of a strict positive correlation between $u - \bar{u}$, $u = Y/Y^p$ and $e - \bar{e}$, $e = L^d/L$. Yet, the coefficient in front of the traditional PC would still be a mixture of the $\beta' s$ and $\kappa' s$ of the two original PCs, and thus represent a synthesis of goods and labour market characteristics.

With respect to the investment climate we proceed similarly and assume that this climate is adaptively following the current risk premium $\varepsilon (= \rho - (r - \hat{p}))$, that is the excess of the actual profit rate over the actual real rate of interest (which is perfectly foreseen). This gives

$$\dot{\varepsilon}^m = \beta_{\varepsilon^m}(\varepsilon - \varepsilon^m) \quad \text{with} \quad \varepsilon = \rho + \hat{p} - r \tag{2.8}$$

which is directly comparable with

$$\dot{\pi} = \beta_\pi(\hat{p} - \pi) \tag{2.9}$$

It seems natural to assume that economic climate expressions evolve sluggishly towards their observed short-run counter-parts. The investment function of the model is then simply given by

$$\hat{K} = \frac{I}{K} = i(\varepsilon^m) \quad \text{with} \quad \dot{\varepsilon}^m = \beta_{\varepsilon^m}(\varepsilon - \varepsilon^m) \tag{2.10}$$

in place of Sargent's investment function $i(\varepsilon) + n$. One may consider the expression ε^m as measuring the state of confidence of the economy (which is updated on the basis of new observation on excess profitability).

The DAS–AD model in intensive form

We have now introduced the first modifications needed to overcome the extreme conclusions of the traditional AS–AD approach as they were discussed in Sargent (1987, Ch.5). In Sargent's approach to Keynesian dynamics, β_{ε^m}, β_π, β_p are all set equal to infinity and $\bar{u}$ set equal to one. This implies that only current inflation rates and excess profitabilities matter for the evolution of the economy and that prices are perfectly flexible, so that full capacity utilization (and not only normal capacity utilization) is always achieved. This extreme (structurally unstable) limit case has however little in common with the properties of the DAS–AD model.

One point that still needs definition and explanation is the concept of rate of capacity utilization that is used here since we now allow for Keynesian over- or under-employment of the capital stock (in place of Sargent's price-taking profit-maximizing firm behaviour). Capacity utilization u is measured by the ratio of the actual output to the potential output Y^p:[2]

$$u = Y/Y^p \tag{2.11}$$

with $Y^p = F(K, L^p)$ and $\omega = F_L(K, L^p)$.

Y is determined from the IS–LM equilibrium block in the usual way. We have assumed in the price PC a normal rate of capacity utilization that is less than one, implying that demand pressure leads to price inflation before potential output has been reached (in line with what is assumed in the wage PC). The idea behind this assumption is that there is imperfect competition on the market for goods so that firms raise prices before profits become zero at the margin.

Sargent (1987, ch.5) does not only assume myopic perfect foresight ($\beta_\pi = \infty$), but also that the price level is given by marginal wage costs ($\beta_p = \infty, \bar{u} = 1$). This 'limit case' of the DAS–AD model does not represent a meaningful model, in particular since its dynamic properties are not consistent with situations of very fast adjustment of prices and climate expressions to currently correctly observed inflation rates and excess profitability. One can show that in a such a model there is a dichotomy between a supply side of Solow (1956)–Goodwin (1967) type and an appended IS–LM block that determines the dynamics of the price level in a Friedmanian way.[3]

We note that the steady state of the considered Keynesian dynamics is the same as the one of the traditional AS–AD dynamics (with

$\varepsilon_o^m = 0, u_o = \overline{u}, e_o = \overline{e}, y_o^p = y_o/u_o, l_o^p = f^{-1}(y_o^p)$ in addition). The intensive form of all resulting static and dynamic equations is presented below.

We can reduce the dynamics of the model to an autonomous system of five predetermined state variables: the real wage, real balances per unit of capital, full employment labour intensity, and the expressions for the inflation and the investment climate. When the model is subject to explosive forces, it requires extrinsic non-linearities in economic behaviour (assumed to come into affect far off the steady state) in order to bound the dynamics to an economically meaningful domain in the 5D state space.[4]

The model consists of the following five laws of motion for real wages $\omega = w/p$, real balances $m = M/(pK)$, the investment climate ε^m, labour intensity $l = L/K$ and the inflationary climate π:

$$\hat{\omega} = \kappa[(1-\kappa_p)\beta_w(l^d/l - \overline{e}) - (1-\kappa_w)\beta_p(y/y^p - \overline{u})] \tag{2.12}$$

$$\hat{m} = \hat{M} - (\hat{K} + \hat{p}) = -\hat{p} - i\varepsilon^m \tag{2.13}$$

$$\dot{\varepsilon}^m = \beta_{\varepsilon^m}(\rho + \hat{p} - r - \varepsilon^m) \tag{2.14}$$

$$\hat{l} = \hat{L} - \hat{K} = -i\varepsilon^m \tag{2.15}$$

$$\dot{\pi} = \beta_\pi(\hat{p} - \pi) \tag{2.16}$$

with $\hat{p} = \kappa[\beta_p(y/y^p(\omega) - \overline{u}) + \kappa_p\beta_w(l^d/l - \overline{e})] + \pi$ and $\hat{L} = n$.

We employ reduced-form expressions throughout and consider the dynamics of the real wage, ω, real balances per unit of capital, m, the investment climate ε^m, labour intensity, l, and the inflationary climate, π on the basis of the simplifying assumptions that natural growth n determines also the trend growth term in the investment function as well as money supply growth. The above dynamical system is to be supplemented by the following static relationships for output, potential output and employment (all per unit of capital), the rate of interest and the rate of profit:

$$y = \frac{1}{1-c}[i\varepsilon^m + n + g - t] + t \tag{2.17}$$

$$y^p = f((f')^{-1}(\omega)) \tag{2.18}$$

with $F(1, L^p/K) = f(l^p) = y^p$ and $F_L(1, L^p/K)) = f'(l^p) = \omega$

$$l^d = f^{-1}(y) \tag{2.19}$$

$$r = r(y, m) \tag{2.20}$$

$$\rho = y - \omega l^d \tag{2.21}$$

We assume, as in Sargent (1987), that government expenditures per unit of capital g, and taxes net of interest per unit of capital t, are given magnitudes, just as the marginal propensity to consume c. The expression $f((f')^{-1}(\omega))$ gives the potential output per unit of capital. Labour demand per unit of capital, l^d, is calculated by inverting the production function. The expression $r(y, m)$ gives the traditional LM curve in inverted form (with $r_y > 0, r_m < 0$).

Stability analysis

The static equations have to be inserted on the right-hand sides of the above-mentioned laws of motion in order to obtain an autonomous system of five differential equations that is non-linear in a natural or intrinsic way. We note however that there are many items that reappear in various equations, or are similar to each other, implying that stability analysis can exploit a variety of linear dependencies in the calculation of the conditions for local asymptotic stability. This approach and the subsequent analysis of the dynamical system will be considered in an informal way.[5]

Proposition 1: stability of balanced growth

Let us assume that $\beta_\pi > 0, \beta_w > 0, \beta_p > 0$ are sufficiently small. Let us assume furthermore that the weight parameters κ_w, κ_p do not equal to 1 (so that the inflationary climate expression is involved in the dynamics). Let us assume finally that money demand is sufficiently inelastic with respect to the nominal rate of interest. Then, the interior steady state of the considered 5D dynamical system is surrounded by damped oscillations or even subject to monotonic convergence.

We formulate, as a corollary to this proposition, that, due to the always negative sign of the 5D determinant of the dynamic system at the steady state, loss of stability can only occur by way of Hopf bifurcations, i.e., through the generation of cycles.

Corollary 1: roads to instability

Let us assume an asymptotically stable steady state on the basis of the preceding proposition. Then, the interior steady state of the 5D dynamical system will lose its stability (generally) by way of a sub-critical Hopf bifurcation (loss of a corridor of stability) or supercritical Hopf bifurcation (generation of a persistent business cycle) if the parameters β_p *or* β_π *are chosen sufficiently large.*

Since the model is a non-linear one, we know from the Hopf-bifurcation theorem that a loss of stability will occur through the death of an unstable limit cycle (the subcritical case) or the birth of a stable one (the supercritical case), when destabilizing parameters pass through their bifurcation values. Such loss of stability is possible if prices become sufficiently flexible compared to wage flexibility, hence leading to an adverse type of real wage adjustment, or if the inflationary climate expression is updated sufficiently fast, i.e., if the system loses its inflationary inertia to a sufficient degree. These are typical feedback structures of a properly formulated Keynesian dynamics that may give rise to global instability (directly in the case of subcritical Hopf bifurcations, with a delay in the case of supercritical bifurcations) and require adding further *extrinsic behavioural non-linearities* to the model in order to bound the generated business fluctuations.

We conclude from this section that our Keynesian disequilibrium dynamics can generate damped oscillations, persistent fluctuations or even explosive oscillations. Moreover it is necessary to introduce certain behavioural non-linearities in order to allow for viable business fluctuations.

We have already discussed the stock-flow dynamics of the AS–AD model of Sargent (1987) to a certain degree. Concerning private savings the budget equations of households imply that the new issue of equities by firms is indeed absorbed if the new issue of money and bonds is accepted by households.[6] Since money and bonds are perfectly liquid this assumption is not a problematic one as the model is currently formulated. Note that money and bond financing of government expenditure are present here, since the central bank buys government bonds through its open market operations and since it – by assumption – transfers the interest they generate back into the government sector. The model therefore exhibits flow consistency in the described form.

The inflow of new financial asset feeds back into the stock already held by the private households. However, it is infinitesimally small and therefore does not impact the current reallocation of stocks which, independently of these flows, determine the rate of interest and the share price at each moment in time. Yet, in the considered form of traditional AS–AD analysis, there is no feedback of share prices into the real sector, since they do not have an impact on the rate of interest. The interest rate is determined by a standard LM-equation that depends on the state of activity Y of the economy. This rate determines, via the real interest rate and the rate of profit, the investment decision of firms which therefore is completely independent from the stock market. Monetary policy is very powerful in this model (in particular in the form of an interest rate policy rule) since it directly impacts investment behaviour without any detour through the financial markets of the economy. In short, the DAS–AD growth model overcomes the logical inconsistency of the AS–AD framework, as put in evidence by Barro, but its stock-flow interactions are far from being convincing due to the poor representation of the financial markets in this model.

Tobin's portfolio approach to macrodynamics

Sargent's textbook (1987) considers three financial markets: money M (issued by the central bank), bonds B (issued by the government) and equities E (issued by firms). The money market is the only one that is explicitly modelled. The financial markets are represented by a single equilibrium condition, the traditional LM curve. To support this approach, equities and bonds are assumed to be perfect substitutes, which is puzzling given that the latter have a fixed price and thus represent a type of money. In the models of the present book we therefore prefer to treat bonds and equities as imperfect substitutes by using Tobin's (1969) portfolio approach to financial markets.

In this section we present Tobin's portfolio choices in a very basic macroeconomic framework that ignores inflation and growth and represents the quantity adjustment process by a simple dynamic multiplier approach as in Blanchard (1981).

Tobinian portfolio choice

From now on, we assume that financial assets are imperfect substitutes and that capital gain expectations are also imperfect and work in a portfolio structure as in Tobin (1969). Moreover we assume that the stocks of the financial assets M, B, E are exogenously given:[7]

$$\overline{M} = M^d = f_m(r, r_e^e)W_c^n \tag{2.22}$$

$$\overline{B} = B^d = f_b(r, r_e^e)W_c^n \tag{2.23}$$

$$p_e\overline{E} = p_eE^d = f_e(r, r_e^e)W_c^n \tag{2.24}$$

$$W_c^n = \overline{M} + \overline{B} + p_e\overline{E} \text{ and } f_m(r, r_e^e) + f_b(r, r_e^e) + f_e(r, r_e^e) \equiv 1 \tag{2.25}$$

$$r_e^e = \frac{pY - wL^d}{p_e\overline{E}} + \overline{\pi}_e^e = r/q + \overline{\pi}_e^e \tag{2.26}$$

The expression r_e^e defines the rate of return on equities that is, as shown in equation (2.26), the sum of the dividend rate of return ρ/q and expected capital gains on equities π_e^e. Since all profits are assumed to be paid out as dividends, the dividend rate of return is obtained by dividing the rate of profit of firms by Tobin's q.

Equations (2.22) to (2.24) state that the demand for a given financial asset depends positively on its own rate of return and negatively on the rate of return of other assets, i.e. in particular, money demand depends negatively on the rate of interest and the rate of return on equities. Asset holders, for example, intend to increase their short-term bond holdings in the case of an increase in the short-term interest rate r as in a Baumol cash-management process. Changing interest rates therefore affect the cash management of asset holders, a fairly trivial and tranquil component of their whole portfolio choice, but also affect the equity demand of asset holders, since they consider their bond holdings as alternative to their equity holdings (in particular when the stock market is under pressure). Money holdings $M2 = M(r) + B(r)$ and equities E are imperfect substitutes, but the internal restructuring of $M2$ determines the transactions demand for money at each moment in time.

Equation (2.25) is the *stock* constraint of households which states that households 'must allocate their entire wealth, but no more, among bonds, equities, and money' (Sargent, 1979, p.67). Due to this constraint, only two of the three equations (2.22) to (2.24) are independent from each other. Therefore one of these three equations should be left aside in order for the model not to be overdetermined. This principle is referred to by Sargent (1979, p.67) as Walras' law of stocks when he observes:

> Note that the constraint can be rearranged to read:
>
> $$M^d - M = (B - B^d) + (E - E^d)$$

which states that the excess demand for money equals the sum of the excess supplies for bonds and equities. This is the form of Walras' law for stocks of paper assets in our model.

In our model, the missing equation will be (2.23). As for equations (2.22) and (2.24) they will be used to determine the variables r, p_e since we assume a given supply of high-powered money $M2 = \overline{M} + \overline{B}$. If we assumed instead that the central bank sets the rate of interest r at each moment in time we would have a change in causality on the financial markets. In such a case, M, B and of course p_e would be determined through the above portfolio equations, since the central bank would have to adjust the supply of the two assets M, B to the demands of households through open market policies. One can note that both versions of the model imply that the sum of money and bond holdings $M2$ will remain fixed unless the central bank is buying equities in place of fixed-price bonds through its open market operations.

In view of this, we now postulate the following hierarchy of asset markets:

$$
\begin{aligned}
p_e\overline{E} &= f_e(0, r_e^e)W_c^n \\
\overline{M} &= f_m(r, 0)W_c^n \\
\overline{B} &= f_b(r, r_e^e)W_c^n \\
& \quad f_e(0, r_e^e) + (f_m + f_b)(0, r_e^e) \equiv 1
\end{aligned}
$$

We assume that the first decision of asset holders concerns the decision between equities and $M2$ holdings (hoarding) and that this decision is independent of the nominal rate of interest (around the steady state of the economy). The latter is only important for the cash management of asset holders, when they determine how much of their money $M2 = \overline{M} + \overline{B}$ they intend to hold as cash and how much as saving deposits. Pure money hoarding would be reduced if the rate of interest on savings deposits was increased, but this would not lead to any change in the total amount of liquid assets demanded by asset holders. Their relevant decision is therefore the choice between illiquid and liquid assets rather than the one between saving deposits and cash. This means that the share price is independent of the nominal rate of interest.

The change in stock prices p_e induces that, at each moment in time, asset holders hold exactly the amount of their initial stocks, which means in particular that $M2$ is given unless the central bank trades in equities. In times of stress (for the equity market), when people want to go into money (=bond) hoarding, the equity price will thus fall significantly without the possibility for asset holders to modify their actual stock of equities. As for the stock market equilibrium, we get again $E = \overline{E}$, but due to trading processes in the background of this situation a new share price p_e appears and thus a new money demand $M2$. At the end of the process, the supply of equities is again held by asset holders and the demand for $M2$ is back to its initial level.

It is easy to show that excess demand on the asset markets is a negative function of the share price p_e. In disequilibrium, the share price is therefore adjusting towards its equilibrium value (all other variables beeing fixed for the moment). The equilibrium share price represents, therefore, an attractor of disequilibrium share prices. We assume that this ultra short-run process occurs in virtual time so that the market for equities is always cleared. Comparative static exercises then easily show that the equilibrium value of the stock price depends positively on the rate of profit and also positively on capital gains expectations.

The equity market equilibrium condition implies:

$$q = f_e(0, \rho(\cdot)/q + \pi_e^e)(m + b + q) \tag{2.27}$$

with $m = M/(pK)$ and $b = B/(pK)$

This relationship defines a function $q = q(\rho, \pi_e^e, m, b)$, whose partial derivatives are given by the implicit function theorem through a comparative static exercise:

$$\frac{\partial q}{\partial \rho} = \frac{f_{e2}(\cdot)(m + b + q)/q}{N} > 0$$

$$\frac{\partial q}{\partial \pi_e^e} = \frac{f_{e2}(\cdot)(m + b + q)}{N} > 0$$

$$\frac{\partial q}{\partial m} = \frac{f_e(\cdot)}{N} = \frac{\partial q}{\partial b} > 0$$

with $N = 1 - f_e(\cdot) + f_{e2}(\cdot)\rho/q^2(m + b + q) > 0$

We note that the partial derivative with respect to ρ, π_e^e are approaching zero if the partial derivative f_{e2} of the (relative) equity demand function is going to zero, for a given value of f_e at the steady state of the economy.

Multiplier dynamics and capital gains expectations

With regards to the real side of the economy, we take into account the stock market effect on investment (and consumption) behaviour (and hence on aggregate demand). We consider that the share price is now measuring the state of confidence in the economy and thus we use it in the investment function in place of the short-term rate of interest. This gives the following law of motion for the real side of the economy:

$$\hat{Y} = \beta_y[(Y^d - Y)/Y] = \beta_y[(a_y Y + a_q(q_s - q^o) + \overline{A} - Y)/Y] \qquad (2.28)$$

where $a_y \in (0, 1), a_q > 0$ and where $\overline{A}$ summarizes autonomous expenditures (fiscal policy and more).

This is a standard textbook dynamic multiplier process but Tobin's average q, in its deviation from its steady state value q^o, is now used in the aggregate demand function in place of the excess returns in the firm sector. Since prices, capital and the equity stock are considered as given in this section, we can assume $\frac{E}{pK}$ to be equal to one, so that Tobin's average q is equal to the share price p_e.

We now add two laws of motions corresponding to the formation of capital gain expectations. We assume a nested process that is formally described by two differential equations:

$$\hat{p}_s = \beta_s\left(\frac{p_e}{p_s} - 1\right) \qquad (2.29)$$

$$\dot{\pi}_e^e = \beta_{\pi_e^e}(\hat{p}_s - \pi_e^e) \qquad (2.30)$$

We assume a chartist type of behaviour where chartists use as the reference share price p_s a smoothed value of the actual share price p_e, that adjust to the actual share prices with a delay measured by $1/\beta_s$. The growth rate of these intermediate, or smoothed, share price $\hat{p}_s$ then gives the reference path for the adjustment of share price expectations π_e^e.

Blanchard's (1981) analysis of the interaction of the stock market with the goods market considers the limit case where $\beta_s, \ \beta_{\pi_e^e} = \infty$ holds, where bonds and equities are again perfect substitutes and expectations are perfect. Moreover he treats the resulting saddlepoint dynamics between the dynamic multiplier process and the stock market dynamics by means of the rational expectations assumption that turns the variable q into a jump variable.[8] The obtained dynamics are then very different from the real and stock market interaction considered below and thus should not be considered as a limit case of the following stability analysis.

We couple the asset dynamics of our reformulation of Blanchard (1981) model (with nested adaptive capital gains expectations) with the above-mentioned multiplier dynamic:

$$\dot{Y} = \beta_Y[(a_y - 1)Y + a_q(q_s - q^o) + \overline{A}] \tag{2.31}$$

$$\hat{q}_s = \beta_s\left[\frac{q(\rho(\cdot), \pi_e^e, m+b)}{q_s} - 1\right] \text{ with } q_s = p_s \tag{2.32}$$

$$\dot{\pi}_e^e = \beta_{\pi_e^e}(\hat{q}_s - \pi_e^e) \tag{2.33}$$

In order to make the 3D dynamics in Y, q_s, π_e^e. complete we calculate that:

$$\rho = \rho(\cdot) = \frac{pY - wL^d}{pK} = \frac{Y}{K}(1 - \omega/z)$$

$$\omega = w/p < z = Y/L^d = const$$

assuming a constant value for the labour productivity coefficient $z > w/p$.

Stability analysis

Given the multiplier formula, we get $Y^o = \frac{\overline{A}}{1-a_y}$ as the steady state value of the output and $\rho^o = \frac{Y^o}{K}(1 - \omega/z)$ as the rate of profit. The steady state value of q is then the solution of the equation:

$$\frac{q}{m+b+q} = f_e(\rho^o/q) \tag{2.34}$$

since capital gain expectations are zero in the steady state. The left hand side of this equation is upward sloping and ranging from 0 to ∞, while the right hand side is downward sloping with values between zero and one. There is therefore a unique intersection which defines the steady state value q^o that appears in the aggregate demand function Y^d. We assume that the parameters behind the asset demand functions are such that $r^o < \rho^o/q^o$ holds, i.e., the dividend rate of return is higher than the interest rate on savings deposits in the steady state.

Assuming that f_{e2} is chosen sufficiently small, we get the following sign distribution of the Jacobian matrix J at the steady state:

$$J = \begin{pmatrix} - & + & 0 \\ J_{21} & - & J_{23} \\ \beta_{\pi_e^e} J_{21} & - & \beta_{\pi_e^e}(J_{23} - 1) \end{pmatrix}$$

where J_{21}, J_{23} are positive and sufficiently small.

The structure of this Jacobian matrix is therefore dominated by

$$J = \begin{pmatrix} - & + & 0 \\ 0 & - & 0 \\ 0 & - & -\beta_{\pi_e^e} \end{pmatrix}$$

which obviously is a stable matrix according to the Routh–Hurwitz conditions.[9] This implies the following proposition:

Proposition 2: stable real-financial market interaction

Let us assume that the sensitivity parameter f_{e2} is chosen sufficiently small (at the steady state), i.e., the equity market is in a sufficiently tranquil state there. Then, the steady state of the considered 3D dynamical system is surrounded by damped oscillations (or even subject to monotonic convergence).

With respect to the abstract representation of the Jacobian J:

$$J = \begin{pmatrix} J_{11} & J_{12} & J_{13} \\ J_{21} & J_{22} & J_{23} \\ J_{31} & J_{32} & J_{33} \end{pmatrix}$$

one can in fact show that a value of $\beta_s > 0$ (chosen sufficiently small) that implies $J_{33} <$ also implies

$$|J_2| = \begin{vmatrix} J_{22} & J_{23} \\ J_{32} & J_{33} \end{vmatrix} > 0$$

while the minor J_1 of order 2 is always positive. The minor

$$|J_3| = \begin{vmatrix} J_{11} & J_{12} \\ J_{21} & J_{22} \end{vmatrix}$$

finally is positive if

$$\frac{\partial q(\rho(\cdot))}{\partial Y} = \frac{f_{e2}(\cdot)(m+b+q)\rho'/q}{N} < \frac{1-a_y}{a_q \rho'}$$

holds. Since $0 > |J| > J_3 J_{33}$, this implies the validity of the Routh–Hurwitz stability conditions.

Corollary 2: policy roads to stability

Assume that there is a Tobin tax τ_t levied on capital gains: $\tau_t \hat{p}_e$, implying that $\dot{\pi}_e^e = \beta_{\pi_e^e}(\tau_t \hat{q}_s - \pi_e^e)$ holds for the adjustment of capital gain expectations, so that $J_{33} < 0$. Let us assume moreover that raising such a tax gives rise to

$$\frac{f_{e2}(\cdot)(m+b+q)/q}{1 - f_e(\cdot) + f_{e2}(\cdot)(\rho/q)(m+b+q)/q} < \frac{1-a_y}{a_q}$$

as the stock market reaction to a changing rate of profit. Then, the steady state of the considered 3D dynamical system is surrounded by damped oscillations (or even subject to monotonic convergence).

The stability for the stock market can be improved if government expenditures are adjusted in a countercyclical way, i.e., if a fiscal policy reaction function of the type

$$A = \overline{A} - g_y(Y - Y^o) \tag{2.35}$$

is added to the model. By contrast, a Taylor rule of the type[10] $r = r_o + g_y(Y - Y^o)$ would be completely ineffective, since it would only alter the cash-management process of asset holders. Monetary policy, in order to be efficient, must influence the composition of $M_2 + p_e\overline{E}$, by appropriate open market operations in the stock market.

Outlook

In this chapter we have presented in a model of disequilibrium adjustment processes on the market for goods and for labour and a model of portfolio choices on the financial markets where imperfect substitution is interacting with imperfect capital gain expectations. In the next chapter, these two models will be integrated in a single framework illustrating the interaction of the wage–price spiral on the real markets with portfolio adjustments on the financial markets. Moreover the simple dynamic multiplier will be expanded towards a Metzlerian treatment of goods market adjustment and a Harrodian treatment of investment accelerator processes.

3
Tobinian Stock-Flow Interactions in the KMG Framework

Introduction

This chapter presents the 'KMG–Tobin' portfolio model and studies its (in)stability properties. This macrodynamic model is an 'old Keynesian' extension of the Keynes–Metzler–Goodwin (KMG) model of Chiarella and Flaschel (2000a) and its aim is to improve the financial side of the latter. In the KMG model, three asset markets are considered (equities, bonds and money) but they are depicted in a rudimentary way and have little influence on the real side of the model. The equities market is presented only in nominal terms and the mechanism through which the price of equities is determined is left in the background. This price does not play any role in the KMG model, due to the absence of wealth and capital gains income effects on aggregate demand. In the same way, asset-holding households are supposed to hold government bonds, but the feedback of their rate of change – determined by government budget constraint – is suppressed via a suitably chosen taxation rule such that there is no interest income effect on asset holders' consumption. The only financial market used to influence the real side of the economy is the money market (providing an LM curve theory of interest) through the negative effect of the interest rate on the rate of investment. However, this financial market does not explicitly interact with the two others since the demand for money is here simply providing a LM curve giving rise to a stable relationship between the nominal rate of interest, the output-capital ratio and supplied real balances per unit of capital.

The KMG–Tobin model presented here attempts to remedy such defaults by using the insights of James Tobin's 'old Keynesianism'. First, although wealth and interest income effects are still ignored, bond and equity stock dynamics now feed back into the real part of the economy through the introduction of Tobin's q into the function defining the investment behaviour of firms. Second, the three financial markets now interact with each other thanks to the introduction of Tobinian portfolio choices. From now on the demand for each asset varies positively with its own real rate of return and negatively with the rates of other assets. In particular the demand for bonds, and hence the interest rate on bonds,[1] are now influenced by variations in the price of equities.

In Tobin's portfolio choices theory the demand for each asset is defined in such a way that the total amount of assets that households want to hold is equal to their net wealth. This *stock constraint* attached to portfolio choices is one of the two pillars of Tobin's approach to macroeconomic modelling. The second pillar, or *flow constraint*, states that the net amount of assets accumulated (liabilities issued) by one sector must equal its net savings (expenditures). In the KMG–Tobin model the stock constraint concerns only capital holders, while the flow constraint has to be fulfilled for all the sectors of the considered economy (namely capital holders, workers, firms and the government).

Given the complexity of the KMG–Tobin model, which contains more than 50 equations in its extensive form, the best way to make sure that its accounting framework is consistent is to build the *social accounting matrix* (SAM) of the model. This type of accounting table, which was also used by Tobin in one of his models (Backus *et al.*, 1980, p.264), synthesizes all the flow constraints attached to a given model:

> There is only one fundamental law of economics: for every income there is a corresponding outlay of expenditure. The law is equivalent for economists of the physicists' law of energy conservation. It plays a similar role in defining the completeness of a model or analytical formulation: no theory or model can be correct unless it is complete in the sense that all incomes and outlays are fully accounted for. A social accounting matrix, or SAM, is a simple and efficient way of representing this fundamental law. (Pyatt, 1988, p.329)

To propose a model based on Tobinian portfolio choices and a SAM is not highly original. At least two types of models share the same features, namely *stock flow consistent* (SFC) and *financial computable general equilibrium* (FCGE) models. At the end of the chapter we will briefly present these two bodies of literature and compare them with our own research programme.

The outline of this chapter is as follows. The next section presents the SAM of the KMG–Tobin Model. We then develop the extensive form of the model and give a detailed explanation of its structure. The following section discusses the accounting consistency of the model and then move on to investigate the various feedback channels that the model exhibited in its real and its financial part and their interactions. Next, we perform some preliminary stability considerations. and the final section proposes a comparison of our model with other macroeconomic models based on Tobin's methodology.

The accounting framework

A social accounting matrix (SAM) represents the national accounting framework in a matrix form.[2] SAMs were developed by R. Stone in the early 1960s for the *Cambridge Growth Project*[3] and were originally used for building applied macroeconomic models. In a SAM, every transaction by one sector implies an equivalent transaction by another sector (every purchase implies a sale) and every entry on the balance sheet of one sector has a counterpart in another entry on the same balance sheet. With such a framework 'everything comes from somewhere and everything goes somewhere' so that 'there is no black hole'.[4]

Table 3.1 gives the SAM of our theoretical model or, to be more precise, its *transactions flow matrix*. A transactions flow matrix is a type of SAM which was first used by Tobin and his Yale colleagues (Backus *et al.*, 1980, p.264) and was later made popular by the work of Wynne Godley (1999). Its main advantage compared to a traditional SAM is to facilitate the representation of firms' inventories which play a great role in the KMG model.[5] In such a SAM, every row represents a monetary transaction, and every column corresponds to a sector account. The latter is divided into a current and a capital account, except for sectors which have no savings (in this case workers).[6] Sources of funds appear with plus signs and uses of funds are indicated by negative signs. The sum of every row must equate to zero as each transaction

Table 3.1 Transactions flow matrix of the KMG–Tobin model

Sector / Flows	Workers	Asset holders		Firms		Government		Σ
		Current	Capital	Current	Capital	Current	Capital	
Consumption	$-pC_w$	$-pC_c$		$+pC$				0
Government expenditures				$+pG$		$-pG$		0
Gross investment				$+pI + p\delta K$	$-pI - p\delta K$			0
Change in inventories				$+p\dot{N}$	$+p\dot{N}$			0
Wages	$+wL^d$			$-wL^d$				0
Taxes	$-\tau_w wL^d$	$-pT_c$				$+pT$		0
Interest on bonds		$+rB$				$-rB$		0
Firms' profits		$+\rho^e pK$		$-\Pi$	$+pS_f$			0
Asset holders' savings		$-pS_p$	$+pS_p$					0
Government savings						$-pS_g$	$+pS_g$	0
Δ money			$-\dot{M}^d$				$+\dot{M}$	0
Δ bonds			$-\dot{B}^d$				$+\dot{B}$	0
Δ equities			$-p_e\dot{E}^d$		$+p_e\dot{E}$			0
Depreciation of Capital				$-p\delta K$	$+p\delta K$			0
Σ	0	0	0	0	0	0	0	0

always simultaneously corresponds to a source and a use of funds. Equally, the sum of each column must be zero as each account (or sub-account) is balanced. Workers receive wage income from firms and spend all their income buying consumption goods pC_w and paying taxes $\tau_w wL^d$ so that they do not have savings. Assets holders receive dividends from firms $\rho^e pK$ and interest on government bonds rB. Like workers they buy consumption goods pC_c and pay taxes pT_c but they also have savings which are invested into bonds $\dot{B}^d$, money holdings $\dot{M}^d$ and equities $p_e\dot{E}^d$. Their purchases of equities help firms to finance their net investment in fixed capital[7] pI and the changes in the stock of inventories $p\dot{N}$. Firms' income is generated through households' consumption pC $(= pC_w + pC_c)$ and government's purchases of services pG. The real savings of firms pS_f, that are their retained profits, equate the difference between their gross profits Π and the dividends distributed to asset holders.

The KMG model considers three sectors; households (disaggregated into workers and capital holders), non-financial firms and the government (which includes the central bank). Workers receive wages wL^d, government experiences a budget deficit $-pS_g$ since the amount of taxes $pT\,(=\tau_w wL^d + pT_c)$ is smaller than the sum of its expenditures $(rB + pG)$. This deficit is financed through issues of money (by the open market operations the central bank) and bonds.

For the KMG portfolio model to be stock-flow consistent, it must integrate properly the accounting identities issued from its SAM. The transcription of Table 3.1 into equations gives thirteen accounting identities corresponding to the seven columns and the six non-tautological rows.[8] In other words, for the accounting of the KMG model to be right, we will have to integrate in its equations twelve of the thirteen accounting identities issued from the matrix. In this case, according to *Walras's law of flows*, the 'missing' thirteenth identity will always be verified. Of course, the matrix and its twelve associated accounting identities provide only the skeleton of the KMG–Tobin model. For this accounting framework to come to life as an economic model, we will also have to introduce behavioural equations explaining all the entries of the matrix not defined through accounting identities.

The extensive form of the model

In this section we provide the extensive or structural form of our growth model of KMG type, now exhibiting a portfolio equilibrium block in the place of the LM block. We split the model into appropriate modules corresponding to the various sectors of the economy (namely households, firms, and the government), the wage–price interaction and the asset markets.

Households

We disaggregate the households sector into workers and asset holders. We begin with the description of workers' behaviour:

Workers

$$\omega = w/p \tag{3.1}$$

$$C_w = (1 - \tau_w)\omega L^d \tag{3.2}$$
$$S_w = 0 \tag{3.3}$$
$$\hat{L} = n = \text{const.} \tag{3.4}$$

Equation (3.1) gives the definition of the real wage ω before taxation, where w denotes the nominal wage and p the actual price level. We operate in a Keynesian framework with sluggish wage and price adjustment processes, hence we take the real wage to be given exogenously at each moment in time. Furthermore we follow the Keynesian framework by assuming that the labour demand of firms can always be satisfied out of the given labour supply.[9] Then, according to (3.2), real income of workers equals the product of real wages times labour demand, which net of taxes $\tau_w \omega L^d$, equals workers' consumption, since we do not allow for savings of the workers as postulated in (3.3).[10] The absence of savings means that the wealth of workers remains nil at every point in time. In other words, workers do not hold any money and they consume instantaneously their disposable income.[11] As usual in theories of economic growth, we finally assume in equation (3.4) a constant growth rate n of the labour force L based on the assumption that labour is supplied inelastically at each moment in time. The parameter n can be easily reinterpreted as the growth rate of the working population plus the growth rate of labour augmenting technical progress.

The modelling of asset holders' income, consumption and wealth is described by the following set of equations:

Asset holders

$$\rho^e = (Y^e - \delta K - \omega L^d)/K \tag{3.5}$$
$$C_c = (1 - s_c)[\rho^e K + rB/p - T_c], \quad 0 < s_c < 1 \tag{3.6}$$
$$C = C_w + C_c \tag{3.7}$$
$$S_p = s_c[\rho^e K + rB/p - T_c] \tag{3.8}$$
$$= (\dot{M} + \dot{B} + p_e \dot{E})/p \tag{3.9}$$
$$W_c = (M + B + p_e E)/p, \quad W_c^n = pW_c \tag{3.10}$$

The first equation of this module defines the expected rate of return on real capital ρ^e as the ratio of the currently expected real cash flow to the real stock of business fixed capital K. The expected cash flow is given by expected real revenues from sales Y^e diminished by the real depreciation of capital δK and the real wage sum ωL^d.

We assume that firms pay out all expected cash flow in form of dividends to the asset holders. These dividend payments are the first source of income for asset holders. A second source of income is given by real interest payments on short term bonds (rB/p), where r is the nominal interest rate and B the stock of such bonds. Summing up these sources of income, and taking account of lump sum taxes T_c in the case of asset holders, we get the disposable income of asset holders within the square brackets of equation (3.6). taken together with a postulated fixed propensity to consume $(1 - s_c)$ out of this income, this gives us the real consumption of asset holders. Equation (3.7) states that total consumption is given by the sum of expenditures of both classes of households.

The real savings of pure asset owners are their real disposable income minus their consumption, as exposed in equation (3.8). They can allocate it in form of money $\dot{M}$, or buy other financial assets, namely short-term bonds $\dot{B}$ or equities $\dot{E}$ at the price p_e, the only financial instruments that we allow for in the present reformulation of the KMG growth model. Hence, savings of asset holders must be distributed to these assets as stated in equation (3.9). Real wealth of pure asset holders is defined on this basis in equation (3.10) as the sum of the real cash balance, real short-term bond holdings and real equity holdings of asset holders. Short-term bonds are assumed to be fixed price bonds with a price of one, $p_b = 1$, and a flexible interest rate r.

We describe the demand equations in financial assets of asset owners along the lines Tobin's (1969) general equilibrium approach:

$$M^d = f_m(r, r_e^e)W_c^n \tag{3.11}$$

$$B^d = f_b(r, r_e^e)W_c^n \tag{3.12}$$

$$p_e E^d = f_e(r, r_e^e)W_c^n \tag{3.13}$$

$$W_c^n = M^d + B^d + p_e E^d \tag{3.14}$$

The demand for money balances of asset holders M^d is determined by a function $f_m(r, r_e^e)$ that depends on the interest rate on short-run bonds r and the expected rate of return on equities r_e^e. The product of this function and the nominal wealth W^n gives the nominal demand for money M^d (i.e., f_m describes the portion of nominal wealth that is allocated to pure money holdings). This formulation of money demand is not based on a transaction motive, since the holding of transaction balances is limited to firms.

By using this block of equations we assume that financial assets are imperfect substitutes. What is the motive for asset holders to hold a fraction of their wealth in the form of money, when there is a riskless interest bearing asset? It seems reasonable to refer to a speculative motive: asset holders want to hold money in order to *be able* to buy other assets or goods with zero or very low transaction costs. This of course assumes that there are (implicitly given) transaction costs when fixed price bonds are turned into money.

The nominal demand for bonds is determined by $f_b(r, r_e^e)$ and the nominal demand for equities by $f_e(r, r_e^e)$, which describe the fractions allocated to these forms of financial wealth. From equation (3.10) we know that the actual nominal wealth equals the stocks of financial assets held by asset holders. We assume, as usual in portfolio approaches, that the asset holders do demand assets of an amount that equals their nominal wealth, as stated in equation (3.10). In other words, they simply reallocate their wealth in view of new information on the rates of returns on their assets.

We now come to the expected rate of return on equities r_e^e which consists of real dividends per equity $(\rho^e pK/p_e E)$, and expected capital gains, π_e, the latter being the expected growth rate of equity prices:

$$r_e^e = \frac{\rho^e pK}{p_e E} + \pi_e \tag{3.15}$$

We assume that there are two types of asset holders which differ with respect to their expectation formation of equity prices π_e. There are *chartists* who in principle employ an adaptive expectations mechanism:

$$\dot{\pi}_{ec} = \beta_{\pi_{ec}}(\hat{p}_e - \pi_{ec}) \tag{3.16}$$

where $\beta_{\pi_{ec}}$ is the adjustment speed towards the actual growth rate of equity prices. The other type of asset holders, *fundamentalists*, employs a forward looking expectation formation mechanism:

$$\dot{\pi}_{ef} = \beta_{\pi_{ef}}(\bar{\eta} - \pi_{ef}) \tag{3.17}$$

where $\overline{\eta}$ is the fundamentalists' expected long run inflation rate of share prices. Assuming that the aggregate expected inflation rate is a weighted average of the two expected inflation rates, where the weights are determined according to the sizes of the groups, we postulate:

$$\pi_e = \alpha_{\pi_{ec}}\pi_{ec} + (1 - \alpha_{\pi_{ec}})\pi_{ef} \tag{3.18}$$

Here $\alpha_{\pi_{ec}} \in (0, 1)$ is the ratio of chartists to all asset holders.

Firms

We consider the behaviour of firms by means of two submodules. The first one describes the production framework and firms' investment in business fixed capital. The second one introduces the Metzlerian approach of inventory cycles with regards to expected sales, actual sales and the output of firms.

Firms: production and investment

$$\rho^e = (pY^e - wL^d - p\delta K)/(pK) \tag{3.19}$$

$$Y^p = \overline{y}^p K \tag{3.20}$$

$$u = Y/Y^p \tag{3.21}$$

$$L^d = Y/\overline{x} \tag{3.22}$$

$$e = L^d/L = Y/(xL) \tag{3.23}$$

$$q = p_e E/(pK) \tag{3.24}$$

$$I = i_1(q-1)K + i_2(u - \overline{u})K + nK \tag{3.25}$$

$$\hat{K} = I/K \tag{3.26}$$

$$p_e\dot{E} = pI + p(\dot{N} - IN) \tag{3.27}$$

Firms are assumed to pay out dividends according to expected profits (expected sales net of depreciation and minus the wage sum), see the above module of the asset-owning households. The rate of expected profits ρ^e is expected real profits per unit of capital as stated in equation (3.19). For producing output firms utilize a production technology that transforms demanded labour L^d combined with business fixed capital K into output. For convenience we assume that the production takes place by a fixed proportion technology.[12] According to (3.20) potential output Y^p is therefore given in each moment of time by the fixed coefficient $\bar{y}^p$ times the existing stock of physical capital. Accordingly, the utilization of productive capacities is given by the ratio u of actual production Y and the potential output Y^p. The fixed proportions in production also give rise to constant output-labour coefficient $\bar{x}$, by means of which we can deduce labour demand from goods market determined output as in equation (3.22). The ratio L^d/L thus defines the rate of employment of the model.

The economic behaviour of firms also comprises the investment decision into business fixed capital, which is determined independently from households savings decision. We here model investment decisions per unit of capital as a function of the deviation of Tobin's q, see Tobin (1969), from its long run value *1*, and the deviation of actual capacity utilization from a normal rate of capital utilization, and add an exogenously given trend term, here given by the natural growth rate n in order to allow this rate to determine the growth path of the economy in the usual way. We employ here Tobin's average q which is defined in equation (3.24). It is the ratio of the nominal value of equities and the reproduction costs for the existing stock of capital. Investment in business fixed capital is enforced when q exceeds one, and is reduced when q is smaller then one. This influence is represented by the term $i_1(q-1)$ in equation (3.25). The term $i_2(u-\bar{u})$ models the component of investment which is due to the deviation of utilization rate of physical capital from its non-accelerating inflation value $\bar{u}$. The last component, nK, takes account for the natural growth rate n which is necessary for steady state analysis if natural growth is considered as exogenously given. Equation (3.27) is the budget constraint of the firms. Investment in business fixed capital and unintended changes in the inventory stock $p(\dot{N}-IN)$ must be financed by issuing equities, since equities are the only financial instrument of firms in this paper. Capital stock growth finally is given by net investment per unit of capital I/K in this demand determined modelling of the short-run equilibrium position of the economy.

Next we model the inventory dynamics in the model following Metzler (1941) and Franke (1996). This approach is a very useful concept for describing the goods market disequilibrium dynamics with all of its implications:

Firms' output adjustment

$$
\begin{aligned}
N^d &= \beta_{n^d} Y^e && (3.28)\\
IN &= nN^d + \beta_n(N^d - N) && (3.29)\\
Y &= Y^e + IN && (3.30)\\
Y^d &= C + I + \delta K + G && (3.31)\\
\dot{Y}^e &= nY^e + \beta_{y^e}(Y^d - Y^e) && (3.32)\\
\dot{N} &= Y - Y^d && (3.33)\\
\Pi &= pY^d + p\dot{N} - w.L^d && (3.34)\\
S_f &= \Pi/p - \rho^e K = Y - Y^e = IN && (3.35)
\end{aligned}
$$

where $\beta_{n^d}, \beta_n, \beta_{y^e} \geq 0$.

As stated in equation (3.28), the desired stock of physical inventories is denoted by N^d and is assumed to be a fixed proportion of the expected sales. The planned investments IN in inventories follow a sluggish adjustment process towards the desired stock N^d according to equation (3.29). Taking account of this additional demand for goods we write the production Y to be set equal to the expected sales of firms plus IN in equation (3.30). For explaining the expectation formation for good demand, we need the actual total demand for goods which is given by consumption (of private households and the government) and gross investment by firms (3.31). By knowing the actual demand Y^d, which is always served, the dynamics of expected sales is given in equation (3.32). It models these expectations to be the outcome of an error correction process, that incorporates also the natural growth rate n in order take account of the fact that this process operates in a growing economy. The adjustment of sales expectations is driven by the prediction error $(Y^d - Y^e)$, with an adjustment speed that is given by β_{y^e}. Actual changes in the stock of inventories are given by the deviation of production from goods demanded (3.33). Equation (3.34) states that gross accounting profits of firms Π are equal to the value of sales pY^d, less wages wL^d plus the change in the stock of inventories $p\dot{N}$. The real savings of firms, that is their real retained profits, are equal to the difference between their real gross profits Π/p and the real dividends distributed to asset holders $\rho^e K$. Plugging in the definitions of $\Pi, \dot{N}$ and ρ^e (as they appear in equations (3.19), (3.33), and (3.34)), we compute that $S_f = Y - Y^e$ or equivalently that $S_f = IN$ as stated in equation (3.35).

The government sector

The role of the government in this chapter is to provide the economy with public (unproductive) services within the limits of its budget constraint. Public purchases (and interest payments) are financed through taxes, through newly printed money, or newly issued fixed-price bonds ($p_b = 1$). The budget constraint gives rise to some repercussion effects between the public and the private sector:

$$T = \tau_w \omega L^d + T_c \tag{3.36}$$

$$T_c = \bar{t}_c^n K + rB/p, \qquad \bar{t}_c^n = \text{const.} \tag{3.37}$$

$$G = \bar{g}K, \qquad \bar{g} = \text{const.} \tag{3.38}$$

$$S_g = T - rB/p - G \tag{3.39}$$

$$\hat{M} = \bar{\mu} \tag{3.40}$$

$$\dot{B} = pG + rB - pT - \dot{M} \tag{3.41}$$

The tax income consists of taxes on wage income and lump sum taxes on capital income T_c. The latter assumption makes aggregate demand independent of the interest payments of the government, which simplifies steady state calculations significantly.[13]

As in Sargent (1987), we assume that the government provides services as a fixed proportion $\bar{g}$ of real capital, which enables it to represent fiscal policy by means of simple parameters in the intensive form of the model.

Real savings of the government, that are a deficit when negative, are defined in equation (3.39) by real taxes diminished of real interest payments and real public services. Once again, the growth rate of money is given by a constant $\bar{\mu}$.

Equation (3.40) is the monetary policy rule of the central bank. Money is assumed to enter the economy via open market operations of the central bank, which buys short-term bonds from the asset holders when issuing new money. Changes in the short-term bonds supplied by the government are given as a residue in equation (3.41), that is the budget constraint of the government.

Wage–price dynamics

We now turn to the last module of our model which provides the wage–price spiral picking up the Rose (1967) approach of two short-run Phillips curves, (i) the wage Phillips curve and (ii) the price Phillips curve:

$$\hat{w} = \beta_w(e - \overline{e}) + \kappa_w\hat{p} + (1 - \kappa_w)\pi \tag{3.42}$$

$$\hat{p} = \beta_p(u - \overline{u}) + \kappa_p\hat{w} + (1 - \kappa_p)\pi \tag{3.43}$$

$$\dot{\pi} = \beta_\pi(\alpha\hat{p} + (1 - \alpha)(\overline{\mu} - n) - \pi) \tag{3.44}$$

where $\beta_w, \beta_p, \beta_\pi \geq 0$, $0 \leq \alpha \leq 1$, and $0 \leq \kappa_w, \kappa_p \leq 1$. This approach makes use of the assumption that relative changes in money wages are influenced by demand pressure in the market for labour and price inflation (cost-pressure) terms and that price inflation in turn depends on demand pressure in the market for goods and on money wage (cost-pressure) terms.

In equation (3.42) wage inflation depends on a demand pull term $\beta_w(e - \overline{e})$, that is on the gap between actual employment e and its NAIRU value $\overline{e}$. It also depends on a cost push element that is the weighted average of short-run (perfectly anticipated) price inflation $\hat{p}$ and medium run expected overall inflation π, with weights given by κ_w and $1 - \kappa_w$.

The price Phillips curve is quite similar. The demand pull term is given by the gap between capital utilization and its NAIRU value, $(u - \overline{u})$, and the cost push element is the weighted average of short-run wage inflation $\hat{w}$ and expected medium run overall inflation π.

We postulate in equation (3.44) that changes in expected medium-run inflation π are due to an adjustment process towards a weighted average of the current inflation rate and the steady state inflation. By doing so we introduce a simple kind of forward-looking expectation into the economy that is driven by the adjustment velocity β_π.

Although the model is a broad description of macroeconomic dynamics, it is dependent on specific assumptions, in particular with respect to financial markets and the government sector. The latter are however the ones usually used when one wants to provide a complete description of a closed monetary economy with labour, goods markets and three markets for financial assets.[14]

Capital markets

We have not discussed yet the determination of the nominal rate of interest r and the price of equities p_e and thus we still have to explain how capital markets are organized. Following Tobin's (1969) portfolio approach, we postulate that the following equilibrium conditions always hold and thus determine the prices of bonds and equities as endogenous variables of the model. Let us note that all asset supplies are of given magnitudes at each moment in time and that r_e^e is given by $\frac{\rho^e pK}{p_e E} + \pi_e$ so that it varies only with variations in the share price p_e:

$$M = M^d = f_m(r, r_e^e)W_c^n \tag{3.45m}$$

$$B = B^d = f_b(r, r_e^e)W_c^n \tag{3.45}$$

$$p_e E = p_e E^d = f_e(r, r_e^e)W_c^n \tag{3.46}$$

In our model, the prices (or interest rates) of the financial assets are determined on the secondary markets, that are cleared at all moments in time. This implies that newly issued assets do not have a (significant) effect on these prices.

Trade between asset holders induces a process that makes asset prices fall or rise in order to equilibrate demands and supplies. In the short run (in continuous time) the structure of wealth of asset holders, W_c^n is given, disregarding of changes in the share price p_e. This implies that the functions $f_m(\cdot)$, $f_b(\cdot)$, and $f_e(\cdot)$, introduced in equations (3.11) to (3.13) must satisfy the following well known conditions:

$$f_m(r, r_e^e) + f_b(r, r_e^e) + f_e(r, r_e^e) = 1 \tag{3.47}$$

$$\frac{\partial f_m(r, r_e^e)}{\partial i} + \frac{\partial f_b(r, r_e^e)}{\partial i} + \frac{\partial f_e(r, r_e^e)}{\partial i} = 0, \quad \forall\, i \in \{r, r_e^e\} \tag{3.48}$$

These conditions guarantee that the number of independent equations is equal to the number of statically endogenous variables (r, p_e) that the asset markets are assumed to determine at each moment in time.

We postulate that the financial assets display the gross substitution property, which means that the demand for all other assets increase whenever the price of another asset rises. For a formal definition see for example Mas-Colell, Whinston, and Green (1995, p. 611).

$$\frac{\partial f_b(r, r_e^e)}{\partial r} > 0, \quad \frac{\partial f_m(r, r_e^e)}{\partial r} < 0, \quad \frac{\partial f_e(r, r_e^e)}{\partial r} < 0 \tag{3.49}$$

$$\frac{\partial f_e(r, r_e^e)}{\partial r_e^e} > 0, \quad \frac{\partial f_m(r, r_e^e)}{\partial r_e^e} < 0, \quad \frac{\partial f_b(r, r_e^e)}{\partial r_e^e} < 0 \tag{3.50}$$

Stock-flow consistency

With equations (3.45m) to (3.46) we have considered three asset market equilibrium conditions. If the KMG model is consistent, one of them is thereby redundant. Indeed *Walras's law of stocks* states that if two of these markets clear, so does the last one. Here one can consider, as usual in macroeconomic models, that the equilibrium on the money market is the one which is determined by the other two equilibria. When the model is solved equation (3.45m) must therefore be left aside in order to avoid the model being overdetermined.

An important feature of Tobin's approach to financial markets is that the two remaining equations should be understood as defining the value of the interest rate r and of the price of equities p_e. The values of r and p_e are defined through equations (3.45) and (3.46) so that the two corresponding markets (and also the money market) are cleared at all moments in time.

This means that, from a mathematical point of view, if we want our model to have as many equations as unknowns, we still have to introduce equations which define asset holders flow demands for financial assets $\dot{M}^d$, $\dot{B}^d$ and $p_e\dot{E}^d$.[15] Indeed, since r and p_e are the explained (endogenous) variables in equations (3.45) and (3.46), these flow demands are left unexplained. In order to define these variables, and thus to achieve a complete model, one can note that a consequence of market-price clearing at all moments in time is that flow demand must adjust to flow supply for every types of financial assets:

$$\dot{M}^d = \dot{M} \tag{3.51}$$

$$\dot{B}^d = \dot{B} \tag{3.52}$$

$$p_e\dot{E}^d = p_e\dot{E} \tag{3.53}$$

Once again, due to *Walras' law of flows*, one of these three equations should be left aside. Indeed, as shown in the margins of Table 3.2, all of the 13 accounting identities issued from the transactions flow matrix appear among the equations of the KMG model presented in the previous section. Therefore our model is overdetermined and one of these equations is redundant. One can consider that this redundant equation is the equation (3.52m) relative to the (flow) equilibrium condition on the market of equities.

Table 3.2 Transactions flow matrix and corresponding equations

Sector / Flows	Workers	Asset holders		Firms		Government		Σ	
		Current	Capital	Current	Capital	Current	Capital		
Consumption	$-pC_w$	$-pC_c$		$+pC$				0	(3.7)
Government expenditures				$+pG$		$-pG$		0	
Gross investment				$+pI + p\delta K$	$-pI - p\delta K$			0	
Change in inventories				$+p\dot{N}$	$-p\dot{N}$			0	
Wages	$+wL^d$			$-wL^d$				0	
Taxes	$-\tau_w wL^d$	$-pT_c$				$+pT$		0	(3.36)
Interest on bonds		$+rB$				$-rB$		0	
Firms' profits		$+\rho^e pK$		$-\Pi$	$+pS_f$			0	(3.35)
Asset holders' savings		$-pS_p$	$+pS_p$					0	
Government savings						$-pS_g$	$+pS_g$	0	
Δ money			$-\dot{M}^d$				$+\dot{M}$	0	(3.51)
Δ bonds			$-\dot{B}^d$				$+\dot{B}$	0	(3.52)
Δ equities			$-p_e\dot{E}^d$		$+p_e\dot{E}$			0	(3.52m)
Depreciation of Capital				$-p\delta K$	$+p\delta K$			0	
Σ	0	0	0	0	0	0	0	0	
	(3.2)	(3.6)	(3.9)	(3.34)	(3.27)	(3.39)	(3.41)		

Proposition 1

The equation (3.52m) is implied by the first 52 equations of the KMG model taken together, meaning that every new issued amount of equities of firms will be met by the demand for equities by the asset holders.

Proof

To prove this proposition we refer to the definitions of nominal savings of the three considered sectors, as they appeared in equations (3.9), (3.41) and (3.35):

$$pS_p \equiv \dot{M}^d + \dot{B}^d + p_e\dot{E}^d \tag{3.54}$$

$$pS_g \equiv -\dot{M} - \dot{B} \tag{3.55}$$

$$pS_f \equiv pIN \tag{3.56}$$

Let us assume that the issue of new bonds and money of the government are absorbed by the asset holders so that equations (3.51) and (3.52) both hold. By definition we know that ex-post investments equal savings. Investment is given by the investment into business fixed capital plus actual inventory investment. Savings are the sum of the savings of all sectors:

$$
\begin{aligned}
& pI + p\dot{N} = pS_p + pS_g + pS_f \\
\Leftrightarrow\ & pI + p\dot{N} = \dot{M}^d + \dot{B}^d + p_e\dot{E}^d - \dot{M} - \dot{B} - pIN \\
\Leftrightarrow\ & pI + p\dot{N} = p_e\dot{E}^d + pIN \\
\Leftrightarrow\ & pI + p(\dot{N} - IN) = p_e\dot{E}^d
\end{aligned}
$$

From equation (3.27) we conclude that equation (3.52m) holds, which means that the demand for new equities equals its supply $p_e\dot{E} = p_e\dot{E}^d$. Therefore, the KMG model fulfils the accounting consistency requirements imposed by Tobin's general equilibrium methodology.

The feedback channels of the model

As the model is formulated it exhibits three fundamental feedback chains that interact with each.

On the real part of the model there are Harrodian and Metzlerian quantity adjustment processes on the market for goods. There is also a Goodwin–Rose type wage–price spiral, augmented by an expression of the inflationary climate. They both interact with income-driven quantity adjustment processes (and capital accumulation) on the market for labour and for goods.

Within the financial markets, there is a positive feedback loop between capital gains on equities and capital gains expectations (that is fed by the goods markets through the dividend rate of return obtained by firms) which, in turn, influences goods markets via the investment behaviour of firms and Tobin's q.

In addition, the model uses an LM theory of the short-term rate of interest (or can alternatively be based on an interest rate policy rule) and a stable dynamic multiplier process, whose results are linked to the labour market through a Leontief-type production function. Figure 3.1 summarizes these aspects of our KMGT dynamics.

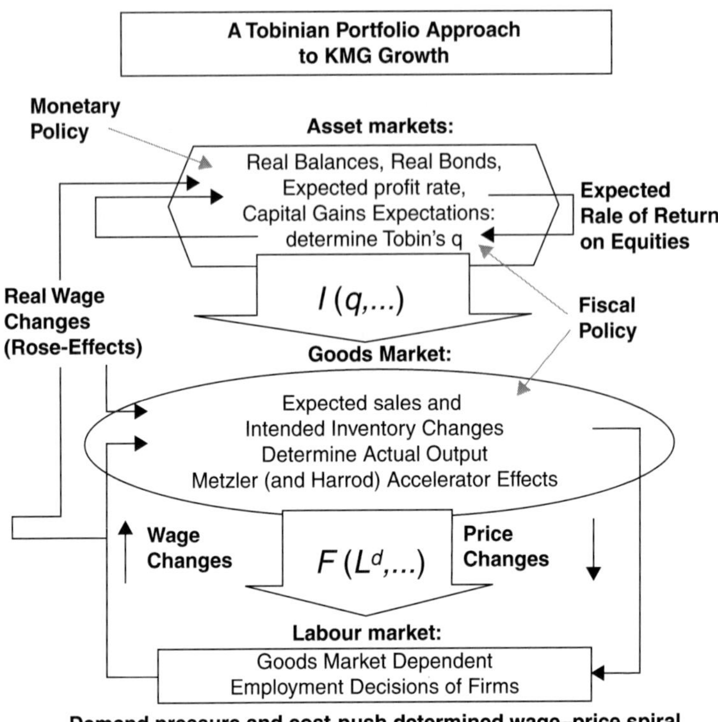

Figure 3.1 The market hierarchy and the repercussions of the model

A Harrodian multiplier-accelerator mechanism is obtained in this model. Investment depends positively on the rate of capacity utilization of firms and can lead to increases in goods demand and firms' sales expectations. This can generate output increases and thus further increases in the capacity utilization rate, if the impact of this rate on investment is sufficiently strong. This mechanism operates at business cycle frequency, while the Metzlerian sales expectations-inventory dynamics may operate at a higher frequency (and is perhaps not as an important accelerating quantity adjustment process as the Harrodian one).

The Metzlerian quantity adjustment process is as follows: increased sales expectations lead to increases in planned inventories and to increased inventory adjustment, increased output and income. This feeds aggregate demand and increases sales expectations further which may lead to an unstable adjustment process if the inventory adjustment process is sufficiently fast. As already stated, we do not expect this process to interfere with the normal behaviour of the economy.

The described positive quantity feedback chains are of a simple nature as compared to the wage–price spiral of the model and can be tamed by a counter-cyclical fiscal policy, as shown in the next chapter. The wage–price dynamics by contrast is multifaceted, since the thereby implied law of motion for the real wage can depend positively or negatively on economic activity, cases labelled respectively labour-market-led and goods-market-led from now on. In the labour-market-led case money wages respond stronger than the price level to changes in economic activity while this is the opposite in the goods-market-led case. In addition to this distinction, aggregate demand can depend positively or negatively on the real wage, giving rise to the distinction wage-led versus profit-led, respectively. In a wage-led economy consumption is reacting stronger (positively) than investment (negatively) to real wage increases so that consumption determines the direction of change when the real wage is increasing. In a profit-led economy the opposite occurs.

In sum this allows for four cases; two stabilizing ones, given by the combinations, (1) profit-led and labour-market-led, and (2) wage-led and goods-market-led; and two accelerating ones, that are given by the combinations, (3) profit-led and goods-market led, and (4) wage-led and labour-market-led.

Feedback chain (1) is stabilizing since increases in real wages are limited by decreases in aggregate demand (since they provide a profit squeeze). In the same way, chain (2) is stabilizing, since increases in real wages do stimulate aggregate demand. This is accompanied by stronger price than money wage reaction which provides a limit to the initially rising real wages.

Of course, everything said so far also holds for recession in place of booms though the mechanism may then not be as strong due to downward rigidities (to be introduced in the next section). From an empirical point of view, one may in addition expect scenario (1) to be more relevant than scenario (2), since it is commonly argued that real wages move pro-cyclically with economic activity, i.e. are labour-market-led.[16] Situation (2) where positive (negative) real wage shocks are limited by subsequently higher price than wage inflation (deflation) is not what one would expect to happen in OECD countries.

A similar statement may apply to scenario (3) where a profit-led improvement of the economy leads to real wage decreases and further increases in profits, and thus to partial instability, possibly tamed by other feedback chains and thus not visible in isolation. Yet we have already argued that – if at all – real wages should move pro-cyclically (maybe somewhat concealed through a quarter phase displacement if the growth rate of real wages is what is moving pro-cyclically). In a goods-market-led economy real wages – or their growth rate – should fall when economic activity is increasing which is the opposite of what is described in the literature.

Scenario 4 finally considers again a pro-cyclical behaviour of real wages (or their rate of growth), but couples it with an aggregate goods demand schedule which is positively sloped with respect to real wages. Rising real wages therefore stimulate the economy and lead to further increases in real wages since wage inflation exceeds price inflation. In our view this scenario could describe what happened before the occurrence of stagflation in the 1970s. There was an accelerating wage–price spiral which was counteracted for example by President Nixon in the USA by way of a wage–price freeze and by restrictive monetary policy. Thus, due to its accelerating nature, scenario (4), is only a temporary one while scenario (1) characterized not only most of the business cycles in the US economy after the Second World War, but also the long wave that led from prosperity to stagnant economic activity during this period.[17]

Figure 3.2 portrays two of the four scenarios we discussed above for the case of a depressed economy and indicates by two arrows the variables which are reacting stronger to changes in economic activity and to changes in the real wage in comparison to its counterpart in aggregate demand or wage/price adjustment.

From a purely theoretical perspective one has, however, to cope with the fact that the wage–price spiral can have four faces and may therefore be much more difficult to control than the quantity adjustment processes on the real side of the economy. Moreover its working in the boom may be different in magnitude from its working in the bust (due to changes in adjustment speeds). Meade (1982) wrote a whole book on wage fixing or wage management policies (in addition

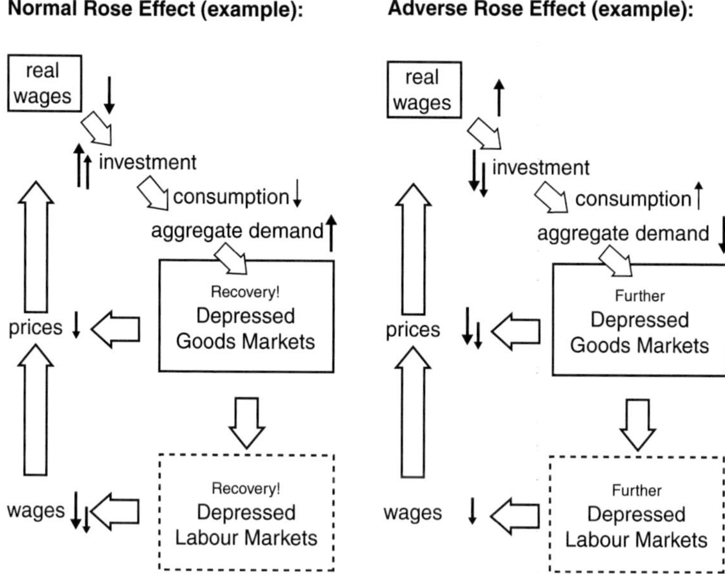

Figure 3.2 Real wage feedback chains 1 and 3 for a depressed economy

to demand management policies), a topic that is however very much neglected in the academic literature. We will show in the next chapter that a wage inflation policy that is oriented towards an inflationary compensation, and close to reaching it, is one step towards a control of the wage–price spiral (since it removes the role of demand pressure on the labour market), the other step being a fiscal and monetary policy that controls demand pressure in the market for goods.

Turning now to the financial markets, i.e. the stock market, we have a simple positive feedback loop between capital gains and capital gain expectations, as far as chartist behaviour is concerned and if all other influences on this spiral are considered as fixed. This feedback loop drives share prices in an accelerating way until some outside element stops this process or reverses it in the opposite direction. As we have seen in preceding sections, the law of motion of share prices is difficult to handle. It is influenced by the expected rate of return on real capital since this rate is here assumed to equal the dividend rate of return component in the rate of return on equities. Our simple adaptive modelling of chartists' capital gain expectations is only one example for such a process which – though only backward looking – can be technically refined in many ways.

Accelerating stock price dynamic implies an accelerating motion for Tobin's q which thus exercises rectified influence on investment behaviour and thus on the business cycle, since q acts as some measure of the state of confidence. The stock market may therefore destabilize the real markets in addition to their own feedback channels and should therefore be made less volatile. We shall see in the next section that a Tobin tax on the capital gains in the stock market may be an appropriate tool to make these markets more tranquil and less short-sighted.

Summing up, the tools for tranquilizing the wage–price spiral in its unstable configurations might seem difficult to design in detail. However, we will see in the next chapter, that it is relatively simple to make the balanced growth path of the economy become an attractor through a well-designed anti-cyclical fiscal policy, a monetary policy oriented towards a stabilization of Tobin's q, or a Tobin tax on capital gains in the equity market.[18]

Unleashed capitalism

We will show in the next chapter that the steady state of the KMGT system loses its stability by way of a Hopf bifurcation, i.e., in a cyclical fashion. Such Hopf bifurcations in particular occur when the stabilizing parameters that we assume in the next chapter to be sufficiently small are made sufficiently large. The instability proof essentially rests on the fact that the determinant of the Jacobian matrix at the steady state of the considered dynamic system is always negative, so that eigenvalues have to cross the imaginary axis (excluding zero) when stability gets lost. With respect to the actual loss of stability one has to study the principal minors of the Jacobian of the dynamics at the steady state, or alternatively to use numerical methods (such as eigenvalue diagrams; see Figure 3.3). From such tools one then gets the result that significant flexibilities in the wage–price spiral or in the financial markets (including high money demand elasticities) will indeed lead to loss of stability by way of persistent or explosive business fluctuations (see also Asada *et al.*, 2010a).

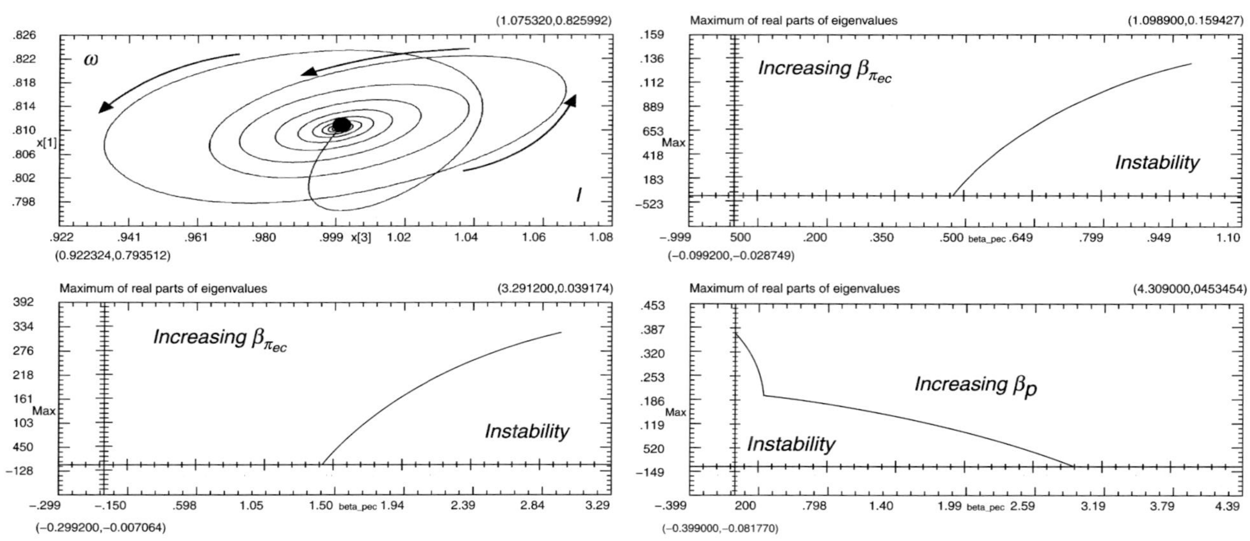

Figure 3.3 Damped oscillations (top left) and the loss of local stability via Hopf bifurcations with respect to β_{π^c}, $\beta_{\pi_{ec}}$ and β_p

As numerical simulations have shown, the range for which such local Hopf-bifurcation matters is much narrowed. This requires the need for global changes (regime switches) in behaviour if the economy is locally explosive and departs too much from its steady state. There is indeed at least one important example for such a behavioural switch that in many situations (as far as the real markets are concerned) is sufficient to restrict the trajectories of the dynamics to an economically meaningful domain of their whole phase space. This non-linearity relates to the fact, already observed by Keynes (1936), that money wages may be flexible in an upward direction, but are rigid (or at least considerably less flexible) in the downward direction.

Let us assert without proof that the normal or adverse Rose effect of changing real wages leads to changing aggregate demand and thereby to further changes in money wages, the price level and the real wage.[19] Either wage or price flexibility will, through their effects on the expected rate of profit and from there on asset markets, be destabilizing and lead to Hopf bifurcations, limit cycles or eventually purely (locally) explosive behaviour. The Mundell or real rate of interest effect is not so obviously present in the considered dynamics as there is no longer a real rate of interest involved in investment (or consumption) behaviour. Increasing expected price inflation does neither directly increase aggregate demand nor economic activity and thus the actual rate of price inflation. This surely implies that the model needs to be extended in order to take account of the role that is generally played by the real rate of interest in macrodynamic models. There are finally two accelerator effects involved in the dynamics, the Metzlerian inventory accelerator mechanism and the Harrodian fixed business investment accelerator. We expect that increasing the parameters β_n and i_u will also be destabilizing and also lead to Hopf bifurcations and other complex dynamic behaviour.

We finally provide two numerical examples that illustrate damped oscillations, a loss of stability via Hopf bifurcation, the generation of limit cycles as business fluctuations from a global perspective by the addition of downward money wage rigidity to the money wage Phillips curve, and finally – through this kinked wage Phillips curve – the generation of complex dynamics if increases in certain adjustment speeds make the steady state strongly repelling.[20]

The simulations in the top-left of Figure 3.3 show damped oscillations when the parameter choices of our stability propositions are applied. The other three figures show eigenvalue diagrams that plot the maximum real part of eigenvalues against crucial parameters of the dynamical system under consideration namely β_{π^c}, $\beta_{\pi_{ec}}$ and β_p. These show the expected results that increasing speeds of adjustments in the movements of the inflationary climate and the capital gain expectations of chartists will be destabilizing, while price flexibility is stabilizing (and correspondingly: wage flexibility is destabilizing).

In Figure 3.4 we show an example of a period (cycle) doubling route to complex dynamics (but not chaos) from the economic point of view, since the cycles that are generated are fairly similar to each other. We increase the speed of adjustment of money wages from $\beta_w = 1.4$ to $\beta_w = 2.0$ and from there to $\beta_w = 2.82$ and then to $\beta_w = 3.0$. The first thing to note is that the dynamics remain viable over such a broad range of adjustment speeds for money wages, due to the kink in the money wage Phillips curve and despite a strong local instability around the steady state described above. To the right of the shown attractors the trajectories are of a fairly smooth type, yet in the top left they are going through some turbulence which makes the attractor more and more complex with the increasing adjustment speed of money wages.

We do not go into the details of such simulations any further here, but only present them as evidence that the considered model type is capable of producing various dynamic outcomes and is thus a very open one with respect to possible business cycle implications (and thus needs empirical estimation of its parameter values in order to get more specific results).

Related literature

The KMG–Tobin model presented in this chapter is characterized by (a) an old Keynesian way of depicting financial markets and (b) a consistent accounting framework which features in a transactions flow matrix. As such our model can be viewed as the heir of the 'general equilibrium' models developed by Tobin (1969) at Yale. More generally the KMG research programme is related to the tradition of accounting-based macroeconomic models issued from the work of R. Stone at the *Department of Applied Economics* (DAE) of the University of Cambridge. As already mentioned, Tobin's transactions flow matrix is simply a variation of the original SAM developed by Stone in the early

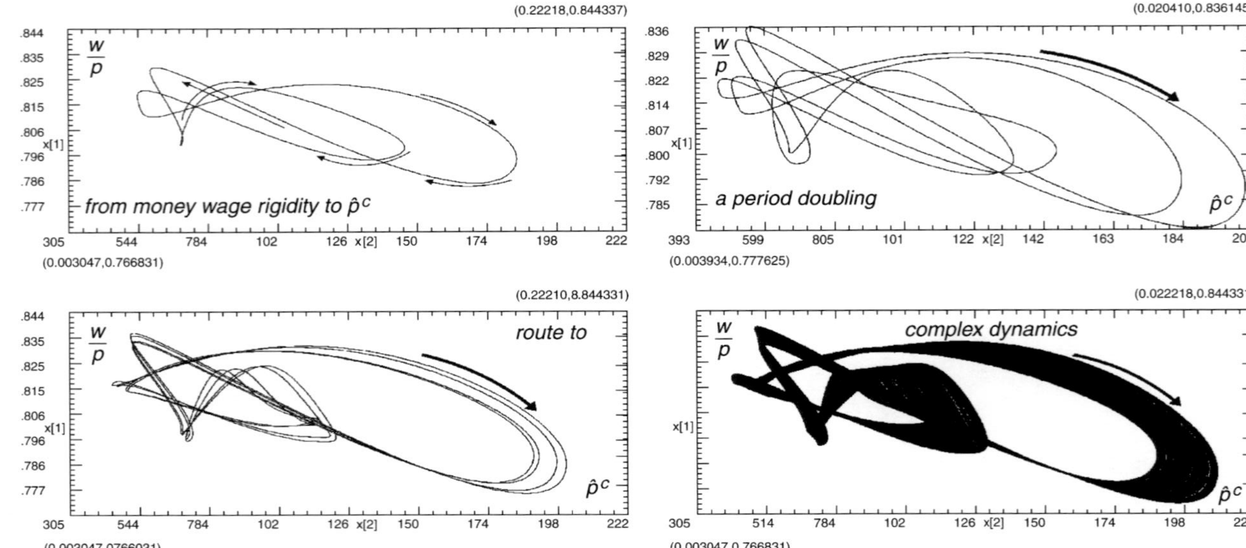

Figure 3.4 A period doubling route to complex dynamics through an accelerating wage–price spiral, augmented by downward money wage rigidity (with financial market accelerators still tranquil)

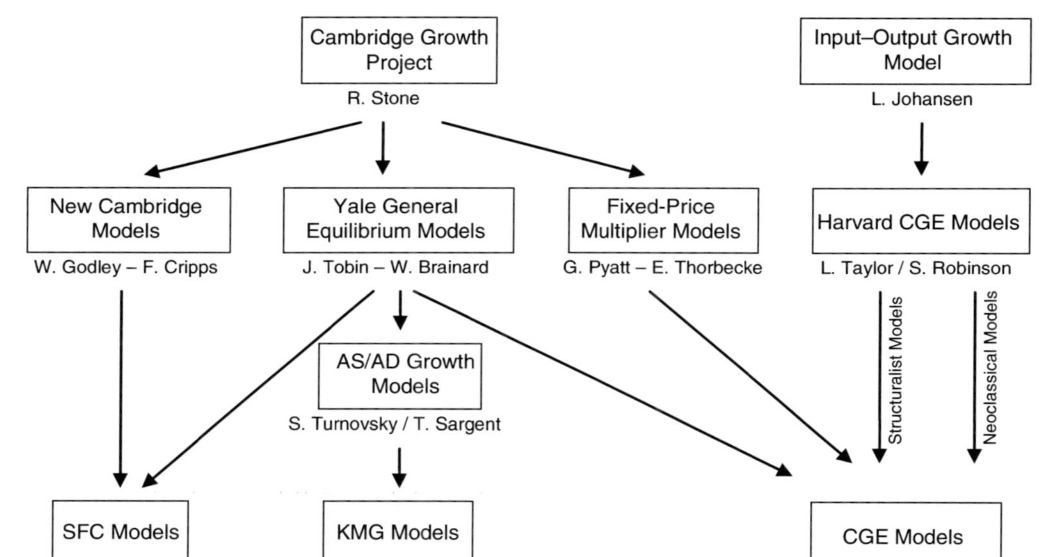

Figure 3.5 A family tree of accounting-based macromodels

1960s and there is little doubt that Tobin's concern for the accounting consistency of his models came from his one-year stay at the DAE in 1949–50. Figure 3.5 shows that at least two other recent research programmes are part of the Stone–Tobin lineage, namely *stock-flow consistent* and *computable general equilibrium* models.

Stock-flow consistent models

Stock-flow consistent (SFC) models have been developed over the past few years following the seminal post-Keynesian growth model of Lavoie and Godley (2001–2).[21] These models are the descendants of the accounting-based *New Cambridge* models developed in the late 1970s and early 1980s by Godley and Cripps at the DAE.[22] Although New Cambridge models did not make any reference to Tobin's methodology, SFC models make now a systematic use of Tobinian transactions flow matrices and portfolio choices equations. Like New Cambridge models, SFC models are written in discrete time and are strongly rooted in the Kaldorian theory of endogenous money. Therefore they depart from our research programme regarding the modelling of time intervals and the representation of the money market. However, aside from these two elements, the similarities between growth SFC models, in particular the ones proposed in Lavoie and Godley (2001–2) and Godley and Lavoie (2007, ch.11), and the KMG–Tobin model are striking. For instance, both types of models dismiss mainstream microfoundations of macroeconomics based on optimization behaviour, which lead them to use Keynesian-style consumption or investment functions. Moreover, in these models, market clearing through prices does not occur on the real side of the economy and an important role is given to the inventories of produced goods held by firms.

The lack of representative agent-based behavioural equations in KMG and SFC models is in line with Tobin's (1982, p.173) own rejection of mainstream microfoundations for macroeconomic modelling:

> Macroeconomics models of the type I am advocating are, I admit, only loosely linked to optimizing behaviour of individual agents. Following an older tradition, economy-wide structural equations are an amalgam of individual behaviour and aggregation across a multitude of diverse individuals.

In an earlier section of this chapter we have explained the consumption behaviour of households by using a Kaldorian framework (equations 3.2 and 3.6) where consumption is a fixed proportion of (net) wages and the income of asset holders (Kaldor, 1966). As for the behaviour of firms, we have used what can be described as a 'Tobin-Kalecki' investment function (equation 3.25) where the rate of accumulation of capital depends positively on the deviation of Tobin's q from one and on the deviation of the utilization rate from its normal level $\overline{u}$. Such choices are very similar to the assumptions adopted by Godley and Lavoie in their reference model. They have also used a Kaldorian function relating consumption to wages, dividends and interest payments. The only differences are that their function, which is similar to the one proposed by Kaldor (1966), also takes into account capital gains and does not differentiate households' behaviour between workers and asset holders. Moreover, Godley and Lavoie's investment function can be considered as an extended version of our own function, since it includes the leverage ratio and the rate of profits of firms on top of Tobin's q and the utilization rate. The main difference in this case is that there is nothing in their model to force the q ratio towards unity or the utilization rate towards a predetermined level (whereas $q=1$ and $u=\overline{u}$ at the steady state of the KMG model).

The behaviour of real markets (those for labour and products) is another common feature of KMG-style and SFC models. In both approaches financial markets are the only ones which clear through price adjustment. Real markets are demand-led: demand is always satisfied by a higher supply at the actual price of the market (the wage rate or the price of goods). In particular, there is nothing in these models which leads towards an equality between supply and demand of labour; that is, to full employment. As for the market of products, we adopt a Metzlerian approach where firms hold inventories which are assumed to be always large enough to absorb any discrepancy between production and demand. In their reference model Lavoie and Godley (2001–2) used instead the typical Keynesian assumption that supply instantaneously adjusts to demand. However, they have later developed more realistic models where it takes time for firms to adapt their production capacities (Godley and Lavoie, 2007) and where they cannot forecast with perfect precision the amount of future demand so that they are forced to hold inventories.

The representation of inventories in these models is then very similar to the process described in equations (3.28) to (3.33), although Godley and Lavoie (2007, pp. 251–2) do not make any reference to Meltzer's work:[23]

> Based on their ... experience and best-practice management techniques, firms will set a target inventories to sale ratio, which should allow them to respond fully to any peak in demand ... Firms are continuously building up or reducing the size of their inventories, in an attempt to achieve their inventory targets. In addition, when forecasting mistakes occur, there is a discrepancy between what is sold and what was expected to be sold when the production decision had to be taken. This implies a change in actual inventories, even if the target inventories to sale ratio had been previously reached.

The way of linking the behaviour of real markets to changes in prices is also, to some extent, similar in both types of models. Indeed, the absence of a price-clearing mechanism does not mean that conditions in real markets have no impact on prices: in the KMG model an increase in the levels of employment or capacity utilization will generate an increase in wages and prices. A rise in the level of employment will have a direct effect on the nominal wage inflation rate (equation 3.42) and an indirect effect on the inflation rate (through wage cost in equation 3.43). In the same way, a higher rate of capacity utilization has both a direct effect on the inflation rate and an indirect effect on the rate of growth of nominal wages. In the most elaborated models of Godley and Lavoie (2007), where inflation is taken into account, there is a similar mechanism in place, since a higher rate of employment leads to an increase in the wage inflation rate (through a rise in the level of real wage targeted by workers) and hence in the inflation rate.[24] In other words, as with our approach, Godley and Lavoie use a standard Phillips curve where a higher rate of employment simply leads to a higher rate of inflation. Such a view is different from the monetarist conception based on a vertical Phillips curve where a higher rate of employment generates an *acceleration* of inflation (that is, where *changes* in inflation rise with the employment rate).[25] What we called NAIRU (and which does not appear in Godley and Lavoie's models) is thus simply a 'normal' rate of employment (in the sense that prices increase when the current employment rate is above this level and decrease when it is below), and this is compatible with the post-Keynesian theory endorsed by these authors. The same may not be said of our integration of price expectations in the modelling of wage–price dynamics. In equation (3.42) we assumed that changes in expected inflation were partly determined by the long-run steady-state inflation rate, given by the money growth rate minus the long-term equilibrium growth rate of the economy. Such a concept of steady-state inflation is consistent with the monetarist tradition and our own assumption of an exogenous money growth rate controlled by the central bank (equation 3.40). The quantity theory of money however is fiercely rejected by post-Keynesian authors.

In SFC models, the central bank cannot control the money supply directly but can only set the level of the key interest rate, hoping that higher rates will slow down the economy and money demand. The causality is reversed in comparison with our model since the LM device assumes an exogenous money supply and represents the interest rate as the price issued from the money market equilibrium. In the KMG–Tobin model the use of an LM curve is only a matter of convenience and a way to stick to Tobin's old Keynesianism. However we are aware that this view is out of step with contemporary macroeconomics since most economists now agree on the fact that central banks use the interest rate as their policy variable and pay little attention to monetary aggregates (Romer, 2000). This is the reason why, in a book co-authored with R. Franke, Chiarella and Flaschel proposed another version of the KMG model, known as 'Keynes–Metzler–Goodwin–Taylor'. In this model the LM curve is replaced by a Taylor interest rate policy rule, which comes down to adopting the post-Keynesian assumption of endogenous money (Chiarella *et al.*, 2005).

Aside from this point, it is worth noting that there are no private banks in the KMG–Tobin model so that investment is ultimately financed by savings in the form of purchases of equities by asset holders. Such an assumption is at odds with the post-Keynesian concept of *monetary production economy* according to which production is made possible by initial loans from banks and occurs before any collection of savings. SFC models therefore usually integrate private banks which are fully accommodating in the same way as the central bank: they set an interest rate on loans (applying a mark-up on the key rate of the central bank) and provide all loans required by creditworthy borrowers at this rate. Once again, the absence of private banks in our model is not related to a fundamental disagreement to this post-Keynesian view but comes simply from our will to keep the core KMG model as simple as possible. In their recent monograph Godley and Lavoie (2007, p.57) have made a similar choice for their simplest model:

> We have reluctantly come to the conclusion that it is impossible to deploy a really simple model of a complete monetary economy in which inside and outside money both make their appearance at the outset. We have therefore decided to start by constructing and studying a hypothetical economy in which there is no private money at all, that is, a world where there are no banks, where producers need not borrow to produce, and hence a world where there are no interest payments. We have done this while fully recognising that money generated by loans from private banks (e.g. to finance inventories when production takes time) is of the utmost importance in the real world of monetized economies.

Starting with a simple model with government money only and then introducing private banks is what we have done in Flaschel and Hartmann (2011). In this paper, a simplified version of the KMG–Tobin model is extended in order to integrate a banking system which is in line with the conception of endogenous money mentioned above. In this model, all short-term bonds issued by firms[26] or the government that are not held by workers and asset holders are purchased by the banking system. In addition, money supply follows money demand in an accommodating way and the central bank is assumed to set the short-term interest rate by following a Taylor's rule. As for the loan rate (the rate on short-term bonds held by private banks), it is determined by an endogenous mark-up on the key rate (which is negatively correlated to the state of the business cycle). Of course the representation of the banking system in this model remains uneven, since private banks and the central bank are aggregated together, and loans are assimilated to purchases of short-term bonds. Charpe (2008, ch.5) has however proposed a model which integrates more realistic commercial banks in the KMG model along the lines of Godley and Lavoie's work. Thus it seems to us that the issue of the representation of the monetary side of the economy, although an important one, is not an element which makes a significant difference between KMG and SFC approaches.

Actually we claim that the real difference between both modelling methodologies is not to be found at the level of the theoretical assumptions adopted for behavioural equations, but rather at the level of the period length used for writing models and studying their properties. Most of the SFC models are written in discrete time and thus are not solved analytically but simply studied through computing simulations. Godley and Lavoie (2007, p.9) consider that the results of these simulations are instructive enough to be able to 'build up, knowledge, or "informed intuition", as to the way monetary economies must and do function'. However we trust that the use of continuous time is the better choice to approach macroeconomic issues.[27] In particular the absence of an analytical solution can be a problem when the aim of the model is to capture the economic mechanisms that generate business cycles. For instance Lavoie (2006) tried to use the results of the simulations made in the reference paper he wrote with Godley (Lavoie and Godley, 2001–2) in order to tackle the issues brought up by Minsky (1986) with his *financial instability hypothesis*.[28] Such an attempt is not really convincing since all the simulations used by Lavoie were made for a stable steady state which is at odds with Minsky's concept of endogenous financial instability. Taylor (2004, ch.8) proposed another interpretation of Godley and Lavoie's model which is certainly closer to Minsky's writings. This interpretation is based on a version in continuous time of the model which allows a mathematical analysis of the conditions that are likely to generate an unstable regime similar to the one described by Minsky.

Financial computable general equilibrium models

Figure 3.5 shows that *computable general equilibrium* (CGE) models are another type of accounting-based macromodels which belong to the Stone/Tobin lineage. They differ from SFC and KMG models on two aspects. First, while SFC and KMG models are *theoretical* models, CGE models are *applied* macroeconometric models used by policy analysts and international institutions such as the World Bank, the IMF or the International Food Policy Research Insititute.[29] These models, written in discrete time are *calibrated*[30] and subjected to simulations whose results help to deal with issues surrounding economic development and international trade. Second, the first CGE models were not inspired by the work of Stone but by Leontief Input–Output models.[31] The originators of these models, S. Robinson and L. Taylor, were Harvard PhD students of H. Chenery (himself a former PhD student of Leontief) who tried to build models similar to the Input–Output growth model of the Norwegian economy proposed by L. Johansen (1960). Johansen's work, based on an input–output accounting matrix, was however very close to Stone's work and the latter heavily influenced the subsequent CGE literature.[32] In particular, following the work of Pyatt[33] at the World Bank, SAMs became, in the 1980s, the cornerstone of the CGE methodology. Like SFC models, 'CGE models are always based on a SAM framework' (Robinson, 2003, p.1).

The CGE literature is too huge to be properly reviewed here but a good way to present it is to distinguish between *structuralist* and *neoclassical* models (Robinson, 1991). Structuralist CGE models, pioneered by Taylor and Black (1974), trace their intellectual roots to Marx, Kalecki, Kaldor and Keynes, and, although they were developed independently, they can be described to some extent as applied open-economy versions of the theoretical post-Keynesian SFC models mentioned above.[34] Therefore they have obvious links with our research programme which will not be investigated further here.

Neoclassical CGE models, initiated by Adelman and Robinson (1978), are allegedly based on Walras' general equilibrium[35] and they assume profit-maximizing behaviour by producers, utility maximization by consumers, and markets which clear through flexible adjustments in wage and prices. The link with our research programme is therefore less obvious than in the case of structuralist models. However there is a particular type of neoclassical CGE model, labelled *financial* computable general equilibrium models (FCGE), which is worth mentioning here with regards to the way it specifies the interactions between financial variables and the real side of the economy. These models began in the 1990s following the 'Maquette' model of the OECD (Bourguignon *et al.*, 1991), can to some extent be depicted as 'Old Keynesian'.

First, like our model, they represent the behaviour of financial markets through Tobinian portfolio choices.[36] These portfolio decisions are usually only expressed in terms of *flows*. However one of the reference FCGE models, the Integrated Macroeconomic Model for Poverty

Analysis (IMMPA) of the World Bank (Agénor *et al.*, 2003), provides a full *stock* treatment of portfolio decisions similar to equations (3.11) to (3.13).

Second, FCGE models usually integrate various channels through which the economic sectors' balance sheet (or net worth) can impact financial and real flows. For instance in the IMMPA, banks set the loans interest rate as a premium over the average cost of funds and this premium decreases with the ratio of the stock of private capital to the stock of debt. Moreover, the loans interest rate, which represents the cost of borrowing to finance investment, has a negative impact on the rate of accumulation.

The financial side of neoclassical FCGE models usually departs from 'old Keynesianism' in respect of the role given to the market of equities or the behaviour of banks. Equities markets usually do not feature in FCGE models since most of these models represent developing countries where bank loans still finance most of the capital accumulation. As for the behaviour of banks and the money market, FCGE models are traditionally based, like SFC models, on the theory of endogenous money.

4
Analysis and Policy Implications of the KMG–Tobin Model

Introduction

In this chapter we study analytically the properties of the KMG–Tobin model and use them to make some policy proposals. First, the intensive form of the dynamics is derived in order to allow for steady state considerations (in the following section) on the basis of nine autonomous laws of motion that exhibit a unique point of rest or steady state. The next section focuses on the short-run comparative statics of the financial markets module of the system. The stability of the full 9D dynamical system is then analysed by way of a sequence of subsystems of increasing dimension. Following this, the next section analyses the dynamical behaviour of the system when it is displaced from its steady state position, but still remains in a neighbourhood of the steady state. Conclusions are drawn in the final section.

The intensive form of the model

In this section we derive the intensive form of the model. We express all stock and flow variables in the laws of motion to be derived per unit of capital. We thus divide nominal stock and flow variables by the nominal value of the capital stock pK and all real ones by K, the real capital stock. This enables to determine a (unique) steady state solution under the form of an interior point of rest of the state space considered.

We begin with the intensive form of some necessary definitions or identities, that we need for representing the dynamic system in an intelligible way. The function q used in this block of equations will be determined and discussed later on, when the comparative statics of the portfolio part of the model will be investigated:

$$Y/K = y = (1 + \beta_{n^d}(n + \beta_n))y^e - \beta_n \nu$$

$$L^d/K = l^d = y/\overline{x}$$

$$e = l^d/l$$

$$u = y/y^p$$

$$\rho^e = y^e - \delta - \omega l^d$$

$$C/K = c = (1 - \tau_w)\omega l^d + (1 - s_c)(y^e - \delta - \omega l^d - \overline{t}_c^n)$$

$$I/K = i = i_1(q - 1) + i_2(u - \overline{u}) + n$$

$$Y^d/K = y^d = c + i + \delta + \overline{g}$$

$$p_e E/(pK) = q = q(m, b, \rho^e, \pi_e)$$

$$r_e^e = \rho^e/q + \pi_e$$

$$\pi_e = \alpha_{\pi_e}\pi_{ec} + (1 - \alpha_{\pi_e})\pi_{ef}$$

The above equations describe output and employment per unit of capital, the rate of utilization of the existing stock of labour and capital, the expected rate of profit, consumption, investment and aggregate demand per unit of capital, Tobin's average q, and the expected rate of return on equities (including expected capital gains π_e^e).

Let us translate the laws of motion of the dynamically endogenous variables into capital intensive form. The law of motions for the nominal wages and price level stated in equations (3.42) and (3.43) are interacting instantaneously and thus depend on each other. Solving these two linear equations for $\hat{w}$ and $\hat{p}$ gives:

$$\hat{w} = \kappa(\beta_w(e - \overline{e}) + \kappa_w\beta_p(u - \overline{u})) + \pi \tag{4.1}$$

$$\hat{p} = \kappa(\beta_p(u - \overline{u}) + \kappa_p\beta_w(e - \overline{e})) + \pi \tag{4.2}$$

with $\kappa = (1 - \kappa_w\kappa_p)^{-1}$. For a detailed computation see Chiarella and Flaschel (2000a) and in Appendix I. From these two inflation rates one can compute the growth law of real wages $\omega = w/p$ by means of the definitional relationship $\hat{\omega} = \hat{w} - \hat{p}$. This gives us

$$\hat{\omega} = \kappa[(1 - \kappa_p)\beta_w(e - \overline{e}) + (\kappa_w - 1)\beta_p(u - \overline{u})] \tag{4.3}$$

where κ is $(1-\kappa_w\kappa_p)^{-1}$. The next set of equations explains the dynamic laws of the expected rate of inflation, the labour capital ratio, the expected sales, and the stock of inventories in intensive form:

$$\dot{\pi} = \alpha\beta_\pi\kappa[\beta_p(u - \overline{u}) + \kappa_p\beta_w(e - \overline{e})] + (1 - \alpha)\beta_\pi(\overline{\mu} - n - \pi) \tag{4.4}$$

$$\hat{l} = n - i = -i_1(q - 1) - i_2(u - \overline{u}) \tag{4.5}$$

$$\dot{y}^e = \beta_{y^e}(y^d - y^e) + (n - i)y^e \tag{4.6}$$

$$\dot{\nu} = y - y^d - i\nu \tag{4.7}$$

Equation (4.4) is almost the same as in the extensive modelling, but here the term $\hat{p}-\pi$ is substituted according to equation (4.2). Equation (4.5), the law of motion of relative factor endowment, is given by the (negative of the) investment function as far as its dependence on asset markets and the state of the business cycle are concerned. Equation (4.6) is obtained by way of the time derivative of y^e as follows:

$$\dot{y}^e = \frac{d(Y^e/K)}{dt} = \frac{\dot{Y}^eK - Y^e\dot{K}}{K^2} = \frac{\dot{Y}^e}{K} - y^e i = \beta_{y^e}(y^d - y^e) + y^e(n - i)$$

In the same way, one gets equation (4.7). The laws of motion governing the expectations about the equity prices are not changed by the intensive form modelling and thus are once again as follows:

$$\dot{\pi}_{ef} = \beta_{\pi_{ef}}(\overline{\eta} - \pi_{ef}) \tag{4.8}$$

$$\dot{\pi}_{ec} = \beta_{\pi_{ec}}(\hat{p}_e - \pi_{ec}) \tag{4.9}$$

In the following, only the value of aggregate capital gains expectations is needed. In order to compute the latter we need the historic values of actual inflation in equity prices $\hat{p}_e$, for which we lack a law of motion, because the general equilibrium approach tells us that $\hat{p}_e$ is such that asset markets are in equilibrium. We follow Sargent (1987, p.117), in using the integral representation of the expectation about equity price inflation, which leads us to the following definition of aggregate expectation of equity price inflation:

$$\pi_e(t) = \alpha_{ec}\left[\pi_{ec}(t_0)e^{-\beta_{\pi_{ec}}(t-t_0)} + \beta_{\pi_{ec}}\int_{t_0}^{t} d^{-\beta_{\pi_{ec}}(t-s)}\hat{p}_e(s)ds\right]$$
$$+ (1-\alpha_{ec})[(\pi_{ef}(t_0)-\overline{\eta})e^{-\beta_{\pi_{ef}}t} + \overline{\eta}] \tag{4.10}$$

where $\pi_{ec}(t_0)$ and $\pi_{ef}(t_0)$ are the initial values of the expectations about growth in equity prices, performed by the chartist and the fundamentalists at time t_0. The details for obtaining this equation are given in the mathematical Appendix I. Such an integral equation for expectations formation could be avoided if the nested adaptive expectations procedure we considered in the second section of Chapter 2 was applied in place of the simple adaptive expectations scheme used here.

Finally, the laws of motion for real balances and real bonds per unit of capital have to be derived. Based on the knowledge of the laws for inflation $\hat{p}$ and investment i we can derive the differential equation for bonds per unit of capital shown in equation (4.11) from the following expression:

$$\dot{b} = \frac{d(B/pK)}{dt} = \frac{\dot{B}}{pK} - b(\hat{p}+i)$$

where $\dot{B}$ is given by equation (3.41). The same idea is used for the changes in the money supply. Therefore, we get the following two differential equations:

$$\dot{b} = \overline{g} - \overline{t}_c^n - \tau_w\omega l^d - \overline{\mu}m$$
$$- b(\kappa[\beta_p(u-\overline{u}) + \kappa_p\beta_w(e-\overline{e})] + \pi + i) \tag{4.11}$$
$$\dot{m} = m\overline{\mu} - m(\kappa[\beta_p(u-\overline{u}) + \kappa_p\beta_w(e-\overline{e})] + \pi + i) \tag{4.12}$$

The dynamics in extensive form can be reduced to nine (eight) differential equations, where however the law of motion for share prices has not been determined yet, or alternatively to seven differential and one integral equation, which is easier to handle (since there is no longer a law of motion for the development of future share prices to be calculated). Economic policy (fiscal and monetary) is still represented in very simple terms here, since money supply is growing with a given rate and both government expenditures and taxes on capital income (net of interest payments per unit of capital) are given parameters. This makes the dynamics of the government budget constraint[1] a very trivial one and thus remains a matter for future research. The main advantage is that fiscal policy can be discussed here in a very simple way by means of three parameters only.

Contrary to what occurs in the KMG model of Chiarella and Flaschel (2000a), there are now two variables from the financial sector that feed back to the real dynamics in this extended system: the bond to capital ratio b representing the evolution of government debt, and Tobin's average q. The first one influences the statically endogenous variable q, that in turn enters the investment function as a measure of the firms' performance. However, government bonds do not influence the economy in other ways, since there are no wealth effects in consumption and the interest income channel to consumption has been suppressed (by the assumption on tax collection concerning capital income). In addition, the interest rate channel of the earlier KMG approaches, where the real rate of interest entered the investment function, is now absent from this function. Therefore, the nominal interest rate, determined by portfolio equilibrium, does not matter in the present formulation of the model, where Tobin's q provides the channel through which investment behaviour is reacting to the results brought in by the financial markets.

Price inflation (via real balances and real bonds) and the expected rate of profit (via the dividend rate of return) influence the behaviour of asset markets via their respective laws of motion, while the reaction of asset markets feeds back instantaneously into the real part of the economy through the change in Tobin's q that they generate (and the dynamics of expected capital gains).

Steady state considerations

In this section we put in evidence the existence of a steady state in the considered economy. This can be done independently of the knowledge supplied in the next section on the comparative statics of the asset market equilibrium system. Indeed, Tobin's q is given by 1 in the steady state, via the real part of the model, and the portfolio equations can be solved in conjunction with the government budget constraint for the three variables r, m, b which they then determine.

Let us note that m, b are data in the short-run analysis of the behaviour of asset markets of the next subsection (where q, r are determined on their basis as the variables that bring the asset markets to equilibrium), while m, b are variables in the long run that are to be derived from asset market equilibrium conditions and the government budget constraint.

In the following, variables x with $\breve{x}$ on top denote the steady state value of the corresponding variable.

Proposition 1

Let us assume that $s_c > \tau_w$ and $s_c \breve{\rho}^e > n + \overline{g} - \overline{t}_c^n$. *Let us assume furthermore that the parameter ϕ used below has a positive numerator, (so that the government runs a primary deficit in the steady state) and is between zero and one if money supply is growing. The dynamic system given by equations (4.3) to (4.12) possesses a unique interior (meaningful steady state solution) if the fundamentalists long run reference inflation rate of equity prices equals the steady state inflation rate of good prices*

$$\overline{\eta} = \breve{\hat{p}}$$

and if

$$\begin{aligned} &\lim_{r \to 0}(f_m(r, \breve{\rho}^e + \breve{\pi}_e) + f_b(r, \breve{\rho}^e + \breve{\pi}_e)) < \overline{\varphi} \\ \text{and} \quad &\lim_{r \to \infty}(f_m(r, \breve{\rho}^e + \breve{\pi}_e) + f_b(r, \breve{\rho}^e + \breve{\pi}_e)) > \overline{\varphi} \end{aligned}$$

holds true with $\overline{\varphi} = \frac{\overline{g} - \overline{t}_c^n - \tau_w \breve{\omega} \breve{l}^d}{\overline{g} - \overline{t}_c^n - \tau_w \breve{\omega} \breve{l}^d + \overline{\mu}} 2$

Proof

If the economy stays in a steady state, then all intensive variables stay constant and all time derivatives of the system become zero. Therefore, by setting the left hand side of the system of equations (4.3) to (4.12), at the exception of (4.10), equal to zero, we can deduce the steady state values of the variables. From equation (4.5) we can derive that $\breve{i} = n$ holds. From (4.6) we get $y^e = y^d$. From (4.12): $\overline{\mu} = (\kappa[\beta_p(u - \overline{u}) + \kappa_p \beta_w (e - \overline{e})] + \pi + i)$. By plugging in the last relation into equation (3.44), and using $\breve{i} = n$ and $\alpha\beta_\pi \neq -(1-\alpha)\beta_\pi$, we get that

$\bar{\mu} - n - \pi = 0$ and $\kappa[\beta_p(u - \bar{u}) + \kappa_p\beta_w(e - \bar{e})] = 0$. Thus, we have the following two equations for $u - \bar{u}$ and $e - \bar{e}$:

$$u - \bar{u} = -\kappa_p\beta_w(e - \bar{e})/\beta_p$$
$$u - \bar{u} = (1 - \kappa_p)\beta_w(e - \bar{e})/[(1 - \kappa_w)\beta_p]$$

By assumption, we have $\beta_p, \beta_w > 0$ and $0 \le \kappa_p, \kappa_w \le 1$. Therefore $e - \bar{e}$ must equal zero in order to fulfil the last two conditions. When $e = \bar{e}$, according to (4.3), we know that $u = \bar{u}$. Therefore equation (4.5) leads to $\breve{q} = 1$.

From these relations, one can easily compute the unique steady state values of the variables y^e, l, π, ν, ω:

$$\breve{y}^e = \frac{\breve{y}}{1 + n\beta_{n^d}}, \quad \text{with } \breve{y} = \overline{uy}^p \tag{4.13}$$

$$\breve{l} = \breve{y}/(\overline{ex}) \tag{4.14}$$

$$\breve{\pi} = \bar{\mu} - n \tag{4.15}$$

$$\breve{\nu} = \beta_{n^d}\breve{y}^e \tag{4.16}$$

$$\breve{\omega} = \frac{\breve{y}^e - n - \delta - \bar{g} - (1 - s_c)(\breve{y}^e - \delta - \bar{t}_c^n)}{(s_c - \tau_w)\breve{l}^d} \tag{4.17}$$

$$\breve{\rho}^e = \breve{y}^e - \delta - \omega\breve{l}^d \tag{4.18}$$

All these values are determined on the good and labour markets. In particular, the steady state value of the real wage has been derived from the goods market equilibrium condition that must hold in the steady state. It is positive under the assumptions made in Proposition 2.

We now take into account the asset markets which determine the values of the short-term interest rate r (which is now uniquely in charge to clear the asset markets). In conjunction with the determination of the steady state for m, b, where $m + b$ is determined through the government budget constraint. This is the case because the steady state rate of return on equities relies, on the one hand, on $\breve{\rho}^e$ (since q has been determined through the condition $i = n$ and shown to equal one in steady state) and, on the other hand, on the expected inflation rate of share prices. The latter equals the goods price inflation rate in the steady state as shown below:

$$r_e^e = \breve{\rho}^e + \breve{\pi}_e$$

The steady state values of the two kinds of expectations about the inflation rate of equity prices (of chartists and fundamentalists) are

$$\breve{\pi}_{ef} = \overline{\eta} \text{ and } \breve{\pi}_{ec} = \overline{\eta} \qquad (4.19)$$

from which one can derive that $\pi_e = \overline{\eta} = \hat{p} = \pi = \overline{\mu} - n$ holds. We have seen that, in the steady state, Tobin's q equals to one and its time derivative equals to zero, $\dot{q} = 0$:

$$\begin{aligned} & \dot{q} && = 0 \\ \Rightarrow\ & \frac{(\dot{p}_e E + p_e \dot{E})pK - p_e E(\dot{p}K + p\dot{K})}{p^2K^2} && = 0 \\ \Rightarrow\ & \frac{\dot{p}_e E + p_e \dot{E}}{pK} && = \hat{p} + n \end{aligned}$$

According to equation (3.27) we have that $p_e\dot{E} = pI + p(\dot{N} - IN)$. We thus get in the steady state $p_e\dot{E} = pI$. By inserting this into the last identity, we get that $\hat{p}_e = \hat{p}$ and thus, as an important finding, that $\overline{\eta} = \overline{\mu} - n$ must hold in order to allow for a steady state.

We can now determine the steady state values of the stocks of real cash balances and the stock of bonds. These values have to be determined in conjunction with the steady state interest rate r which is now responsible only for clearing the asset markets, because Tobin's $q = 1$ has already been determined on the real markets.

The budget constraint of the government is given in intensive form by

$$\dot{b} + \dot{m} = \overline{g} - \overline{t}_c^n - \tau_w \omega l^d - (b + m)(\hat{p} + i) \qquad (4.20)$$

One therefore obtains in the steady state that:

$$\breve{b} + \breve{m} = (\overline{g} - \overline{t}_c^n - \tau_w \omega l^d)/\overline{\mu} \qquad (4.21)$$

Let us consider the asset demand functions (3.11) and (3.12):

$$m = f_m(r, r_e^e)(m + b + q), \quad q = 1 \tag{4.22}$$

$$b = f_b(r, r_e^e)(m + b + q), \quad q = 1 \tag{4.23}$$

The left side of the last two equations are the supplied amounts and the right sides represent the demand for the assets m, b.

Let us use now equation (4.21):

$$\overline{\mu}(\breve{m} + \breve{b}) = \overline{g} - \overline{t}_c^n - \tau_w \omega l^d \tag{4.24}$$

From this system of three linear independent equations (4.22) to (4.24) one can deduce the three unique steady state values r, $\breve{b}$, and $\breve{m}$.

Beginning with the steady state interest rate we sum equations (4.22) and (4.23) and multiply by $\overline{\mu}$:

$$\overline{\mu}(\breve{m} + \breve{b}) = (\breve{f}_m + \breve{f}_b)\overline{\mu}(\breve{m} + \breve{b} + 1)$$

where $\breve{f}_m$ and $\breve{f}_b$ denote the values of $f_m(r, \breve{\rho}^e + \breve{\pi}_e)$ and $f_b(r, \breve{\rho}^e + \breve{\pi}_e)$ respectively. By plugging in the budget constraint in the form of equation (4.24) we get that:

$$\breve{f}_m + \breve{f}_b = \overline{\varphi}$$

with $\overline{\varphi} = \frac{\overline{g} - \overline{t}_c^n - \tau_w \breve{\omega} \breve{l}^d}{\overline{g} - \overline{t}_c^n - \tau_w \breve{\omega} \breve{l}^d + \overline{\mu}}$. From properties (3.48) and (3.50), we can conclude that:

$$\frac{\partial (f_m + f_b)}{\partial r} > 0 \tag{4.25}$$

which implies that the cumulated demand for money and bonds is a strictly increasing function in the variable r.

If $\lim_{r \to 0} (f_m(r, \breve{\rho}^e + \breve{\pi}_e) + f_b(r, \breve{\rho}^e + \breve{\pi}_e)) < \overline{\phi}$ and $lim_{r \to \infty}(f_m(r, \breve{\rho}^e + \breve{\pi}_e) + f_b(r, \breve{\rho}^e + \breve{\pi}_e)) > \overline{\varphi}$, then by monotony and continuity there must be a value of r that equilibrates the asset markets in the above aggregated form. Therefore, the steady state supplies of m, b can be calculated through equations (4.22) and (4.23) in a unique way, based on the steady state interest rates $r = r$ and $r_e^e = \breve{\rho}^e + \pi_e$. This concludes the uniquely determined derivation of steady state values for our dynamical system (4.3) to (4.12).

We observe finally that the calculation of the steady state value of the rate of wage and the rate of profit can be simplified when it is assumed that government expenditures are given by $\overline{g}+\tau_w\omega l^d$ in place of $\overline{g}$. alone.

Comparative statics of the asset markets

After having specified the extensive and intensive form of the model and having shown the existence and uniqueness of an interior steady state solution of the intensive form, we now focus on the short-run comparative statics of the financial markets module of the system. We thus now derive the function $q=q(m, b, \rho^e, \pi_e)$ that was already used in the intensive form presentation of the model. This function is now needed to investigate the stability properties of the model close to its steady state solution.[3]

Let us assume that the asset demand functions display the property which gave us a unique interior steady state solution in the preceding section.[4] It is now possible to approximate these demand functions by linear functions in a neighbourhood of the steady state in order to derive the stability properties of the next subsection. These linearized versions of the asset demand functions can be written as:

$$
\begin{aligned}
f_m^l(r, r_e^e) &= \alpha_{m0} - \alpha_{m1} r - \alpha_{m2}(\rho^e/q + \pi_e) \\
f_b^l(r, r_e^e) &= \alpha_{b0} + \alpha_{b1} r - \alpha_{b2}(\rho^e/q + \pi_e) \\
f_e^l(r, r_e^e) &= \alpha_{e0} - \alpha_{e1} r + \alpha_{e2}(\rho^e/q + \pi_e)
\end{aligned}
$$

where the superscript l denotes the linearized form and where:

$$\alpha_{ij} \geq 0 \quad \forall i \in \{b, m, e\}, j \in \{0, 1, 2\}$$

Thanks to proposition 1, it is sufficient to focus on the first two asset market equilibrium conditions in all subsequent equilibrium considerations. These two equilibrium conditions are:

$$m = (\alpha_{m0} - \alpha_{m1}r - \alpha_{m2}(\rho^e/q + \pi_e))(m + b + q) \tag{4.26}$$

$$b = (\alpha_{b0} + \alpha_{b1}r - \alpha_{b2}(\rho^e/q + \pi_e))(m + b + q) \tag{4.27}$$

Solving (4.26) and (4.27) for the interest rate r we obtain:

$$r_{\mathrm{LM}} = \frac{\alpha_{m0} - \alpha_{m2}(\rho^e/q + \pi_e) - m/(m + b + q)}{\alpha_{m1}} \tag{4.28}$$

$$r_{\mathrm{BB}} = \frac{-\alpha_{b0} + \alpha_{b2}(\rho^e/q + \pi_e) + b/(m + b + q)}{\alpha_{b1}} \tag{4.29}$$

The *LM*–subscript denotes the interest rate that equates the demand for real balances and the real money supply. The *BB*–subscript denotes the interest rate that equates real bond demand and supply. Figure 4.1 displays examples of these two functions. The intersection of the *LM*–curve and the *BB*–curve then provides the equilibrium values for the short-term interest rate r and Tobin's q. The figure shows examples of such functions. Since we know that the functions are not linear in q, we do not know yet whether the equilibrium exists and is unique. However, we are only considering a neighbourhood of the steady state solution for $r, q, m, b, \rho^e, \pi_e$ where the latter must of course fulfil the above equilibrium conditions for the asset markets. In order to show that r, q exists and is uniquely determined for all m, b, ρ^e, π_e sufficiently close to this steady state solution we therefore have to show that the assumptions of the implicit function theorem are valid at the steady state.

Proposition 2

Let us adopt the assumptions of proposition 1. There is a unique solution (r, q) to the equations (4.22) and, (4.23), which thus clears the asset markets, for all values of m, b, ρ^e, π_e in an appropriately chosen neighbourhood of the interior steady state solution of the dynamics (4.3) to (4.12).

Proof

We have to show that the Jacobian of the system

$$f_m(r, q)(m + b + q) - m = 0$$

$$f_b(r, q)(m + b + q) - b = 0$$

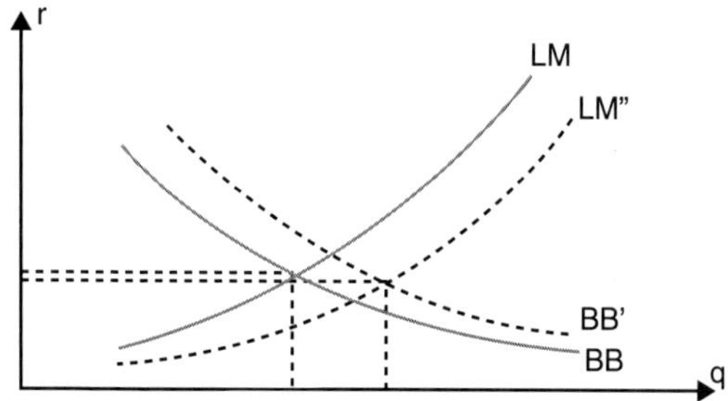

Figure 4.1 *LM–BB* curves

Note: The dashed lines show the simultaneously shifted curves of the *LM* and *BB* curve when one of the statically exogenous variables ρ^e, π_e q, m rises or b falls.

is regular with respect to the variables r, q, which means that

$$\begin{vmatrix} \frac{\partial}{\partial r}(f_m(r,q)(m+b+q)-m) & \frac{\partial}{\partial q}(f_m(r,q)(m+b+q)-m) \\ \frac{\partial}{\partial r}(f_b(r,q)(m+b+q)-b) & \frac{\partial}{\partial q}(f_b(r,q)(m+b+q)-b) \end{vmatrix} \neq 0$$

must hold true. As for the signs of the entries in this Jacobian, we know that:

$$\begin{pmatrix} - & + \\ + & + \end{pmatrix}$$

which immediately implies the regularity of this Jacobian.

We have thus shown that the financial markets can always be cleared through adjustments of the short-term interest rate and Tobin's q. But how do these two variables react in the short-run when the above given statically exogenous variables change (in time)? We consider this question first on the level of the partial equilibrium curves shown in Figure 4.1. We can derive as dependencies of the two-short run interest functions r_{LM}, r_{BB} from ρ^e, π_e, q, m and on this level also from q the following relationships:

$$\underset{}{r_{\mathrm{LM}}}(\underset{-}{\rho^e}, \underset{-}{\pi_e}, \underset{-}{m}, \underset{+}{b}, \underset{+}{q}) \text{ and } r_{\mathrm{BB}}(\underset{+}{\rho^e}, \underset{+}{\pi_e}, \underset{-}{m}, \underset{+}{b}, \underset{-}{q}) \tag{4.30}$$

These results come directly from the partial derivatives of the functions in equations (4.28) and (4.29). Equations (4.28) and (4.29) together build up an equilibrium condition by $r_{\mathrm{LM}} = r_{\mathrm{BB}}$:

$$\frac{\alpha_{m0} - \alpha_{m2}(\rho^e/q + \pi_e) - m/(m+b+q)}{\alpha_{m1}} - \frac{-\alpha_{b0} + \alpha_{b2}(\rho^e/q + \pi_e) + b/(m+b+q)}{\alpha_{b1}} = 0 \tag{4.31}$$

To apply the implicit function theorem then gives the following qualitative dependencies of Tobin's q^*:

$$\begin{aligned} &\underset{+\quad +\quad +\quad +}{q^*(\rho^e, \pi_e, m, b)} \qquad \forall q > \left(\frac{\alpha_{b1}}{\alpha_{m1}} - 1\right) m \\ &\underset{+\quad +\quad +\quad -}{q^*(\rho^e, \pi_e, m, b)} \qquad \forall q > \left(\frac{\alpha_{b1}}{\alpha_{m1}} - 1\right) m \end{aligned} \tag{4.32}$$

We thus know that the first situation must apply locally around the steady state if $(\frac{\alpha_{b1}}{\alpha_{m1}} - 1)\check{m} < 1$ holds, while the second one occurs in the opposite case.[5] We thus get the results that an increase in ρ^e unambiguously increases Tobin's q, as an increase in the expected capital gains π_e. An increase in m also pushes q upwards and thus increases investment, as an increase in m would do in the presence of a negative dependence of the rate of investment to the rate of interest (the Keynes effect of traditional models of the AS–AD variety). The positive influence of m on q thus mirrors the Keynes effect of traditional Keynesian short-run equilibrium analysis. The nominal rate of interest is however no longer involved in the real part of the model as it is here formulated, which enables to ignore the comparative statics of this interest rate here.

Results with respect to the influence of bonds b on a change in Tobin's q are however ambiguous and depend on the steady state value of real balances m as well as on the parameters that determine the interest rate sensitivity of money and bonds demand. But we get more insights into the formation of Tobin's q by means of the following proposition:

Proposition 3

In a neighbourhood around the steady state, the partial derivative of Tobin's q with respect to cash balances exceeds the partial derivative of q with respect *to bond holdings:*

$$\frac{\partial q}{\partial m} > \frac{\partial q}{\partial b}$$

Proof

According to Appendix II we can rewrite the inequality of the proposition as

$$-\frac{\det \frac{\partial(F_1,F_2)}{\partial(r,m)}}{\det \frac{\partial(F_1,F_2)}{\partial(r,q)}} > -\frac{\det \frac{\partial(F_1,F_2)}{\partial(r,b)}}{\det \frac{\partial(F_1,F_2)}{\partial(r,q)}}$$

Since we know that the denominator is negative, we get equivalently:

$$\begin{aligned}
\det \frac{\partial(F_1,F_2)}{\partial(r,m)} &> \det \frac{\partial(F_1,F_2)}{\partial(r,b)} \\
\Leftrightarrow \; -\alpha_{m1}b + \alpha_{b1}(b+q) &> \alpha_{m1}(m+q) - \alpha_{b1}m \\
\Leftrightarrow \quad \alpha_{b1}(m+b+q) &> \alpha_{m1}(m+b+q) \\
\Leftrightarrow \quad \alpha_{b1} &> \alpha_{m1}
\end{aligned}$$

which is true since this inequality is an implication of equation (4.24).

This proposition tells us that open market policy of the government, when the central bank buys bonds by means of issuing money ($dm = -db$), has an expansionary effect on Tobin's q:

$$\frac{\partial q}{\partial m}dm + \frac{\partial q}{\partial b}(-dm) > 0 \qquad (4.33)$$

Let us note finally that the effect of ρ^e on q can be related to the Rose effect of the KMG model of Chiarella and Flaschel (2000a). There is no longer a Mundell effect in the model as there is no influence of the real rate of interest on aggregate demand.

Local stability and instability

In the following we assume that all assumptions stated in Proposition 2 are met. What remains to be analysed is the dynamic behaviour of the system, when it does not rest in the steady state but is in a small neighbourhood of the steady state. In the following we show that there must be a locally stable steady state if some sufficient conditions are met.

We begin with an appropriate subsystem of the full dynamics for which the Routh–Hurwitz conditions can be shown to hold. Setting $\beta_p = \beta_w = \beta_{\pi_{ef}} = \beta_{\pi_{ec}} = \beta_n = \beta_\pi = 0$, $\beta_{y^e} > 0$, and keeping π, π_e, ω, ν at their steady state values, we get the following subdynamics of state variables m, b and y^e which is then independent from the rest of the system:[6]

$$\begin{aligned} \dot{m} &= m(\overline{\mu} - (\pi + i)) \\ \dot{b} &= \overline{g} - \overline{t}_c^n - \tau_w \omega \frac{y}{x} - \overline{\mu} m - b(\pi + i) \\ \dot{y}^e &= \beta_{y^e}[c + i + \delta + \overline{g} - y^e] + y^e(i - n) \end{aligned} \tag{4.34}$$

Proposition 4

The steady state of the system of differential equations (4.34) is locally asymptotically stable if β_{y^e} is sufficiently large, the investment adjustment speed i_2 concerning deviations of capital utilization from the normal capital utilization is sufficiently small and the absolute values of the partial derivatives of desired cash balances with respect to the interest rate $\partial f_m/\partial r$ and the rate of return on equities $\partial f_m/\partial r_e^e$ are sufficiently small. Moreover the equity market must be in a sufficiently tranquil state, i.e., the partial derivative $\partial f_e/\partial r_e^e$ must also be small enough.

Proof

The proof makes use of the Routh–Hurwitz conditions (see Gantmacher (1971) for example) and is given in detail in mathematical Appendix III.

In other words the proposition asserts that local asymptotic stability at the steady state of the considered sub-dynamics is given, when the demand for cash is very little influenced by the rates of return on the financial asset markets,[7] the accelerating effect of capacity utilization on the investment behaviour is sufficiently small, and the adjustment speed of expected sales towards actual demand is fast enough. Moreover an important condition is that the stock markets must be sufficiently tranquil in the reaction to changes in the rate of return on equities, and in particular not close to a liquidity trap.

We now consider the same system but allow for β_p to become positive, though still small. This means that ω, which has entered the m, b, y^e–subsystem so far only through its steady state value, now becomes a dynamic variable that gives rise to a 4D dynamics:

$$\begin{aligned}
\dot{m} &= m\left(\overline{\mu} - \left(\kappa\beta_p\left(\frac{y}{y^p} - u\right) + \pi + i\right)\right)\\
\dot{b} &= \overline{g} - \overline{t}_c^n - \tau_w\omega\frac{y}{x} - \overline{\mu}m - b\left(\kappa\beta_p\left(\frac{y}{y^p} - u\right) + \pi + i\right)\\
\dot{y}^e &= \beta_{y^e}[c + i + \delta + \overline{g} - y^e] + y^e(i - n)\\
\dot{\omega} &= \omega\kappa(\kappa_w - 1)\beta_p\left(\frac{y}{y^p} - \overline{u}\right)
\end{aligned} \tag{4.35}$$

Proposition 5

The interior steady state of dynamic system (4.35) is locally asymptotically stable if the conditions in proposition 4 are met and β_p is sufficiently small.

Proof

The proof is left to Appendix III.

We enlarge the system (4.35) by letting β_w become positive and we get the following subsystem:

$$\begin{aligned}
\dot{m} &= m\left(\overline{\mu} - \left(\kappa\left[\beta_p\left(\frac{y}{y^p} - u\right) + \kappa_p\beta_w\left(\frac{y}{xl} - \overline{e}\right)\right] + \pi + i\right)\right)\\
\dot{b} &= \overline{g} - \overline{t}_c^n - \tau_w\omega\frac{y}{x} - \overline{\mu}m - b\left(\kappa\left[\beta_p\left(\frac{y}{y^p} - u\right) + \kappa_p\beta_w\left(\frac{y}{xl} - \overline{e}\right)\right] + \pi + i\right)\\
\dot{y}^e &= \beta_{y^e}[c + i + \delta + \overline{g} - y^e] + y^e(i - n)\\
\dot{\omega} &= \omega\kappa\left[(1 - \kappa_p)\beta_w\left(\frac{y}{xl} - \overline{e} + \kappa_w - 1\right)\beta_p\left(\frac{y}{y^p} - \overline{u}\right)\right]\\
\dot{i} &= l\left[-i_1(q - 1) - i_2\left(\frac{y}{y^p} - \overline{u}\right)\right]
\end{aligned} \tag{4.36}$$

Proposition 6

The steady state of the dynamic system (4.36) is locally asymptotically stable if the conditions in proposition 5 are met and β_w is small enough.

Proof

The proof is left to mathematical Appendix III.

Once again, we enlarge the system by letting $\beta_n > 0$. We get then:

$$
\begin{aligned}
\dot{m} &= m\left(\overline{\mu} - \left(\kappa\left[\beta_p\left(\frac{y}{y^p} - u\right) + \kappa_p\beta_w\left(\frac{y}{xl} - \overline{e}\right)\right] + \pi + i\right)\right) \\
\dot{b} &= \overline{g} - \overline{t}_c^n - \tau_w\omega\frac{y}{x} - \overline{\mu}m - b\left(\kappa\left[\beta_p\left(\frac{y}{y^p} - u\right) + \kappa_p\beta_w\left(\frac{y}{xl} - \overline{e}\right)\right] + \pi + i\right) \\
\dot{y}^e &= \beta_{y^e}[c + i + \delta + \overline{g} - y^e] + y^e(i - n) \\
\dot{\omega} &= \omega\kappa\left[(1 - \kappa_p)\beta_w\left(\frac{y}{xl} - \overline{e} + \kappa_w - 1\right)\beta_p\left(\frac{y}{y^p} - \overline{u}\right)\right] \\
\dot{l} &= l\left[-i_1(q - 1) - i_2\left(\frac{y}{y^p} - \overline{u}\right)\right] \\
\dot{v} &= y - (c + i + \delta + \overline{g}) - vi
\end{aligned}
\qquad (4.37)
$$

Proposition 7

The steady state of the dynamic system (4.37) is locally asymptotically stable if the conditions in proposition 6 are met and β_n is sufficiently small.

Proof

The proof is left to Appendix III.

We finally let β_π become positive which brings us back to the full differential equation system (though we are still neglecting the integral equation of the model and thus the dynamics of capital gain expectations).

$$
\begin{aligned}
\dot{\omega} &= \omega\kappa[(1 - \kappa_p)\beta_w(e - \overline{e}) + (\kappa_w - 1)\beta_p(u - \overline{u})] \\
\dot{\pi} &= \alpha\beta_\pi\kappa[\beta_p(u - \overline{u}) + \kappa_p\beta_w(e - \overline{e})] + (1 - \alpha)\beta_\pi(\overline{\mu} - n - \pi) \\
\hat{l} &= n - i = -i_1(q - 1) - i_2(u - \overline{u}) \\
\dot{y}^e &= \beta_{y^e}(y^d - y^e) + (n - i)y^e \\
\dot{v} &= y - y^d - iv \\
\dot{b} &= \overline{g} - \overline{t}_c^n - \tau_w\omega l^d - \overline{\mu}m - b(\kappa[\beta_p(u - \overline{u}) + \kappa_p\beta_w(e - \overline{e})] + \pi + i) \\
\dot{m} &= m\overline{\mu} - m(\kappa[\beta_p(u - \overline{u}) + \kappa_p\beta_w(e - \overline{e})] + \pi + i)
\end{aligned}
\qquad (4.38)
$$

Proposition 8

The steady state of the dynamic system (4.38) is locally asymptotically stable if the conditions in proposition 7 are met and β_π is sufficiently small.

Proof

The proof is left to the Appendix III.

In other words, fast sales expectations coupled with sluggish adjustments of wages, prices, inventories and inflationary expectations gives rise to local asymptotic stability if it is furthermore assumed that the investment accelerator term is weak and the real balance effect in the investment equation (via Tobin's q) is sufficiently strong. We conjecture that slow adjustment of capital gain expectations will also preserve the stability of the interior steady state solution of the dynamical system.

Proposition 9

The steady state of the dynamic system (4.38) always loses its stability by way of a Hopf bifurcation if for example the inflationary climate term is adjusted with sufficient speed.

Proof

The proof basically relies on the fact that the determinant of the Jacobian of steady state of the dynamic system (4.38) is always negative[8] so that eigenvalues have to cross the imaginary axis (excluding zero) when stability is lost.

There are further conditions involved when showing the existence of either sub-critical or supercritical Hopf bifurcations. There is first the positive speed condition according to which eigenvalues must cross the imaginary axes. Second, the Liapunov coefficient must be non-zero. Both conditions are purely technical and will almost always hold in a system with non-linear functional relationships such as the ones we have here.

We expect that the above proposition also holds when capital gain expectations of chartists and fundamentalists are made endogenous. In particular, loss of stability can be obtained by increasing the adjustment speed of the backward looking part of the expectations mechanism. Due to the difficulties of treating the 8D integro-differential system, we do not go into a proof of this assertion.

Let us finally assert without proof that the normal or adverse Rose effect (through which changes in real wages lead to changes in aggregate demand and thereby to further changes in money wages, the price level and the real wage)[9] will also be present in the currently considered KMG dynamics. Either wage or price flexibility will therefore be destabilizing and leads us to Hopf bifurcation, limit cycles and eventually purely explosive behaviour. Furthermore, the Mundell or real rate of interest effect is not obviously present in the considered dynamics as there is no longer a real rate of interest involved in investment (or consumption) behaviour. Increasing expected price inflation does not directly increase aggregate demand, economic activity and thus the actual rate of price inflation. This means that the model needs to be extended in order to take into account the role that is generally played by the real rate of interest. There are finally two accelerator effects involved in the dynamics: the Metzlerian inventory accelerator mechanism and the Harrodian fixed business investment accelerator (in level formulation). We therefore expect that increasing the parameters β_n, i_2 will also be destabilizing and lead us to Hopf bifurcations and more.

The emergence of damped business fluctuations under suitable policy measures

In the following analysis, we consider that all assumptions stated in Proposition 3 hold. What remains to be analysed is the dynamical behaviour of the system, when it is displaced from its steady state position, but still remains in a neighbourhood of the steady state. In the following we show that there must be a locally stable steady state, if some sufficient conditions (that are plausible from a Keynesian perspective) are met.

We begin with an appropriate subsystem of the full dynamics for which the Routh–Hurwitz conditions can be shown to hold. Setting $\beta_p = \beta_w = \beta_{\pi_{ef}} = \beta_{\pi_{ec}} = \beta_n = \beta_{\pi^c} = 0$, $\beta_{y^e} > 0$, and keeping $\pi^c, \pi_e, \omega, \nu$ at their steady state values, we get the following subdynamics of state variables m, b and y^e which are then independent of the rest of the system:[10]

$$\begin{aligned} \dot{m} &= m(\mu - (\pi^c + i(\cdot))) \\ \dot{b} &= g - t_c - \tau_w \omega \frac{y}{x} - \mu m - b(\pi^c + i(\cdot)) \\ \dot{y}^e &= \beta_{y^e}[c + i(\cdot) + \delta + g - y^e] + y^e(i(\cdot) - n) \end{aligned} \qquad (4.39)$$

The steady state of the system of differential equations (4.39) was shown to be locally asymptotically stable if β_{y^e} is sufficiently large, the investment accelerator i_u concerning deviations of capital utilization from the normal capital utilization is sufficiently small and the absolute values of the partial derivatives of desired cash balances with respect to the interest rate $\partial f_m/\partial r$ and the rate of return on equities $\partial f_m/\partial r_e^e$ are sufficiently small. The proposition asserts that local asymptotic stability at the steady state of the considered sub-dynamics holds when the demand for cash is not much influenced by the rates of return on the financial asset markets,[11] the accelerating effect of capacity utilization on the investment behaviour is sufficiently small, and the adjustment speed of expected sales towards actual demand (the dynamic multiplier process) is fast enough.

In order to show how policy can enforce the validity of this situation, we need some preliminary observations. In the given structure of financial markets, it is natural to assume that even $\partial f_m/\partial r_e^e = 0$ and $\partial f_e/\partial i = 0$ holds. Indeed fixed-price bonds' properties are equivalent to saving deposits' and bonds and money M taken together form what is named $M2$ in the literature. The internal structure of $M2$ is a matter of simple cash management and should therefore imply that the rate of return r_e^e on equities does not matter. The latter only matters at the stage of the choice between equities and demand for the aggregate $M2$.

Moreover, since the transaction costs for reallocations within $M2$ can be assumed to be small and the speed of adjustment of the dynamic multiplier (which is infinite if *IS*-equilibrium is assumed) large, we only have one critical parameter left in the above proposition which may be the crucial one for the stability of the considered sub-system of the dynamics. This is the investment parameter i_u, that represents a specific kind of investment accelerator of Harrodian type. This suggests that fiscal policy should be used to counteract the working of this accelerator mechanism through which higher capacity utilization leads to higher investment, higher goods demand and finally higher capacity utilization.

The following proposition formulates how fiscal policy should be designed in order to create damped oscillations around the balanced growth path of the model (if they are not yet present).

Theorem 1

Let us assume an independent fiscal authority solely responsible for the control of business fluctuations which implements the following two rules for its activity oriented expenditures and their funding:

$$g^u = -g_u(u - \overline{u}), \quad t^u = g_u(u - \overline{u})$$

The budget of this authority is always balanced and we assume that the tributes t^u that are necessary for this are paid by asset-holding households. The stability condition on i_u is thereby extended to the consideration of the parameter $i_u - g_u$. Therefore, an anti-cyclical policy g_u that is chosen in a sufficiently active way will enforce damped oscillations in the considered sub-dynamics if the savings rate s_c of asset holders is sufficiently close to one and if stock markets are sufficiently tranquil.

Neither the steady state nor the laws of motions are really changed by the introduction of such a self-determined 'business-cycle' authority, if $s_c \approx 1$ holds, which is what we assume to the following for reasons of simplicity.

We now consider the same system but allow for β_p to become positive. This means that ω, which had previously entered the m, b, y^e–sub-system only through its steady state value, now becomes a dynamic variable that gives rise to the 4D dynamical system:

$$\begin{aligned}
\dot{m} &= m\left(\mu - \left(\kappa\beta_p\left(\frac{y}{y^p} - \overline{u}\right) + \pi^c + i(\cdot)\right)\right) \\
\dot{b} &= g - t_c - \tau_w\omega\frac{y}{x} - \mu m - b\left(\kappa\beta_p\left(\frac{y}{y^p} - \overline{u}\right) + \pi^c + i(\cdot)\right) \\
\dot{y}^e &= \beta_{y^e}\left[c + i(\cdot) + \delta + g - y^e\right] + y^e(i(\cdot) - n) \\
\dot{\omega} &= \omega\kappa(\kappa_w - 1)\beta_p\left(\frac{y}{y^p} - \overline{u}\right)
\end{aligned} \tag{4.40}$$

The interior steady state of the dynamical system (4.40) is locally asymptotically stable if the conditions of this 3D case are met and if β_p is sufficiently small.

This result is also obtained for large β_p by the assumption $\kappa_w \approx 1$, i.e. that workers and their representatives should always demand in the money wage negotiation process for a (nearly) full indexation of their nominal wage inflation rate to the rate of price inflation. This implies that:

Theorem 2

Let us assume that the cost-push term in the money wage adjustment rule is given approximately by the current rate of price inflation (which is perfectly foreseen) holds. Then, the considered 4D sub-dynamics implies damped oscillations around the given steady state position of the economy if the conditions of Theorem 1 are met.

This type of *scala mobile* thus implies stability instead of – as might be expected – instability, since it simplifies the real wage channel of the model considerably. However, in order to really tame the wage–price spiral of the model, we need the following additional theorem.

If we enlarge the system (4.40) by letting β_w become positive, we get the following subsystem:

$$\begin{aligned}
\dot{m} &= m\left(\mu - \left(\kappa\left[\beta_p\left(\frac{y}{y^p} - \bar{u}\right) + \kappa_p\beta_w\left(\frac{y}{xl} - \bar{e}\right)\right] + \pi^c + i(\cdot)\right)\right)\\
\dot{b} &= g - t_c - \tau_w\omega\frac{y}{x} - \mu m\\
&\quad - b\left(\kappa\left[\beta_p\left(\frac{y}{y^p} - \bar{u}\right) + \kappa_p\beta_w\left(\frac{y}{xl} - \bar{e}\right)\right] + \pi^c + i(\cdot)\right)\\
\dot{y}^e &= \beta_{y^e}[c + i(\cdot) + \delta + g - y^e] + y^e(i(\cdot) - n) \qquad (4.41)\\
\dot{\omega} &= \omega\kappa\left[(1-\kappa_p)\beta_w\left(\frac{y}{xl} - \bar{e}\right) + (\kappa_w - 1)\beta_p\left(\frac{y}{y^p} - \bar{u}\right)\right]\\
\dot{l} &= l\left[-i_q(q-1) - i_u\left(\frac{y}{y^p} - \bar{u}\right)\right]
\end{aligned}$$

From the preceding section we then get that the steady state of the dynamical system (4.41) is locally asymptotically stable if the conditions in theorem 2 are met and β_w is sufficiently small.

Theorem 3

We assume that the economy is a consensus based one, i.e., labour and capital reach proximate agreement with respect to the scala mobile principle in the dynamic of money wages. Let us assume that they also agree against this background that additional money wage increases should be small in the boom ($u-\bar{u}$) and vice versa in the recession. This makes the steady state *of the considered 5D sub-dynamics asymptotically stable if the conditions of the preceding theorem are met.*

Some sort of wage management process is needed in addition to the demand management process described in theorem 1. Meade (1982) was one of the first who recognized in a very detailed way that a wage and demand management approach is needed for the proper functioning of capitalism in a social and democratic society. Income policy is therefore at least as important and – in this model – more complicated to operate than fiscal policy. The latter only has to tame the Harrodian accelerator dynamic, whereas this income policy must reflect and try to influence in an appropriate way the behaviour of both capital and labour. This policy is therefore interacting with firmly rooted negotiation habits of the two basic agents of our KMGT model and concerns the long run evolution of the economy, not only the business cycle.

We now enlarge the system further by letting β_n, the adjustment speed of planned inventory changes, become positive. One may expect relatively fast adjustment processes implying that the adjustment lag $1/\beta_n$, is probably less than a quarter in length. We now obtain a 6D dynamics from the previously considered 5D system:

$$
\begin{aligned}
\dot{m} &= m\left(\mu - \left(\kappa\left[\beta_p\left(\frac{y}{y^p} - \bar{u}\right) + \kappa_p\beta_w\left(\frac{y}{xl} - \bar{e}\right)\right] + \pi^c + i(\cdot)\right)\right) \\
\dot{b} &= g - t_c - \tau_w\omega\frac{y}{x} - \mu m - b\left(\kappa\left[\beta_p\left(\frac{y}{y^p} - \bar{u}\right) + \kappa_p\beta_w\left(\frac{y}{xl} - \bar{e}\right)\right] + \pi^c + i(\cdot)\right) \\
\dot{y}^e &= \beta_{y^e}[c + i(\cdot) + \delta + g - y^e] + y^e(i(\cdot) - n) \\
\dot{\omega} &= \omega\kappa\left[(1-\kappa_p)\beta_w\left(\frac{y}{xl} - \bar{e}\right) + (\kappa_w - 1)\beta_p\left(\frac{y}{y^p} - \bar{u}\right)\right] \\
\dot{l} &= l[-i_q(q-1) - i_u\left(\frac{y}{y^p} - \bar{u}\right)] \\
\dot{\nu} &= y - (c + i(\cdot) + \delta + g) - \nu i(\cdot)
\end{aligned}
\tag{4.42}
$$

Theorem 4

The Metzlerian feedback between expected sales and output is given by

$$y = (1 + \alpha_{n^d}(n + \beta_n))y^e - \beta_n\nu$$

This static relationship implies that sufficiently small inventory holdings, represented by the parameter α_{n^d} or cautious inventory adjustment β_n (or both) can tame the Metzlerian output accelerator (if the conditions of the preceding theorem are met).

We do not introduce any regulation of this Metzlerian sales-inventory adjustment process, but assume instead that this inventory accelerator process is of a secondary nature in the business fluctuations generated by the dynamics of the KMGT model, in particular if the control of the Harrodian goods market accelerator is working properly.

We now let β_{π^c} become positive so that we are back to the differential equation system:

$$\begin{aligned}
\dot{m} &= m\mu - m(\kappa[\beta_p(u-\overline{u}) + \kappa_p\beta_w(e-\overline{e})] + \pi^c + i(\cdot)) \\
\dot{b} &= g - t_c - \tau_w\omega l^d - \mu m - b(\kappa[\beta_p(u-\overline{u}) + \kappa_p\beta_w(e-\overline{e})] + \pi^c + i(\cdot)) \\
\dot{y}^e &= \beta_{y^e}(y^d - y^e) + (i(\cdot) - n)y^e \qquad (4.43) \\
\dot{\omega} &= \omega\kappa[(1-\kappa_p)\beta_w(e-\overline{e}) + (\kappa_w - 1)\beta_p(u-\overline{u})] \\
\hat{l} &= n - i(\cdot) = -i_q(q-1) - i_u(u-\overline{u}) \\
\dot{\nu} &= y - y^d - i(\cdot)\nu, s \\
\dot{\pi}^c &= \alpha\beta_{\pi^c}\kappa[\beta_p(u-\overline{u}) + \kappa_p\beta_w(e-\overline{e})] + (1-\alpha)\beta_{\pi^c}(\mu - n - \pi^c)
\end{aligned}$$

Theorem 5

Let us assume that the business cycle is controlled in the way we have described so far and that fundamentalist expectations formation about the rate of price inflation become dominant in the adjustment rule for the inflationary climate:

$$\dot{\pi}^c = \beta_{\pi^c}(\alpha\hat{p} + (1-\alpha)(\mu - n) - \pi^c)$$

If the parameter α is sufficiently small so that chartists are only weakly influencing the economy (and if the conditions of the preceding theorem are met) the steady state of the considered dynamics will remain an attractor.

The economy will thus continue to exhibit damped fluctuations if the parameter α, in the law of motion of the inflationary climate expression π^c, is chosen sufficiently small, which is a reasonable possibility if the business cycle is damped and actual inflation is only generated by the market for goods (if theorem 2 is applied with $\kappa_w \approx 1$):

$$\hat{p} \approx \beta_p(u - \overline{u})/(1 - \kappa_p) + \pi^c$$

is moderate. A stronger orientation of the inflation climate towards a return to the steady state rate of inflation thus helps to stabilize the economy.

The consideration of expectation formation on financial markets is still ignored here (assumed as static). It is however obvious that an enlargement of the dynamics by these expectations will not destroy the considered stability properties if only fundamentalists are active, since this only enlarges the Jacobian through a negative entry in its diagonal. In the same way, a relatively small portion of chartists (as compared to fundamentalists) will preserve the damped fluctuations. Therefore the steady state of the dynamic system (4.43) is locally asymptotically stable if the parameter $\alpha_{\pi_{ec}}$ is sufficiently small.

In order to get this result enforced by policy action, independently of the size of the chartist population, we introduce the following type of Tobin tax τ_e on capital gains on equities:

$$\dot{\pi}_{ef} = \beta_{\pi_{ef}}(\eta - \pi_{ef}) \tag{4.44}$$

$$\dot{\pi}_{ec} = \beta_{\pi_{ec}}((1 - \tau_e)\hat{p}_e - \pi_{ec}) \tag{4.45}$$

Such a tax may be monitored through a corresponding tax declaration scheme which not only taxes capital gains, but also subsidizes capital losses (and thus is not entirely to the disadvantage of the asset holders of the model). We may also assume that stock markets will be fairly taxed, which justifies the last assumption made in Theorem 1.

Theorem 6

The Tobin tax parameter τ_e implies that damped business fluctuations remain damped for all tax rates chosen sufficiently large (below 100 per cent).

The financial market accelerator can therefore be tamed through the introduction of an appropriate level of a Tobinian capital gain taxation *rule*. This rule introduces a new sector to the economy which accumulates or decumulates reserve funds R according to the rule

$$\dot{R} = \tau_e \dot{p}_e E$$

In order to keep the laws of motion of the economy unchanged (to allow the application of the stability propositions of the preceding section), we assume that this sector is independent from other public institutions. We get the following steady state value $\breve{\rho}$ of the funds of this new sector expressed per value unit of capital pK:

$$\breve{\rho} = (R/pK) = \tau_e(\mu - n)/\mu < 1$$

This easily follows from the law of motion:

$$\begin{aligned}\hat{\rho} &= \hat{R} - \hat{p} - \hat{K} = \frac{\tau_e \dot{p}_e E}{R} - \hat{p} - \hat{K} \\ &= \frac{\tau_e(p_e E)/(pK)}{R/(pK)} \frac{\dot{p}_e}{p_e} - (\hat{p} + \hat{K}) = \frac{\tau_e q \hat{p}_e}{\rho} - (\hat{p} + \hat{K})\end{aligned}$$

since one have $\hat{p} + \hat{K} = \mu$, $\hat{\rho} = 0$, $q = 1$, and $\hat{p}_e = \hat{p}$ in the steady state. It is assumed that the reserves of this institution are large enough in order not to be exhausted during the damped business fluctuations generated by the model.

The stability results of the propositions of the preceding section and the stability theorems of the present one are appealing in view of what we know about Keynesian feedback structures. Indeed they come to say that: the wage–price spiral must be fairly damped around a cost of living oriented scala mobile; the Keynesian dynamic multiplier process must be (made) a stable one (and not too much distorted by the existence of Metzlerian inventory cycles and Harrodian knife-edge growth accelerator process); inflationary and capital gains expectations are primarily fundamentalist in orientation; and money (cash) demand is subject to only small transaction costs and fairly unresponsive to rate of return changes on risky financial assets. Such assumptions seem to make sense from a Keynesian perspective.

We then obtain from the above theorems that: independently conducted counter-cyclical fiscal policy can limit the fluctuations on the goods market; an appropriate consensus between capital and labour can tame the wage–price spiral; and a Tobin tax can tame the financial market accelerator. Metzlerian inventory dynamics and fluctuations in the inflationary climate may then also be weak and thus not endanger asymptotic stability.

As for monetary policy, in this model we get the extreme result that monetary policy is totally ineffective in the control of the economy between the short and the medium run. It only affects the cash management process of asset holders, but leaves $M2 = M + B$ invariant, unless open market operations are also performed on the equity market. This is of course a demanding policy option that would need to be investigated and discussed in much more details but that is beyond the scope of the present work.[12] Such a monetary policy could however be dangerous in the case of a liquidity trap that would concern the whole of $M2 = M + B$ (where therefore equity owners would attempt to a large degree to sell their equities against the fully liquid assets $M,B,$) since such a situation would imply – as in the financial crisis of 2008/9 – that the public authorities get the bad assets so that the risk of equity holding shifts to the central bank of the country.

In this baseline portfolio approach to Keynesian macrodynamics we will first consider a really tranquil monetary policy as far as the long-run is concerned, i.e. assume a constant growth rate of the money supply $\mu > n$ (as it was assumed so far in our model). This policy is oriented towards the long run and implies here a positive inflation rate in the steady state. This should be a high enough rate to avoid all deflationary tendencies where the above described compromise between capital and labour may break down – since workers might be opposed to money wage reductions.[13]

One can then show that a monetary policy that is only oriented towards the short-term rate of interest is ineffective in this type of KMG–Tobin model in its present form – unless it affects capital gain expectations on the stock market. This result holds for money supply steering as well as for the now fashionable interest rate policy rules, since such policy only affects the cash management process within the given stock of money $M2 = M + B$. This result is a limited case of what Keynes already observed in *The General Theory*, where he wrote:

> Where, however, (as in the United States, 1933–1934) open-market operations have been limited to the purchase of very short-dated securities, the effect may, of course, be mainly confined to the very short-term rate of interest and have but little reaction on the much more important long-term rates of interest. (Keynes, 1936, p.197)

We have not included long-term bonds nor firms' debt, so that equities are the only source of financing for firms' investment. In this model, the following proposal of Keynes should then be read as referring to the stock market:

> If the monetary authority were prepared to deal both ways on specified terms in debts of all maturities, and even more so if it were prepared to deal in debts of varying degrees of risk, the relationship between the complex of rates of interest and the quantity of money would be direct. (Keynes, 1936, p.205)

We take this statement into account by assuming, in extension of the rule $\dot{M} = \mu M$, $\mu = \text{const.}$, that:[14]

$$\hat{M} = \mu - \beta_{mq}(q - \breve{q}), \quad \text{with } \mu M = \dot{B}_c, \dot{M} - \mu M = -\beta_{mq}(q - \breve{q})M = p_e \dot{E}_c \quad (4.46)$$

This additional policy rule of the central bank takes the state of the stock market, as measured by the gap between Tobin's q and its steady state value $\breve{q} = 1$, as a reference point in order to increase money supply above its long-run rate in the bust through purchases of equities. In a boom, it sells stock and decreases the money supply below its long-run trend value. This is clearly a monetary policy that attempts to control the fluctuations in stock prices that the stock market is generating, since it buys stocks when the stock market is weak and sells stocks in the opposite case. Such a policy is meant to be applied under normal conditions on financial markets and may not be of help in cases where a liquidity trap is in operation.

Transferred to the intensive form level this rule, which we call a Tobin rule in the following, now gives rise to the law of motion for real balances per value unit of capital:

$$\hat{m} = \mu - \beta_{mq}(q - \breve{q}) - (\hat{p} + \hat{K}) \quad (4.47)$$

We know that the trend increase in money supply by the central bank (through open market operations in short-term bonds) implies that part of government debt is purchased by the CB, so that the change in government debt is exactly given by the actual change in $M2$. In addition to its holdings of government bonds, we assume that the CB holds equities in a sufficient amount in order to pursue its short-run-oriented stock market policy. This policy is sustainable in the long-run, since the CB buys stocks when they are cheap and sells them when they are expensive. This gives rise to a reformulated law of motion for real balances:

$$\begin{aligned} \dot{m} &= \mu m - \beta_{mq}(q(m+b, r_k^e + \pi_e) - 1) \\ &\quad - (\kappa[\beta_p(u-\overline{u}) + \kappa_p\beta_w(e-\overline{e})] + \pi^c + i(\cdot))m \end{aligned}$$

and thus implies a significant change in the complexity of the dynamics to be investigated. We therefore only conjecture that the above propositions and theorems can again be formulated and proved. We will show that such a policy contributes to the stability of the steady state of the dynamics:

Theorem 7

A *The initially considered 3D subdynamics of the full 9D dynamics:*

$$\begin{aligned} \dot{m} &= m(\mu - \beta_{mq}(q - \breve{q}) - (\pi^c + i(\cdot))) \\ \dot{b} &= g - t_c - \tau_w \omega \frac{y}{x} - \mu m - b(\pi^c + i(\cdot)) \\ \dot{y}^e &= \beta_{y^e}[c + i(\cdot) + \delta + g - y^e] + y^e(i(\cdot) - n) \end{aligned} \tag{4.48}$$

can be additionally stabilized (by increasing the parameter range where damped oscillations are established and by making the originally given damped oscillations even less volatile) by an increasing parameter value β_{mq} *if anti-cyclical fiscal policy is sufficiently active to make the dynamic multiplier process a stable one (by neutralizing the Harrodian investment accelerator) and if the savings rate* s_c *of asset holders is sufficiently close to one (which allows us to ignore effects from taxation on the consumption of asset holders).*

B *The sequence of policy theorems in the present chapter can be applied to this new situation and implies the asymptotic stability of the steady state of the KMGT dynamics when the discussed policy options are put in practice.*

Proof

As for the sketch of the proof of this theorem, see Appendix IV.

The important tools to stabilize the economy, or at least to make it less volatile, are therefore: a Keynesian anti-cyclical demand management; a consensus-based wage management, a Tobin-type management of the financial market accelerating processes; a willingness of the CB to trade equities.

We stress here briefly that this extension is based on the following stock-flow relationships:

$$\begin{aligned}
\dot{B} &= pG + iB - pT - \mu M \\
\dot{E} &= \dot{E}_f - \dot{E}_f \\
p_e\dot{E}_c &= -\beta_{mq}(q - \breve{q})M = \dot{M}_q \\
\dot{M} &= \mu M + \dot{M}_q \\
\dot{\Pi}_c &= r_k^e pKp_eE_c/(p_eE + p_eE_c) + \dot{p}_eE_c \\
\dot{B}_c &= \mu M
\end{aligned}$$

The subscript f stands now for firms and c for central bank in order to distinguish their stock-flow contributions from those of asset holders (for which we do no use any index). Interest payments on B_c are assumed to be transferred back to the government so that part of the government deficit is money financed. Equity prices are determined by current stocks independently on the inflow of new assets. Let us note finally that the central bank accumulates (or decumulates) government bonds B_c, equities E_c, dividend payments and capital gains.[15]

Conclusions and outlook

We have built a high (9D) dimensional model with a real-financial interaction of Tobinian portfolio type. In this model we have proved that, (i) a fiscal authority with a demand management that is independent of the political structure of the economy, (ii) a monetary authority which tailors its Taylor rule to what is needed for stabilizing financial market volatility and therewith investment volatility, (iii) a Tobin tax authority which counteracts destabilizing chartists' capital gain expectations and thus reduces volatility in the stock market or, (iv) a labour market authority or concerted action which tranquillizes the wage–price spiral, can all remove the persistent volatility of the busines cycle observed without policy controls.

These results suggest various ways of getting out of the current form of unleashed capitalism. Monetary policy could turn its focus on impacting the risky assets on the financial markets in a counter-cyclical way so that the volatility of financial markets would be reduced. Inflation and labour market institutions could also be created in order to tame the wage price spiral. The later could range from basic income policies to the erection of a 'flexicurity' system.

5
Tobinian Stock-Flow Interactions in the Mundell–Fleming Model

Introduction

In this chapter we approach the issue of stock-flow interaction in open economies through a slightly modified version of the Mundell–Fleming–Tobin (MFT) model of Rødseth (2000). This model considers IS–LM goods market equilibria in place of the sluggish Metzlerian goods market adjustment processes of the KMG model. The Goodwin component will also be missing here since aggregate demand is not made dependent on income distribution (i.e., the Rose real wage channel is also neglected).

Our model will go significantly beyond the traditional Mundell–Fleming approach. First, we will introduce Tobinian portfolio choices and therefore imperfect substitutability of financial assets in place of an UIP condition. In a first step, this imperfectness will be coupled with the assumption that domestic bonds are non-tradable (i.e., the amount of foreign bonds held domestically will only be changed to the extent that there is a surplus or a deficit in the current account).[1] Second, we will use a standard open economy money wage Phillips curve, i.e we will introduce labour market driven price inflation or deflation dynamics in the Mundell–Fleming framework.

Another important feature of the model presented here is that we will assume regressive exchange rate expectations formation in place of the (questionable) rational expectations assumption. This expectations formation mechanism will allow for maximum stability of the considered dynamics (since only fundamentalist and thus, in principle, only converging expectation revisions are allowed for). This will be helpful for the central objective of the chapter which is to focus on the fundamental destabilizing forces contained in the two accumulation equations for internal and external deficits or surpluses, caused by the government budget equation and the evolution of the current account of the considered economy.

In the next section we will present the accounting framework of the MFT model. The following section will describe its behavioural equations and the subsequent intrinsically generated dynamics (which includes also a Phillips curve approach to inflation dynamics), calculate the steady state position of the dynamics and perform some preliminary stability considerations. We will then study inflation and balance of payments dynamics in the case of an interest rate peg coupled with an exchange rate peg. And the final section will contrast this situation with a regime where the exchange rate is perfectly flexible and the money supply is a given magnitude under the control of the Central Bank of the domestic economy.

The accounting framework

Social accounting matrix and budget equations

Table 5.1 gives the SAM of the MFT model for the non-financial part of the economy. A standard SAM is very similar to Tobin and Godley's transactions flow matrix introduced in previous chapters. The only difference is that a SAM is a square matrix based on the principle of *single-entry* book keeping. In other words every economic transaction has only one entry in the SAM, the originator of the transaction being represented in the corresponding column and the beneficiary in the corresponding row.[2]

Each (sub-)account that needs to be considered in relation to some particular issue has its own row and its own column in the SAM. These rows and columns are identically ordered. Columns represent expenditures and rows show receipts.[3] Totals for corresponding rows and columns are always the same as each account is balanced. There are two types of accounts in a SAM. First, as in Godley's matrix, there are both current and capital accounts for economic sectors. Second there is a 'production' account which, as the name states, contains all the transactions linked to the production activity. Its column represents the 'output costs' and its row shows the 'output uses'. 'As every transaction is, in reality, a transaction between two institutions (A pays B),

Table 5.1 Social accounting matrix of the MFT model

Expenditures / Receipts		Production	Current accounts			Combined capital account	Σ
			Private	Government	Rest of World		
Production			pC	pG	pX	pI	$pY{+}pIM$
Current accounts	Private	pY		iB	$si^{*}F_p$		pY_p
	Gvt		pT		$si^{*}F_c$		pY_g^a
	RoW	pIM					pIM
Capital account			pS_p	pS_g^a	pS_{RoW}	$-pI$	0
Σ		$pY{+}pIM$	pY_p	pY_g^a	pIM	0	

the introduction of the production accounts is essentially an abstraction that allows economic concepts [such as GDP or value-added] to feature in the system' (Pyatt, 1988, p.331).

In its one-country version, the MFT model considers three sectors: the private sector (including both households and non-financial firms), the aggregate government (including the central bank) and the rest of the world or foreign sector. As shown in the first row, the nominal domestic output pY is equal to the sum of consumption pC, government expenditures pG, investment pI and net exports pNX (that are the difference between exports and imports $pX - pIM$):[4]

$$pY \equiv pC + pG + pI + pNX \tag{5.1}$$

Each current account gives the budget equation of the corresponding sector. With respect to the private sector, we assume that all of firms' income is transferred to households. Moreover households provide the credit needed to allow firms to finance their investment expenditures (which is, by and large, the same as the assumption of a direct investment decision by the household sector). Therefore the nominal income of the private sector pY_p comes from the 'value-added' of domestic production pY and the interest payments on domestic bonds iB and foreign bonds $si^{*}F_p$ held by households. Private savings pS_p are defined residually as the part of this income which is not used for consumption purposes or to pay taxes:

$$pY_p \equiv pY + iB + si^*F_p \tag{5.2}$$

$$pS_p \equiv pY_p - pC - pT \tag{5.3}$$

We denote here by B, F_p the domestic and foreign bonds held by the household sector and by F_c the foreign assets held by the central bank (its currency reserves, that can only be changed by open market operations on the domestic market for foreign assets). For domestic bonds we assume, as in Flaschel (2006), that they are non-tradables. We use i for the nominal rate of interest and s for the nominal exchange rate and index by $*$ foreign set variables, which are obviously not under the control of the domestic economy. All other symbols are fairly standard and thus need no explanation here.

Concerning the aggregate government sector, we note that the central bank (CB) may change its government bond holdings by means of an open market policy $dB_c = dM$, and similarly its foreign bond holdings through $dF_c = dM$, without influencing the flow budget equations discussed here, since all interest income from these bond holdings is transferred back to the government sector.[5] The domestic bond holdings of the CB can therefore be neglected in the following and an additional indexation of the magnitude that is held by the household sector can thus be avoided. The aggregate income of the government pY_g^a comes from taxes and interest payments on the foreign reserves of the central bank and is used for government's purchases of services and interest payments on domestic bonds. The value of the government's aggregate savings pS_g^a is usually less than zero since government expenditures tend to be higher than its income:

$$pY_g^a \equiv pT + si^*F_c \tag{5.4}$$

$$pS_g^a \equiv pY_g - pG - iB \tag{5.5}$$

As for the foreign sector, its 'savings' pS_{ROW} are equal to the external current account deficit of the domestic economy, that is the difference between the imports and the money received from abroad (the latter being the sum of exports and interests on foreign bonds):

$$pS_{ROW} \equiv -pNX - si^*F_p - si^*F_c \tag{5.6}$$

As shown in the last row, the standard savings-investment identity holds in this economy:

$$pS_p + pS_g^a + pS_{ROW} = pI$$

which gives for the total domestic savings pS $(= pS_p + pS_g^a)$:

$$pS \equiv pI + pNX + si^*F_p + si^*F_c$$

Financial SAM and saving/financing decisions

A standard SAM, as Table 5.1, does not show transactions on financial assets.[6] To make them appear means turning the SAM into a *financial* SAM (or FSAM). In the case of financial transactions, to use single-entry bookkeeping would lead to a loss of information since a money 'receipt' can come either from an increase in liabilities or a decrease in financial assets. Therefore, to build a FSAM, one has to distinguish between changes in assets and changes in liabilities. One way to do so is to introduce, for every financial asset, a new column labelled 'change in assets and liabilities' and to represent increase in liabilities with a positive sign and increase in assets with a negative sign. This comes down to adopting double-entry book keeping since each financial transaction always simultaneously corresponds to an increase in the assets of one sector and in the liabilities of another. Therefore the sum of every new column must equate to zero. Equally the sum of each row corresponding to a capital account must also be zero as capital accounts are balanced by the savings entries.[7]

Table 5.2 gives the FSAM of the MFT model. The accounting identities issued from the capital account rows describe the saving/financing decisions of the three sectors:[8]

$$\begin{aligned} pS_p &\equiv pI + \dot{M}^d + \dot{B}^d + s\dot{F}_p^d \\ pS_g^a &\equiv -\dot{B} - \dot{M}(+s\dot{F}_c^d) \\ pS_{ROW} &\equiv -s\dot{F} \end{aligned}$$

In the MFT model we will use these equations as follows:

$$\dot{B}^d \equiv pS_p - pI - \dot{M}^d - s\dot{F}_p^d \tag{5.7}$$

$$\dot{B} \equiv -pS_g^a - \dot{M}(+s\dot{F}_c^d) \tag{5.8}$$

$$s\dot{F} \equiv pS_{ROW} \tag{5.9}$$

The first two equations show that the evolution of the *demand* in domestic bonds is implied by households' budget constraint and the evolution of the *supply* derives from the government budget constraint. Equation (5.9) states that the increase (or decrease) in domestic holdings of foreign assets is equal to the external current account surplus (or deficit) of the country (which means that the balance of payments is always balanced, independently of the exchange rate and monetary regimes that are investigated).

The three new columns give the equilibrium conditions on the three financial markets:

$$\dot{M}^d \equiv \dot{M} \tag{5.10}$$

$$\dot{B}^d \equiv \dot{B} \tag{5.11}$$

$$\dot{F} \equiv \dot{F}^d_p(+\dot{F}^d_c) \tag{5.12}$$

With equations (5.10) and (5.11) we assume that the new issues of money and domestic government bonds are always voluntarily absorbed by private households. As for equation (5.12) we use it in two different ways, depending on the exchange rate regime considered. In the case of fixed exchange rates we assume an accommodating supply of foreign bonds by the central bank so that the evolution of its reserves is determined by the evolution of the current account of the economy and private holdings of foreign bonds:

$$\dot{F}^d_c \equiv \dot{F} - \dot{F}^d_p$$

In the case of perfectly flexible exchange rates, we assume that the central bank does not buy (or sell) any new foreign bonds so that $\dot{F}^d_c = 0$. In this second regime, equation (5.12) thus simply gives the equilibrium condition according to which the exchange rate s is determined:

$$\dot{F} \equiv \dot{F}^d_p$$

The FSAM gives all the *flow constraints* that have to be fulfilled in order to build a stock-flow consistent model. In other words, for the accounting of the MFT model to be right, we have to integrate in its equations eleven of the twelve accounting identities issued from the transcription of the FSAM into equations. In this case, according

Table 5.2 Financial SAM of the MFT model

Receipts \ Expenditures		Production	Current accounts			Combined capital account	Δ in assets and liabilities			Σ
			Private	Government	Rest of World		Domestic bonds	Money	Foreign bonds	
Production			pC	$p.G$	$p.X$	pI				$pY+pIM$
Current accounts	Private	pY		$i.B$	si^*F_p					pY_p
	Gvt		pT		si^*F_c					pY_g^a
	RoW	pIM								pIM
Capital accounts	Private		pS_p			$-pI$	$-\dot{B}^d$	$-\dot{M}^d$	$-s\,\dot{F}_p^d$	0
	Gvt			pS_g^a			$+\dot{B}^d$	$+\dot{M}^d$	$(-s\,\dot{F}_c^d)$	0
	RoW				pS_{RoW}				$+s\,\dot{F}$	0
Σ		$pY+pIM$	pY_p	pY_g^a	pIM	0	0	0	0	

to *Walras' law of flows*, the 'missing' twelfth identity will always be verified. In this model the missing identity will be the one relative to the domestic bonds market (equation (5.11)).

Real disposable income and wealth

In order to define the behavioural equations of the model we need to derive expressions for the real disposable income, the real wealth and the debt position of both households and the government. Disposable income is defined, in the conventional Hicksian way, as the level of income that, when consumed, preserves the current level of wealth of the considered sector. Since the rate of inflation $\hat{p} = \dot{p}/p$ is a variable in the following completion of the model, we will use this expression from now on in the definition of the real rates of interest.

The real aggregate government wealth is defined as

$$W_g^a = \frac{-(M+B)+sF_c}{p} = -\frac{(M+B)}{p} + \frac{sF_c}{p} = W_g + W_c \tag{5.13}$$

By definition, the Hicksian real income of the government sector Y_g^H is composed of the tax and receipts of the government plus the inflation and capital gains on government debt and central bank reserves, minus its payments of interests:

$$\begin{aligned} Y_g^H &= Y_g^a - \frac{iB}{p} - \hat{p}W_g + \hat{s}\frac{sF_c}{p} \\ &= T + \frac{si^*F_c}{p} - \frac{iB}{p} + \hat{p}\frac{M+B}{p} + (\hat{s}-\hat{p})\frac{sF_c}{p} \\ &= T - (i-\hat{p})\frac{M+B}{p} + i\frac{M}{p} + (i^* + \hat{s} - \hat{p})\frac{sF_c}{p} \\ &= T + i\frac{M}{p} - (i - i^* - \hat{s})\frac{M+B}{p} + (i^* + \hat{s} - \hat{p})\frac{-(M+B)+sF_c}{p} \\ &= T + i\frac{M}{p} + \xi\frac{M+B}{p} + r^*W_g \end{aligned} \tag{5.14}$$

where $\xi = i^* + \hat{s} - i$ and $r^* = i^* + \hat{s} - \hat{p}$, represent the actual risk premium on foreign bonds and the actual real rate of return on foreign bonds. The third term in equation (5.14) can be ignored if the uncovered interest rate parity condition is assumed to hold. This is however only possible if domestic and foreign bonds are internationally traded.[9]

Concerning the private sector, its wealth is defined as the difference between the wealth of the whole economy W and the aggregate wealth of the government sector W_g^a, i.e.

$$W_p = \frac{M + B + sF_p}{p} = W - W_g^a \quad \left(\text{with} \quad W = \frac{sF}{p}\right) \tag{5.15}$$

The Hicksian real disposable income of the private sector is defined as

$$\begin{aligned} Y_p^H &= Y_p - T - \hat{p}W_p + \hat{s}\frac{sF_p}{p} \\ &= Y - T + (i^* + \hat{s} - \hat{p})\frac{sF_p}{p} + (i - \hat{p})\frac{B}{p} - \hat{p}\frac{M}{p}, \end{aligned}$$

or, after some manipulations,

$$Y_p^H = Y - T + r^*(W - W_g) - \xi\frac{M + B}{p} - i\frac{M}{p} \tag{5.16}$$

From the calculations of the disposable income of households and the government, we finally get:

$$Y_p^H = Y - Y_g^H + r^*W \quad \text{or} \quad Y_p^H + Y_g^H = Y + r^*W$$

as a relationship between the country's total disposable income, its domestic product and the real interest on domestically held foreign bonds.

Dynamics of the model

Output, interest and exchange rate determination

Having described the budget restrictions and disposable income equations of the different sectors in the domestic economy, we follow once again Rødseth (2000) in his description of the temporary equilibrium relationships on the goods and the asset markets, which are given by:

$$\begin{aligned} Y &\overset{IS}{=} C(Y_p^H, W - W_g^a, r, r^{*e}) + I(Y, r, r^{*e}) + G \\ &\quad + NX(\cdot, \sigma, Y^*) \end{aligned} \tag{5.17}$$

$$M/p \overset{LM}{=} m^d(Y, i), m_Y^d > 0, m_i^d < 0 \tag{5.18}$$

$$W \equiv sF/p \stackrel{FF}{=} s(F_p^d + F_c^d)/p = f^d(\xi^e, W - W_g^a) + sF_c^d/p,$$

$$f_{\xi^e}^d > 0, f_{W_p}^d \in (0,1) \tag{5.19}$$

$$B/p = W_p - f^d(\xi^e, W_p) - m^d(Y, i), \quad \xi^e = i^* + \varepsilon(s) - i \tag{5.20}$$

with $r = i - \hat{p}$ and $r^{*e} = i^* + \varepsilon(s) - \hat{p}$ representing the real domestic interest rate and the expected real return on foreign bonds (with $\varepsilon(s)$ representing for example a regressive expectations mechanism). Furthermore, $\sigma = \frac{sp^*}{p}$ denotes the real exchange rate. Equation (5.17) represents an IS curve of an advanced traditional type.[10] The money market equilibrium, a standard LM relationship, is described by equation (5.18), where money demand is assumed to depend positively on the level of output and negatively on the domestic interest rate. Equation (5.19), the FF curve, which represents the equilibrium on the market for foreign bonds (foreign exchange), is determined primarily by the reaction of private households with respect to the risk premium ξ and the marginal wealth effect $f_{W_p}^d$ in foreign (and domestic) bond demand with $F = F_p^d + F_c^d$. According to *Walras' law of stocks*, the market for domestic bonds is always cleared when the money market and the market for foreign bonds are in equilibrium.

We will solve these equations by means of the implicit function theorem for the variables considered as statically endogenous (depending on the monetary and exchange rate regimes that are assumed). We will then insert the results into the laws of motion for p, B and F_p in order to obtain an autonomous system of ordinary differential equations, describing domestic price level dynamic, the dynamic of the government budget constraint, and of the foreign position of the domestic economy. Let us note that the variables M, B, F, i, s may become policy parameters depending on the monetary and exchange regime that is under consideration.[11]

Concerning the interest rate, by applying the implicit function theorem to eq. (5.18) and assuming that money demand is based on the full employment output level $\overline{Y}$, we get that:

$$i = i(p, M, \overline{Y}) \quad \text{with} \quad i_1 > 0, i_2 < 0, i_3 > 0$$

The theory of the nominal rate of interest used here is closely related to the so-called Keynes-effect through which money wage decreases stimulate the economy (when they imply price level changes in the same direction) and lowers the interest rate, which affects consumption and investment via the real rate of interest.

Concerning the nominal exchange rate, inserting the above equation into equation (5.19) gives us an equation for the endogenous variables s and p and thus a theory of the nominal exchange rate, that depends on the dynamically endogenous stock variables B, F_p and the price level p:

$$F_p = pf^d\left(i^* + \varepsilon(s) - i(p, M, \overline{Y}), \frac{M + B + sF_p}{p}\right)/s \tag{5.21}$$

We recall that $f_1^d, f_2^d > 0$ is assumed to hold and that we have $\varepsilon'(s) < 0$.

In the case of a perfectly flexible exchange rate s, when M, F_c remain constant (and under the control of the central bank) as well as $F = F_p + F_c$, we obtain, by means of the implicit function theorem, the following expressions for the partial derivatives:

$$\frac{\partial s}{\partial F_p} = -\frac{s(1 - f_2^d)}{F_p(1 - f_2^d) - pf_1^d\varepsilon'} < 0$$

$$\frac{\partial s}{\partial B} = \frac{f_2^d}{F_p(1 - f_2^d) - pf_1^d\varepsilon'} > 0$$

$$\frac{\partial s}{\partial p} = \frac{f^d - pf_1^d i_1 - f_2^d W_p}{F_p(1 - f_2^d) - pf_1^d\varepsilon'} = \frac{sF_p(1 - f_2^d)/p - pf_1^d i_1 - f_2^d \frac{M+B}{p}}{F_p(1 - f_2^d) - pf_1^d\varepsilon'} < 0$$

with $0 < f_2^d < 1$ (the portfolio choice condition). We note that the last partial derivative is negative if the degree of capital mobility with respect to the risk premium is chosen sufficiently high (which is what we do in the following). The signs of the partial derivatives shown above will also apply to the real exchange rate, due to its definition $\sigma = s(p)p^*/p$. Note finally that the first two partial derivatives will approach zero if capital mobility approaches infinity and that, in this case, the limit of the partial derivative with respect to p is simply given by i_1/ε'. The result $\frac{\partial s}{\partial p} < 0$ reflects the result of the Dornbusch (1976) model, according to which an increase in the domestic interest rate (caused by shrinking real balances) leads to higher depreciation gains expectations and thus a decrease of the nominal exchange rate, that is an appreciation of the currency.

The law of motion for the price level p is determined, under the assumption of constant markup-pricing, by a standard expectations-augmented, open-economy Phillips curve.[12]

$$\begin{aligned}\hat{p} &= \beta_w(Y - \overline{Y}) + \gamma\hat{p} + (1-\gamma)(\pi^* + \varepsilon(s)) \\ &= \beta_w(Y - \overline{Y})/(1-\gamma) + \varepsilon(s), \quad \gamma \in (0,1) \end{aligned} \tag{5.22}$$

where the output gap $Y - \overline{Y}$ measures the demand pressure on the labour market. This form of Phillips curve derives from an expectations-augmented one where the cost-pressure item (relative to the consumer price index) is initially given by a weighted average of domestic and import price inflation of the form: $\gamma\hat{p} + (1-\gamma)(\pi^* + \varepsilon(s))$ and where myopic perfect foresight is assumed (with regards to the evolution of the domestic inflation rate). The foreign rate of inflation, π^*, is assumed to be zero for sake of simplicity.

By inserting the open-economy Phillips curve equation in the IS equilibrium equation described by equation (5.17), we can calculate the signs of the partial derivatives, which, in the case of a sufficiently low speed of adjustment of money wages β_w, are:

$$\frac{\partial Y}{\partial F_p} > 0, \qquad \frac{\partial Y}{\partial B} > 0, \qquad \frac{\partial Y}{\partial p} < 0$$

This holds only if capital mobility is assumed as sufficiently high. We leave the lengthy calculations of the involved partial derivatives to the reader and only state that increases in the wealth of private households stimulate economic activity, while increases in the price level will reduce economic activity through various channels (through real wealth effects in consumption demand, interest rate increases and real exchange rate decreases).

In the case where capital mobility is nearly perfect ($f_\xi^d \approx \infty$) and wages nearly rigid ($\beta_w \approx 0$), we may summarize the comparative static properties – as far as the dynamically endogenous variables are concerned – approximately as follows:

$$i = i(p), i'(p) > 0, \quad s = s(p), s < 0, \quad Y(F_p, B, p), \quad Y_1 > 0, Y_2 > 0, Y_3 < 0$$

Dynamics and the steady state of the economy

Our dynamical representation of the Mundell–Fleming–Tobin model in its general form (with F_c a given magnitude in the considered case of flexible exchange rates and with $p^* = 1$ for simplicity),[13] expressed in nominal terms, consists of the following differential equations:

$$\dot{F}_p = i^*(F_p + F_c) + NX(\cdot, \sigma, Y^*)/\sigma, \quad \sigma = \frac{s}{p}, \; p^* = 1 \tag{5.23}$$

$$\dot{B} = iB + pG - pT - si^*F_c \tag{5.24}$$

These equations will be coupled with the law of motion for the price level p:

$$\dot{p} = [\beta_w(Y - \overline{Y})/(1 - \gamma) + \varepsilon(s)]p \tag{5.25}$$

They will also be integrated with the description of the temporary equilibrium given by equations (5.17) to (5.18) and the definitions of private wealth and real disposable income discussed in the previous section.

In order to allow for a sequential determination of the steady state values of this dynamical system, we proceed as follows.[14] We assume that the steady state value i_o of i is given by i^*, i.e. we have $\xi = 0$ in the steady state. Due to the Phillips curve we know that $Y = Y_o$ must hold. The given quantity of money M then allows to determine the steady state value of p: $p_o = M/m^d(Y_o, i^*)$. To set $\dot{B} = 0$ gives a simple positive relationship between B_o and s_o, which represent the equilibrium in the domestic bond market. The *FFB* – curve implies on this basis:

$$\begin{aligned} F_{po} &\overset{FFB}{=} p_o f^d\left(0, \frac{M + B_o(s_o) + s_o F_{po}}{p_o}\right) \\ &= p_o f^d\left(0, \frac{M}{p_o} + \frac{T - G}{i^*} + \frac{s_o(F_{po} + F_c)}{p_o}\right) \end{aligned}$$

which defines a positive relationship between s_o and F_{po}, as in Figure 5.1 (where we use linear curves for reasons of simplicity).

From $\dot{F} = 0$, the equilibrium in the foreign currency bond market, we get that:

$$i^* F_o + p_o NX(\cdot, s_o/p_o, Y^*) = 0$$

that is, a negative relationship between s_o and F_{po}, represented in Figure 5.1 by the $\dot{F} = 0$ curve. If we assume that $M + B_o$ is non-negative, we have a non-negative demand for foreign bonds at $s_o = 0$ and thus a non-negative value of F_{po} associated with it. In case of linearity, we will then get an intersection of the $\dot{F}=0$ and the *FFB* curve in the positive half plane of the (F, s) space, that gives us positive steady state values for both F_p and s (since one can assume that there is a positive value s where $NX=0$ holds). Under these conditions, the private agents of the domestic economy will hold a positive amount of foreign bonds in the steady state and net exports are therefore negative in the steady state (due to a value of the exchange rate that is below the one that balances the trade balance). In the general case, when both curves of Figure 5.1 are non-linear, one must make sure that (i) the $\dot{F}=0$ curve is not too flat in view of the intersection of the *FFB* – curve with the vertical axis and (ii) both curves are not approaching $+\infty$ for finite values of the nominal exchange rate.

Figure 5.1 illustrates the determination of the steady state values for both the nominal exchange rate and the value of foreign debt held domestically. It also indicates how these values can be influenced by fiscal and monetary policy. It shows that fiscal consolidation will make the currency stronger and increases the amount of foreign debt held domestically. The latter effect is also produced by a monetary expansion, whose effect on the value of s may however be ambiguous,

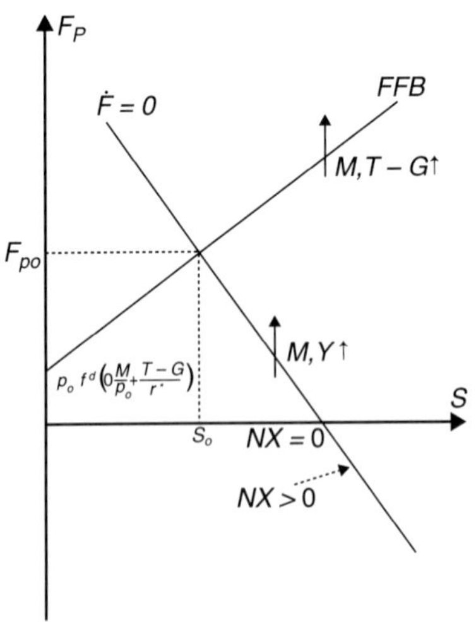

Figure 5.1 Foreign bonds stock equilibrium ($B_o > 0$)

depending on the competitiveness of the considered economy, (i.e. on the elasticity of the net export function with respect to the real exchange rate at the steady state of the economy). At this steady state, we have a negative trade account and a positive interest rate account (and of course a balanced capital account in the balance of payments).

To study closely the IS curve shows however that no endogenous variable is left that allows for IS-equilibrium at the full employment level Y and the foreign interest rate i^*. We therefore now adjust the values T, G such that $T-G$ remains unchanged (that is without impact on the left hand side of the government budget constraint) until the IS curve passes through the determined steady state values. This holds if G, T are, on the basis of a given value for $G-T$, determined by:

$$\overline{Y} = C(\overline{Y} - T_o + i^* s_o F_{po}/p_o + i^* B_o/p_o, i^*, i^*) + G_o + NX(\cdot, s_o/p_o, Y^*)$$

if $I=0$ holds in the steady state (see below).

Note that B_o/p_o, as given by $(T-G)/i^* + \sigma_o F_c$, does not need to be positive, and must in fact be negative. This is due to the fact that interest payments iB_o are positive in the steady state (in the case of a positive value of government debt) which implies that real government income $T + s_o F_c/p_o$ must be sufficiently high relative to G to allow for the given interest obligation of the government (since there is no issue of new government debt in the steady state). We assume the behavioural functions and parameters of the model to be such that disposable income Y_p is positive at the steady state. Moreover our regressive expectations function for exchange rate depreciations or appreciations, is always assumed to fulfil $\varepsilon(s_o)=0$ in the steady state (is assumed to be asymptotically rational) and is therefore shifting with the steady state solution for s_o.

We have determined in advance the steady state values for p, i, Y, r, r^* and then simultaneously the steady state values for s, σ, F_p, B. As for the capital stock K, it was not made explicit since the model's dynamics are in fact treated without any consideration of the law of motion of the capital stock. We justify it by assuming, as an additional consistency condition, that $0=I(Y, i^*, i^*)$ at the steady state. The capital stock will then converge to a certain finite value which is of no importance in the model formulated so far (since we have constant markup pricing by firms, i.e., prices do not react to demand pressure on the market for goods). To measure this demand pressure, by way of Y/K for example, would suggest that this term should enter the investment function in the place of just Y. The dynamics of the capital stock would then feed back into the goods market and become interdependent with the rest of the dynamics, even if prices do not react to such a demand pressure term.

We now consider some features of the 3D MFT dynamics of this chapter by means of the Jacobian matrix calculated at the steady state position of the economy.

Nominal dynamic analysis in the case of perfectly flexible exchange rates

In the following we will investigate the dynamics of the model in nominal terms, provide basic results of comparative statics, consider the steady state of the economy under simplified conditions and finally indicate the range of possibilities that may characterize the considered dynamics.

In its current formulation, the model faces one big difficulty in the case of flexible exchange rates. In this case we have to use the law of motion for the nominal exchange rate in order to calculate the actual real rate of return on foreign bonds $r^* = i^* + \hat{s} - \hat{p}r^* = i^* + \hat{s} - \hat{p}$.[15] That rate enters both the law of motion for W and W_g^a. Due to this complication it is preferable to use the laws of motion for the considered stock magnitudes in nominal terms and to build the subsequent stability analysis, instead of obtaining the law of motion for s by differentiating and transforming the FF curve on the foreign bond market to a sufficient degree.[16]

Local stability analysis

We will first consider a situation where the steady state of the model is surrounded by centrifugal forces (is repelling). In a second step, this case will be contrasted with a situation where an attracting steady state is given. The calculations needed to prove these two results will show that there exists a multiplicity of situations where either stability or instability may prevail around the steady state. The conclusions will be that empirical and numerical methods are needed in order to get a more complete picture of the stock-flow dynamics of the MFT economy. Moreover, it seems that policy must be active (in particular with respect to the government budget) in order to enforce convergent behaviour around the steady state of such a small open economy.

Inserting the functions obtained from our short-term comparative static analysis into the laws of motion for the variables F_p, B, p gives rise to the following eigen-feedbacks of the considered state variables (if $\frac{\partial Y}{\partial F_p}$ is used in explicit form in the first partial derivative):

$$\frac{\partial \dot{F}_p}{\partial F_p} = i^*(1 - C_Y)\frac{-NX_Y}{1 - C_Y - I_Y - NX_Y} - C_{W_p}\frac{-NX_Y}{1 - C_Y - I_Y - NX_Y} > 0$$

$$\text{if} \quad 1 - C_Y - I_Y > 0 \quad \text{and} \quad C_{W_p} \quad \text{sufficiently small}$$

$$\frac{\partial \dot{B}}{\partial B} = i^* > 0$$

$$\frac{\partial \hat{p}}{\partial p} = \varepsilon'(s)s(p) > 0$$

We thus have in such a situation that the trace of the Jacobian of the dynamics at the steady state is positive (as is the determinant). The three state variables taken in isolation are therefore subject to repelling forces as far as their own steady state position is concerned:

$$J = \begin{pmatrix} + & - & \pm \\ 0 & + & \pm \\ 0 & 0 & + \end{pmatrix}$$

with all eigenvalues of this Jacobian being real and positive and thus destabilizing.

Even if one assumes that the first of the above partial derivatives is negative (by allowing a high wealth effect on consumption C_{W_p}) and furthermore that the second partial derivative (in the diagonal of J) is sufficiently low (i.e. that the accumulation of foreign and domestic bonds is not by itself subject to strong destabilizing forces), we get approximately the following sign structure for the considered Jacobian:

$$J = \begin{pmatrix} - & - & \pm \\ 0 & 0 & \pm \\ 0 & 0 & + \end{pmatrix}$$

due to the assumed nearly perfect capital mobility. High capital mobility is therefore problematic for the stability of the balance of payments adjustment process, the evolution of the government debt and for the dynamic price level of the considered small open MFT-type economy. There are some forces, by contrast, that appear to be stabilizing. Further detailed analysis is needed in order to get clear-cut results on local asymptotic stability and thus local convergence towards the steady state. Such stability issues will be approached in the next sections by means of two basic scenarios in the case of fixed as well as flexible exchange rate regimes.

Twin deficit accumulation and inflation dynamics

In order to highlight the role of price-level adjustments, as well as the complications they induce, we now reformulate the model in real terms, with the evolution of the real aggregate wealth of the economy and the government sector instead of the law of motions for F_p and B. On this basis we show that the rate of change of the aggregate wealth of the government sector W_g^a is determined by deducting from its real disposable income the real consumption of this sector. The same applies to the private sector. This gives a simple law of motion for real aggregate wealth of the government sector, besides the one we have determined for the total (foreign) wealth of the domestic economy (see below). These two laws describe the evolution of surpluses or deficits for the government sector and the evolution of current account surpluses or deficits for the economy as a whole. They enable us to deal with the issue of twin deficits in an open economy with a government sector.

As for the rate of change of the aggregate wealth of the government, we get from equation (5.13):

$$\begin{aligned}\dot{W}_g^a &= \frac{-(\dot{M}+\dot{B})+\dot{s}F_c}{p} - \frac{\dot{p}}{p}\frac{-(M+B)+sF_c}{p}\\ &= \frac{-(pG+iB-pT-i^*sF_c)+\hat{s}sF_c}{p} - \hat{p}\frac{-(M+B)+sF_c}{p}\\ &= T - i\frac{B}{p} + \hat{p}\frac{M+B}{p} + (i^*+\hat{s}-\hat{p})\frac{sF_c}{p} - G \quad \text{which finally gives}\end{aligned}$$

$$\dot{W}_g^a = Y_g^a - G = r^*W_g^a + i\frac{M}{p} + \xi\frac{M+B}{p} + T - G \tag{5.26}$$

as the law of motion for the real aggregate wealth or debt that characterizes the government sector as a whole.

Since this debt position is not constant, we adjust the equation for the evolution of total wealth W of the economy. We therefore consider private disposable income Y_p and private wealth W_p in their interaction with the evolution of aggregate government debt and the foreign position of the economy. Let us recall that we assume goods market equilibrium $Y - C - I - G = NX$ in the following derivations.

Concerning the aggregate (foreign) wealth of the domestic economy, we start defining it as

$$W := W_p + W_g + W_c = \frac{sF}{p}, \quad \text{with} \quad F = F_p + F_c$$

or in growth rates

$$\hat{W} = \hat{s} + \hat{F} - \hat{p} \quad \text{or} \quad \dot{W} = \hat{s}W + \frac{s\dot{F}}{p} - \hat{p}W \tag{5.27}$$

Noting that $s\dot{F} \equiv pNX + si^*Fs\dot{F} \equiv pNX + si^*F$,[17] we obtain

$$\begin{aligned} \dot{W} &= \hat{s}W + \frac{p(Y - C - G - I) + si^*F}{p} - \hat{p}W \\ &= (\hat{s} - \hat{p})W + i^*\frac{sF}{p} + Y - C - G - I \end{aligned}$$

or alternatively

$$\dot{W} = (i^* + \hat{s} - \hat{p})W + Y - C - G - I = r^*W + Y - C - G - I, \quad r^* = i^* + \hat{s} - \hat{p}$$

In the following we set foreign inflation equal to zero $\pi^* = 0$ ($\pi^* = 0$),[18] and assume given policy parameters (M, T, G). Inserting the behavioural equations given by equations (5.17)–(5.18), we obtain, together with the law of motion for the price level described by equation (5.22), the following 3D dynamical system:[19]

$$\dot{W} = r^*W + Y - C(Y_p, W - W_g^a, r, r^{*e}) - I(Y, r, r^{*e}) - G \tag{5.28}$$

$$= r^*W + NX(\cdot, \sigma, Y^*) \tag{5.29}$$

$$\dot{W}_g^a = r^* W_g^a + \xi \frac{M+B}{p} + i \frac{M}{p} + T - G \tag{5.30}$$

$$\hat{p} = \beta_w (Y - \overline{Y})/(1-\gamma) + \varepsilon(s), \quad \gamma \in (0,1) \tag{5.31}$$

We assume myopic perfect foresight with respect to inflation on the market for goods, but allow for errors in exchange rate expectations. Let us note that, although laws of motions are based on the actual rate of change of the exchange rate s, we have to use the expected depreciation rate inside behavioural relationships. We have assumed above – following Rødseth (2000, ch.6) – that the total private consumption of domestic and foreign goods depends (positively) on disposable income, private wealth and (negatively) on the real rate of return expected for the two types of bonds. Similarly it is assumed that total net investment depends (positively) on domestic economic activity and (negatively) on the same real rates of return of bonds. The real exchange rate $\sigma = sp^*/p$ enters the goods market equilibrium condition only via exports $X = X(\sigma, Y^*)$.

The above laws of motion for W, W_g^a are based on actual rates of return and thus actual changes in the exchange rate, while some arguments in the consumption function and the investment function are expected ones (relying on our use of a regressive expectations scheme later on) and have thus to be characterized by an index e for 'expected'. Furthermore, we have assumed myopic perfect foresight with respect to the inflation dynamics and therefore do distinguish between expected and actual inflation rates. The former would be used in the behavioural relationships later on while the latter apply to the actual laws of motion for the considered wealth variables. The distinction between actual and perceived rates of return will become important when exchange rate dynamics will be considered (in our representation of the Dornbusch model in an MFT approach to financial markets).

Inflation and capital account dynamics under interest and exchange rate pegs

We are now considering the dynamic implications of a particular regime among the ones that are economically possible in the MFT framework. We follow Rødseth (2000, ch.6.6) and choose a case for which the asset markets are sent into the background of the model, a case which therefore solely studies the interactions of the IS curve with a conventional type of Phillips curve and the dynamics of the capital account. The conventional type of IS–PC analysis (without an LM curve) is therefore here augmented by the change in foreign assets resulting from the excess of domestic savings over domestic investment. This case may be applicable – after some modifications – to the situation of the Chinese economy (at least for certain periods of time).

Assumptions

The assumptions we employ in order to derive this special case from our general framework are the following ones:

- Given Y^*, p^*, i^*: The small open economy assumptions.
- $i = i^*$: An interest rate peg by the central bank (via an accommodating monetary policy).
- $\bar{s} = \text{const.}$ (=1): A fixed exchange rate via an endogenous supply of dollar denominated bonds by the central bank (which is never exhausted).
- W_g^a: A tax policy of the government that keeps the aggregate wealth of the government fixed.
- $G_2, I_2 = 0$: Only consumption goods are import commodities which are never rationed.
- ω: The real wage is fixed by a conventional type of markup pricing.
- r_f^n: The normal rate of return of firms is fixed (since the real wage is a given magnitude) and set equal to i^* for simplicity.
- $Y^p = y^p K, L^d = Y/x$: Fixed proportions in production (y^p, x capital and labour productivity, respectively).
- $K = \text{const.}$: The capacity effect of investment is ignored. Potential output $Y^p(=1)$ is therefore a given magnitude.
- $\overline{Y} = x\overline{L}(=1)$: A given level of the full employment output.

On the basis of these assumptions, the real rates of interest are equalized for the domestic economy: $r^* = i^* + \hat{s} - \hat{p} = i - \hat{p} = r$. Furthermore, the risk premium ξ is zero in the considered situation. Finally, due to the assumed tax policy, the disposable income of the household sector is as follows $Y_p = Y + r^*W - G$. Private wealth W_p is given by $W - W_g^a$ in the considered situation.

The real portfolio demands of the private sector are once again described by the equations:

$$M^d/p = m^d(Y,i), \quad m_Y^d > 0, m_i^d < 0 \tag{5.32}$$

$$sF_p^d/p = f^d(\xi, W_p) = f^d(i^* + \varepsilon(s) - i, W_p), \;\; f_\xi^d > 0, 0 < f_{W_p}^d < 1 \tag{5.33}$$

They are always satisfied by the central bank through open market operations in domestic and foreign bonds, in order to maintain the assumed pegs of the domestic interest rate i and the exchange rate s.

The model

We define again the real exchange rate by $\sigma = (sp^*)/p$, *i.e.*, the amount of domestic goods that is exchanged per unit of foreign good. This rate reduces to $1/p$ due to the above normalization assumptions. Households buy investment goods for their firms and use the normal rate of profit only in order to judge their performance (which is constant due to the above assumptions). Moreover we need to consider only one real rate, r, in the following formulation of the consumption decisions (for domestic and foreign goods) and the investment decision of the household sector. We now distinguish imported from domestic goods in domestic consumption demand and include the real exchange rate on this substructure of total private consumption.

$$\begin{aligned} C_1 &= C_1(Y_p^H, W_p, r, \sigma): \;\; \text{consumption demand for the domestic good} \\ C_2 &= C_2(Y_p^H, W_p, r, \sigma): \;\; \text{consumption demand for the foreign good} \\ C &= C_1(Y_p^H, W_p, r, \sigma) + C_2(Y_p, W_p, r, \sigma)/\sigma: \;\; \text{total consumption} \\ I &= I(Y, r): \;\; \text{investment demand, for domestic goods solely} \end{aligned}$$

The goods market equilibrium or the IS curve of the model is given by:

$$C(Y_p^H, W_p, r, \sigma) + I(Y, r) + G + NX(\cdot) = Y$$

where net exports are based on a standard export function and import demand as determined by C_2. Imports can be suppressed in this equation by reformulating it as follows:

$$\begin{aligned} Y &= C_1(Y + rW - G, W - W_g^a, r, \sigma) + I(Y, r) + G + X(Y^*, \sigma) \\ \sigma &= 1/p, r = i^* - \hat{p} \end{aligned}$$

We have assumed that exports X depend on foreign output and the real exchange rate.

The dynamic equations of the model for nominal wages and wealth are the following ones (the growth of the capital stock is neglected by assumption):

$$\hat{w} = \beta_w(Y-1) + \gamma\hat{p} + (1-\gamma)\widehat{sp}^* \tag{5.34}$$

$$\dot{W} = rW + X(Y^*, \sigma) - C_2(Y + rW - G, W - W_g^a, r, \sigma)/\sigma \tag{5.35}$$

The second law of motion is the usual representation of the balance of payments in real terms, while the first one is a standard money wage Phillips curve where cost-pressure items are represented as a weighted average of actual domestic and import price inflation. On the basis of constant markup pricing, this equation is easily transformed into a reduced form price Phillips curve which can be formulated, with our assumptions, as:

$$\hat{p} = \frac{1}{1-\gamma}\beta_w(Y-1), \text{ and is to be coupled with} \tag{5.36}$$

$$\begin{aligned}\dot{W} &= (i^* - \hat{p})W + X(Y^*, 1/p) \\ &\quad - C_2(Y + (i^* - \hat{p})W - G, W - W_g^a, i^* - \hat{p}, 1/p)/p \end{aligned} \tag{5.37}$$

We have also a reduced form expression for the second law of motion into which the first law has to be inserted in two places in order to get a system of differential equations that depends on the state variables Y, p, and W. The temporary equilibrium output Y depends only on the two state variables p, W by means of the following goods market equilibrium condition:

$$\begin{aligned} Y &= C_1\left(y + \left(i^* - \frac{1}{1-\gamma}(Y-1)\right)W - G, W - W_g^a, i^* \right. \\ &\quad \left. - \frac{1}{1-\gamma}\beta_w(Y-1), p\right) \\ &\quad + I\left(Y, i^* - \frac{1}{1-\gamma}\beta_w(Y-1)\right) + G + X(Y^*, p) \end{aligned} \tag{5.38}$$

We assume for the time being that the parameters of this equilibrium condition are such that the conventional dependency of

IS-equilibrium output on the price level results in: $\partial Y/\partial p < 0$. With respect to aggregate domestic wealth it is obvious that $\partial Y/\partial W > 0$ holds true.

We observe here that we have to add the law of motion for the capital stock K: $\dot{K} = I(Y, i^* - \frac{1}{1-\gamma}\beta_w(Y-1))$ for a complete treatment of the dynamics of this example of a small open economy. However we do not go into such an extended dynamic analysis here. We can also return to an endogenous treatment of the variable W_g^a which would increase the complexity of the analysis further, despite the simple framework that is chosen (where portfolio choice does not matter for the analysis of the dynamics of the real part of the model, T, G given magnitudes):

$$\begin{aligned}
\hat{p} &= \beta_w(Y-1)/(1-\gamma) \\
\dot{W}_g^a &= (i^* - \hat{p})W_g^a + i^* m^d(Y, i^*) + T - G \\
\dot{W} &= (i^* - \hat{p})W + X(Y^*, 1/p) - C_2(Y + (i^* - \hat{p})(W - W_g^a) - i^* m^d(Y, i^*) \\
&\qquad - T, W - W_g^a, i^* - \hat{p}, 1/p)/p
\end{aligned}$$

This extension would again allow for the discussion of the occurrence of twin deficits and other situations of domestic and foreign debt/surpluses.

Steady state determination

For reasons of simplicity we return, however, to the situation where aggregate government wealth (basically the government deficit) stays constant in time (by choosing T appropriately) and thus investigate now the steady state solution and the dynamics of the following system:

$$\begin{aligned}
\hat{p} &= \frac{1}{1-\gamma}\beta_w(Y(p, W) - 1) \\
\dot{W} &= (i^* - \hat{p})W + X(Y^*, 1/p) - C_2(Y(p, W) + (i^* - \hat{p})W - G, W \\
&\qquad - W_g^a, (i^* - \hat{p}), 1/p)/p
\end{aligned}$$

where the properties of the IS-equilibrium are characterized by the standard partial derivatives we have discussed above.

With respect to the steady state solution of this dynamical system we assume[20] that the government pursues – in addition to its tax policy – a constant government expenditure policy that is aimed at fixing the steady state value of exports at the level $\overline{X}$. This implies that the steady state value of the price level, p_o, is to be determined from $\overline{X}=X(Y^*, 1/p_o)$. Assuming that this equation has a (uniquely determined) positive solution for p_o we then can obtain the steady state value of W from the labour market equilibrium equation $1=\overline{Y}=Y(p_o, W_o)$. The solution of this equation may be positive or negative and is again uniquely determined, since the right hand side of this equation is strictly increasing in W_o. The level of government expenditure G that allows for this solution procedure is given by:

$$0 = i^* W_o + \overline{X} - C_2(\overline{Y} + i^* W_o - G, W_o - W_g^a, i^*, 1/p_o)/p_o$$

In this equation, the expenditure level is adjusted so that net imports are equal to the foreign interest income of domestic residents. In other words an excess of imports over exports is needed in the case of a positive foreign bond holdings in the domestic economy at the steady state. This result is based on the assumption that $I(\overline{Y}, i^*)=0$ holds in the steady state, since there must be a stationary capital stock in the steady state of the model.

Stability analysis

Our simplifying assumption on the goods-market equilibrium equation $Y=Y(p, W)$ guarantees that price level increases reduce economic activity (and thus provide a limit to further inflationary tendencies) and induce an increase in economic activity (with dollar denominated wealth). Therefore we have a straightforward sign structure in the partial derivatives of the first law of motion. The second law of motion is however much more difficult to handle. Its partial derivative with respect to W is given by (due to $\hat{p}_o=0$):

$$\frac{\partial \dot{W}}{\partial W} = i^*(1-\sigma_o C_{2Y_p}) - \sigma_o C_{2Y_p}\frac{\partial Y}{\partial W} - \sigma_o C_{2W_p} + \hat{p}_W[(\sigma_o C_{2Y_p}-1)W_o + \sigma_o C_{2r}]$$

where $\hat{p}_W$ stands for the partial derivative of the first law of motion with respect to W.

The remaining partial derivative for local stability analysis is given by:

$$\frac{\partial \dot{W}}{\partial p} = ((\sigma_o C_{2Y_p} - 1)W_o + \sigma_o C_{2r})\hat{p}_p - \sigma_o C_{2Y_p}\frac{\partial Y}{\partial p} + (C_2 + \sigma_o C_{2\sigma} - X_\sigma)/p^2$$

The first two expressions of this equation have a positive sign while the last term in brackets – the reaction of net imports to price level changes via the real exchange rate channel – is generally assumed to be negative ($\sigma = (sp^*)/p = 1/p$). We thus get:

$$J = \begin{pmatrix} \frac{\partial \hat{p}}{\partial p}p & \frac{\partial \hat{p}}{\partial W}p \\ \frac{\partial \dot{W}}{\partial p} & \frac{\partial \dot{W}}{\partial W} \end{pmatrix} = \begin{pmatrix} - & + \\ \pm & \pm \end{pmatrix}$$

The easiest case for a stability result is:

$$J = \begin{pmatrix} \frac{\partial \hat{p}}{\partial p}p & \frac{\partial \hat{p}}{\partial W}p \\ \frac{\partial \dot{W}}{\partial p} & \frac{\partial \dot{W}}{\partial W} \end{pmatrix} = \begin{pmatrix} - & + \\ - & - \end{pmatrix}$$

i.e., the case where interest effects do not dominate the capital account adjustment process and where the normal reaction of the trade balance (based on the so-called Marshall–Lerner conditions) dominates the income, wealth and interest rate effects generated by the general form of a consumption function used here. The steady state is in this case locally asymptotically stable (since trace $J < 0$, $\det J > 0$). In this situation the phase diagram is as shown in Figure 5.2.

When considering this figure one must however keep in mind the very restrictive assumptions made with respect to: the IS curve and its replacement by the evolution of the state variables of the dynamics; the reaction of the balance of payments and the dynamics of the capital account; and the reaction of foreign bond accumulation with respect to price level changes. Therefore it is not clear how dominant the case of stable price level and capital account dynamics are in the set of all possible stability scenarios, even in the special case of an MFT economy considered here. In case of divergence, the question

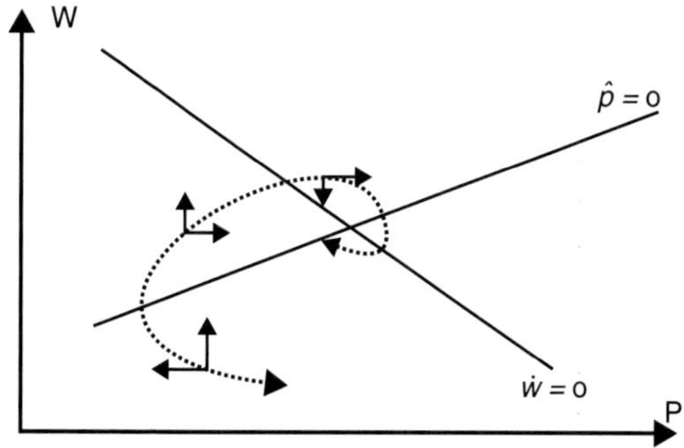

Figure 5.2 The special example of stable inflation and capital account dynamics

would be to determine which private sector mechanisms could keep the dynamics bounded or what policy actions would be needed to ensure this.

The depicted dynamical implications are by and large of the type considered in Rødseth (2000, ch.6.6), although our consumption and investment functions differ to some extent from the ones used there. The reader can refer to this analysis for further details about this stable monetary and exchange rate regime.

By contrast, the worst case scenario (for instability) is given by the situation:

$$J = \begin{pmatrix} \frac{\partial \hat{p}}{\partial p}p & \frac{\partial \hat{p}}{\partial W}p \\ \frac{\partial \dot{W}}{\partial p} & \frac{\partial \dot{W}}{\partial W} \end{pmatrix} = \begin{pmatrix} - & + \\ + & + \end{pmatrix}$$

in which case, the steady state is clearly a saddlepoint. This situation is depicted in Figure 5.3.

Advocates of the jump variable technique would not be able to apply this technique, since both the price level p and the foreign position W of the economy are predetermined variables (despite myopic perfect foresight with regards to domestic inflation rates). The solution to the instability shown in Figure 5.3 can thus not be found in an ad hoc imposition of appropriate jumps in the price level. It must be found through the consideration of private sector or public policy

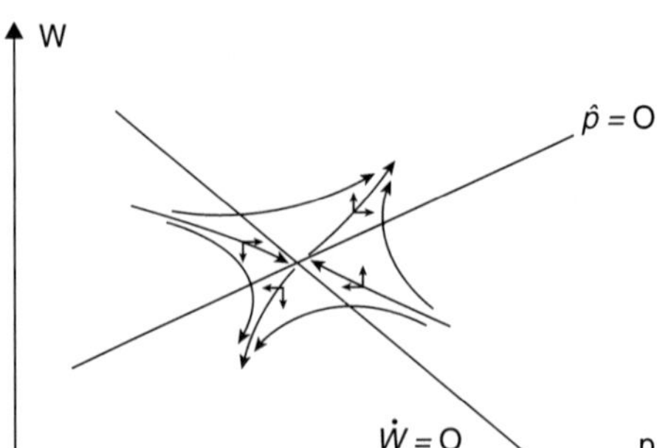

Figure 5.3 The case of centrifugal inflation and capital account dynamics

behavioural changes when the economy has departed too much from its steady state position.

Deficit/surplus accumulation

In order to highlight the important role of price dynamics for the stability of the system, as discussed above, we set foreign inflation equal to zero ($\pi^* = 0$) and assume constant price levels for the domestic economy ($p = p^* = 1$ for notational simplicity). We also assume given policy parameters(M, T, G). By inserting the behavioural equations given by equations (5.17) to (5.19), we obtain the following 2D dynamical system:[21]

$$\begin{aligned}\dot{W} &= i^*W + Y - C(Y_p, W - W_g^a, i^*) - I(Y, i^*) - G \\ &= i^*W + NX(\cdot) \qquad (5.39)\\ \dot{W}_g^a &= i^*W_g^a + i^*\frac{M}{p} + T - G \qquad (5.40)\end{aligned}$$

The corresponding Jacobian at the steady state of the dynamics is characterized by:

$$J = \begin{pmatrix} \frac{\partial \dot{W}}{\partial W} & \frac{\partial \dot{W}}{\partial W_g^a} \\ \frac{\partial \dot{W}_g^a}{\partial W} & \frac{\partial \dot{W}_g^a}{\partial W_g^a} \end{pmatrix} = \begin{pmatrix} (i^* - C_W) & -C_{W_g^a} \\ 0 & i^* \end{pmatrix} = \begin{pmatrix} \pm & + \\ 0 & + \end{pmatrix}$$

with $\det J < 0$ if $i^* < C_W$ and $\operatorname{tr} J > 0$. In the absence of price adjustments, the dynamics of the system become intrinsically unstable in both case (with a saddlepoint in the first situation and an unstable equilibrium in the second one), even if the wealth effect on consumption influences in a larger extent the dynamics of the economy's wealth position than the interest payments. We conclude that the dynamics of twin deficits (or surpluses) are far from being self-correcting.

Overshooting exchange rates and inflation dynamics

As a second case study, we now consider a regime of perfectly flexible exchange rates and given money supply. This implies that supply of foreign bonds is, at each moment in time, given by the stock of these bonds held by the private sector, (since domestic bonds are assumed to be non-tradable). The supply of financial assets is thus constant and its composition can only change via the flows induced in the capital account. The central bank may use open market operations in domestic bonds to modify the composition of the households portfolio, but does not issue money otherwise (in particular to buy foreign bonds from domestic residents). The case considered in this section may be applicable – after some modifications – to an economic situation as represented by the Australian economy (at least for certain time periods of this economy). We stress that we reconsider here Dornbusch (1976) overshooting exchange rate dynamics for imperfect asset substitutability in the case of the, empirically questionable, case of the uncovered interest rate parity condition.

Equilibrium conditions

In our reformulation of the Dornbusch overshooting exchange rate dynamics[22] within the framework of an MFT model, we also assume for simplicity – just as in the original Dornbusch (1976) approach – that transactions demand in the money demand function is based on full employment output $\overline{Y} = 1$. In other words we get from the LM curve of our Tobinian portfolio approach the result that the domestic rate of interest is solely dependent on the price level (positively) and on money supply (negatively):

$$i = \frac{\ln p - \ln M}{\alpha} + \text{const.}$$

as in the case of the Cagan money demand function considered in Flaschel (2006). For full asset markets equilibrium, we need only consider the market for foreign bonds in addition, which in the considered exchange rate regime is:

$$\frac{sF_p}{p} = f^d\left(i^* + \varepsilon(s) - i, \frac{M+B+sF_p}{p}\right) = f^d\left(r^{*e} - r, \frac{M+B+sF_p}{p}\right)$$

$$r^{*e} = i^* + \varepsilon(s) - \hat{p}, \quad r = i - \hat{p}$$

with $F_p, M+B, p$ constant. Since $0 < f_2^d < 1$ holds in a Tobinian portfolio model, we get from this equilibrium condition that the exchange rate s depends negatively on i, F_p and positively on p (when the effect of the price level on the nominal interest rate is ignored). The theory of the exchange rate of the considered Mundell–Fleming regime can thus be represented as follows:

$$s = s(i(p,M), p, F_p), \quad e_1 < 0, e_2 > 0, e_3 < 0, \quad i_1 > 0, i_2 < 0$$

Note that the overall effect of price level changes on the exchange rate may be an ambiguous one.

Next, we consider the IS-equilibrium curve of the presently considered situation:

$$Y = C_1(Y + r^{*e}W - G, W - W_g^a, r, r^{*e}, \sigma) + I(Y, r, r^{*e}) + G + X(Y^*, \sigma)$$

with $\sigma = s/p, p^* = 1$ and G, W_g^a constant. In order to derive conclusions on how the equilibrium output level depends on the price level p., one has to use: our regressive expectations regime; the dependence of the nominal rate of interest and the real exchange rate on the price level; and the functional dependence of the nominal exchange rate on i, p derived above. The outcome is ambiguous, but points up, to a certain degree, to a negative overall dependence of Y on p (as usual). We shall assume that this is true in our following discussion of overshooting exchange rates, since the opposite case would imply a destabilizing feedback of the price level on its rate of change (via the Phillips curve mechanism). The dependence of Y on W is obviously a positive one.

Dynamics and steady state determination

We have determined the statically endogenous variables of the considered MFT regime i, s, Y through the three equilibrium relationships that characterize the model. The state variables of the model are again p, W (the movement of the capital stock is still neglected). The laws of motion for these variables are now given by:

$$\dot{W} = r^*W + X(Y^*, \sigma) - \sigma C_2(Y + r^{*e}W - G, W - W_g^a, r, r^{*e}, \sigma)$$
$$\hat{p} = \beta_w(Y - 1)/(1 - \gamma)$$

where $r^* = i^* + \hat{s} - \hat{p}$ and $r^{*e} = i^* + \varepsilon(s) - \hat{p}$ and $r = i - \hat{p}$. The law of motion for W is now complex, since the static relationships have to be inserted within it. We will therefore not discuss its (in)stability implications in the following and assume that this variable is placed into its new long-run equilibrium position after a shock and kept constant there. We therefore only study the adjustment of the price level p after an open market operation of the central bank (which leaves $M + B$ unchanged). This implies a jump in the variable $W = (sF)/p$ that is neglected in our following analysis of such shocks.

In the construction of a steady state reference solution[23] we proceed as follows. We once again assume that the government pursues an export target $\overline{X}$ by means of its expenditure policy G, besides the tax policy that keeps W_g^a at a constant level $\overline{W}_g^a$. The steady state real exchange rate σ_o is then uniquely determined by the equation $\overline{X} = X(Y^*, \sigma)$. On this basis we can use the equilibrium condition on the market for foreign bonds to determine the steady state level of W, since this equilibrium condition can be rewritten as:

$$f^d(\xi, W - W_g^a) = W - \sigma_o F_c \quad \text{or} \quad 0 = W - \sigma_o F_c - f^d(\xi, W - W_g^a) = g(\xi, W)$$

since money supply and thus F_c is held constant by the central bank. Since $\varepsilon(s_o)$ and ξ_o must be zero at the steady state (see proof below) the above equation can be assumed to have a uniquely determined positive solution if the function f^d is chosen appropriately. We note consider only positive values of W_o, since we assume that households and the central bank hold such assets and firms do not finance their investment expenditures abroad.

From the Phillips curve, we get next that $Y_o = \overline{Y}$ must hold in the steady state ($\hat{p}_o = 0$). Furthermore, the regressive expectations scheme is built in such a way that $\varepsilon(s_o) = 0$ holds for the steady state value s_o of the nominal exchange rate (that remains to be determined). We thus have $r_o = i_o, r_o^* = r^{*e} = i^*$ at the steady state and postulate that $I(Y, i^*, i^*) = 0$ holds for the investment function used in this MFT model. We assume on this basis that the government chooses the level of G and thus $\overline{X}$ so that $i_o = i_o^*$ is enforced by the IS-equation at the steady state:[24]

$$\overline{Y} = C_1(\overline{Y} + iW_o - G, W_o - \overline{W}_g^a, i_o, i^*, \sigma_o) + I(\overline{Y}, i_o, i^*) + G + \overline{X}$$

On this basis we can then get the steady state value of the price level p_o from the LM curve $p_o = M/m^d(\overline{Y}, i^*)$ and thus also the steady state value of the exchange rate $s_o = p_o\sigma_o$.

In the short-run the IS–LM–FF curves determine the variables Y, i, s in this order. The Phillips curve and the balance of payments determine the dynamics of the price level and of domestically held foreign bonds (in real terms). Let us note once again that the dynamics of the capital stock is not considered here. Moreover we will also ignore the complicated adjustment process for $W = sF/p$ and assume instead that this magnitude will immediately jump to its new steady state value after any shock and will be kept frozen there. The aim of the following simplified presentation will be instead to reconsider the Dornbusch (1976) model of overshooting exchange rates in the context of a Tobinian portfolio model of the financial sector (and somewhat advanced formulations of consumption and investment behaviour).

Dornbusch exchange rate dynamics

Let us now consider an open market operation of the central bank $dM = -dB$, that increases the money holdings of private agents by reducing their holdings of domestic bonds (which therefore keeps $M + B$ and F_c constant). Our way of constructing a steady state for the considered dynamics implies that all real magnitudes remain constant (in particular W_o) and that the only steady state changes are as follows:

$$dM/M = dp_o/p_o = ds_o/s_o \quad (\sigma_o = \text{const.}, i_o = i^*)$$

The long-run reaction of the dynamics is, as in the original Dornbusch (1976) model, a very straightforward one: strict neutrality of money and the relative form of the PPP. There is no change in the real exchange rate caused by the monetary expansion that is undertaken.

In the short-run, prices are fixed and the burden of adjustment in the money market falls entirely on the nominal rate of interest i which is decreased below i^* through the monetary expansion. Since the new steady state value e'_o of the nominal exchange rate is above the old level, and since the assumed regressive expectations mechanism is completely rational in this respect, $\varepsilon(s_0'/s), \varepsilon' < 0$ would become positive (generate the expectation of a depreciation) if the short-run exchange rate remained unchanged. Since we ignore – as described above – adjustments in the value of W, the current exchange rate must however depreciate beyond s_0', in order to imply the expectation of an appreciation of the currency so that $\xi = i^* + \varepsilon(s_0'/s) - i = 0$ can remain unchanged (due to the unchanged value of $W_o W_o$,[25] since the adjustment process of W is here ignored).[26] We thus get that i decreases and s increases under the assumed monetary expansion. We expect that goods market equilibrium output increases through these two influences, since $i^* + \varepsilon = i$ has decreased and since σ has been increased (the price level being fixed at p_o). There may be an ambiguous reaction, but we assume here – as before – that goods markets behave normally in this respect.

Therefore, in the short run, the nominal exchange rate overshoots its new long-run level, as in the original Dornbusch model. Due to the increase in the output level beyond its normal level, the price level starts rising in the medium-run according to:

$$\hat{p} = \beta_w(Y - 1)/(1 - \gamma) \quad \text{with} \quad Y = Y(p, W_o),\ \partial Y/\partial p < 0$$

The dynamics therefore converges back to its steady state position with output levels falling back to their normal level, prices rising to their new steady state value p_0', the exchange rate appreciating back to its risen steady state value s_0', and the nominal rate of interest rising again to the unchanged international level i^*. All this takes place in a somewhat simplified portfolio approach to financial markets (in place of the UIP condition under rational expectations) and without any complication arising from possibly adverse adjustments in the balance of payments. One can therefore expect that a treatment of the full model along the lines of Flaschel (2006) would reveal a variety of more complicated situations and, in the worst case, unstable dynamics. The present discussion is therefore only the beginning of a

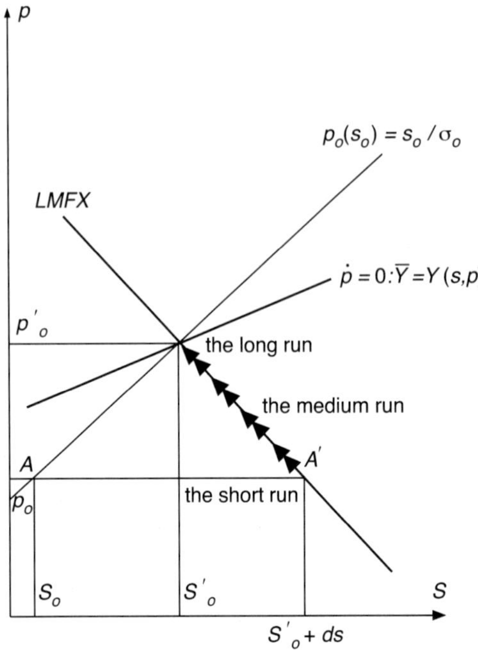

Figure 5.4 The Dornbusch overshooting exchange rate dynamics

detailed discussion of the Dornbusch mechanism in a full-fledged MFT model with inflation and balance of payments adjustment dynamics.

These dynamic adjustment processes are summarized in Figure 5.4. The simple *LMFX* curve describing full portfolio equilibrium is as follows:

$$f^d(i^* + \varepsilon(s) - i(p), W_o - \overline{W}_g^a) = W_o - \sigma_o F_c$$

where all revaluation effects of assets have been ignored, transactions balances are based on normal output still and the dynamics of the state variable W is set aside. The true *LMFX* curve is of course shifting with the changes in W, σ and the output level Y. and is not as simple as shown in this graph (where $\partial Y/\partial s, \partial Y/\partial p < 0$ is assumed).

If the old steady state, A, is disturbed by an expansionary monetary shock that shifts the old *LMFX* curve (not represented) into the new position, the exchange rate adjusts (to A') in the short run (SR) so that full portfolio equilibrium is restored. In the medium run (MR), one can observe rising price levels, rising interest rates and falling exchange rates until the new steady state position (LR) is reached at point B. Let us note that variables W, W_g^a could be subject to jumps in a regime with flexible exchange rates, but would then follow their laws of motion if no further shocks occurred (in the case of W) and remain fixed at their new level (in the case of W_g^a).

Capital account and budget deficit dynamics

We could also return to an endogenous treatment of the variable W_g^a (by making use again of given lump sum taxation T again). This would increase the complexity of the analysis even further and lead us to the consideration the following 3D dynamics:

$$
\begin{aligned}
\hat{p} &= \beta_w(Y-1)/(1-\gamma)\\
\dot{W}_g^a &= (i^* + \hat{s} - \hat{p})W_g^a + (i^* + \hat{s} - i)\frac{M+B}{p} + im^d(Y,i) + T - G\\
\dot{W} &= (i^* + \hat{s} - \hat{p})W + X(Y^*, sp^*/p)\\
&\quad - (sp^*/p)C_2\Big(Y + (i^* + \varepsilon(s) - \hat{p})(W - W_g^a) - im^d(Y,i)\\
&\qquad\qquad - (i^* + \varepsilon(s) - i)\frac{M+B}{p} - T, W - W_g^a, i - \hat{p}, i^*\\
&\qquad\qquad + \varepsilon(s) - \hat{p}, sp^*/p\Big)
\end{aligned}
$$

This extension would again allow for the discussion of the occurrence of twin deficits and other situations of domestic and foreign debt/surplus accumulation. However, the system would be very complex in this case of a perfectly flexible exchange rate. The statically endogenous variables i, s would have to be obtained from the portfolio part of the model, in interaction with the IS curve of the model, and the growth rate of s would have to be calculated in order to insert it into the 3D laws of motion. This would not be an easy task and would make an analysis of the model nearly untractable.

6
International Capital Flows: Two Extensions of the MFTobin Model

Introduction

Over the last decade, the unprecedented increase in the internal and external imbalances of two of the largest economies in the world, the USA and China, has raised serious concerns about the stability of the world economy. Nevertheless, a correction of these imbalances by means of a significant readjustment concerning the US dollar does not seem very likely in the near future, due to a reluctance of some governments to deal with this issue. In light of this, national wage–price adjustments as well as foreign asset in- and out-flows have become important macroeconomic adjustment mechanisms.

We trust that the Mundell–Fleming framework introduced in the previous chapter can help to understand better inflation and balance of payments dynamics in open economies. However this model is still a work in progress and cannot be considered as a definitive version. This chapter considers two possible extensions of the MFT model. The following three sections study how the introduction of international capital flows in the MFT model might alter the results of the previous chapter. The final section provides a framework for a two-country extension of the MFT model.

International capital flows in the MFT model

So far, we have considered a small open economy of Mundell–Fleming–Tobin type that exhibits a Keynesian demand constraint on the market for goods. Moreover, we assumed imperfect substitutability of financial assets in place of the UIP condition. This imperfectness was coupled with the assumption that domestic bonds are non-tradables. The amount of foreign bonds held domestically was only changed to the extent that there is a surplus or a deficit in the current account.

This assumption is now relaxed. Domestic bonds are now assumed to be traded on the international capital market. The main purpose of this extension is to check how our previous results are affected such a change. In the following, we consider a small open economy and assume again that foreign interest and inflation rates, i^*, π^*, as well as foreign output, Y^*, are constant. We present in this section the budget equations of the three sectors of our economy: households, the government and the central bank. With respect to firms, we keep assuming that all their income is transferred to households, which, in return, finance firms' investment expenditures. Our other previous assumptions, especially concerning the central bank and its operations, are maintained.

Financial SAM and accounting identities

From now on, the foreign sector also holds domestic bonds B^*. Moreover we assume, for purpose of simplicity, that there is no money financing of government expenditures (the money stock M remains constant). Table 6.1 gives the FSAM of the MFT model with these new assumptions. The non-financial part of this matrix is almost identical to the SAM presented in Chapter 5 (p. 95). Therefore the goods market equilibrium condition and the budget equations of the three sectors remain mostly unchanged:[1]

$$pY \equiv pC + pG + pI + pNX \tag{6.1}$$

$$pY_p \equiv pY + iB_p + si^*F_p \tag{6.2}$$

$$pS_p \equiv pY_p - pC - pT \tag{6.3}$$

$$pY_g^a \equiv pT + si^*F_c \tag{6.4}$$

$$pS_g^a \equiv pY_g - pG - iB \tag{6.5}$$

$$pS_{ROW} \equiv iB^* - pNX - si^*F_p - si^*F_c \tag{6.6}$$

Table 6.1 Financial SAM with capital flows

Receipts \ Expenditures		Production	Current accounts			Combined capital account	Δ in assets and liabilities		Σ
			Private	Government	Rest of World		Domestic bonds	Foreign bonds	
Production			pC	$p.G$	$p.X$	pI			$pY+pIM$
Current accounts	Private	pY		$i.B_p$	$si^{*}F_p$				pY_p
	Gvt		pT		$si^{*}F_c$				pY_g^a
	RoW	pIM		iB^*					$pIM+iB^*$
Capital accounts	Private		pS_p			$-pI$	$-\dot{B}^d$	$-s\,\dot{F}_p^d$	0
	Gvt			pS_g^a			$+\dot{B}$	$(-s\,\dot{F}_c^d)$	0
	RoW				pS_{RoW}		$+\dot{B}^*$	$+s\,\dot{F}$	0
Σ		$pY+pIM$	pY_p	pY_g^a	$pIM+iB^*$	0	0	0	

The savings-investment identity is the same as in the previous chapter:

$$pS_p + pS_g^a + pS_{ROW} = pI$$

which gives for the total domestic savings pS $(= pS_p + pS_g^a)$:

$$pS \equiv pI - iB^* + pNX + si^*F_p + si^*F_c$$

The financial part of the FSAM now includes changes in foreign holdings of domestic bonds $\dot{B}^*$ whereas changes in money holdings have disappeared (since $\dot{M} = 0$). Therefore the accounting identities describing the saving/financing decisions of the three sectors are now slightly different from the original version of the MFT model:

$$\begin{aligned} pS_p &\equiv pI + \dot{B}^d + s\dot{F}_p^d \\ pS_g^a &\equiv -\dot{B}(+s\dot{F}_c^d) \\ pS_{ROW} &\equiv \dot{B}^* - s\dot{F} \end{aligned}$$

These accounting identities can be rewritten as follows:

$$s\dot{F}_p^d \equiv pS_p - pI - \dot{B}^d \qquad (6.7)$$

$$\dot{B} \equiv -pS_g^a(+s\dot{F}_c^d) \qquad (6.8)$$

$$s\dot{F} \equiv \dot{B}^* - pS_{ROW} \qquad (6.9)$$

Equation (6.7) shows that the evolution of households' holdings of foreign bonds is implied by their budget constraint.[2] Equation (6.8) states that the evolution of the supply of domestic bonds is determined by the evolution of the budget deficit of the government. Equation (6.9) shows that an increase (a decrease) in domestic holdings of foreign assets is equal to the sum of the evolution of foreign holdings of domestic bonds and the external current account surplus (deficit) of the country (which means that the balance of payments is always balanced, independently of the exchange rate and monetary regimes that are investigated).

The new equilibrium conditions on the financial market are the following ones:

$$\dot{B}_p^d \equiv \dot{B} - \dot{B}^* \qquad (6.10)$$

$$\dot{F} \equiv \dot{F}_p^d(+\dot{F}_c^d) \qquad (6.11)$$

With equation (6.10), we will assume that newly issued government bonds that are not bought by the foreign sector are always voluntarily absorbed by households. Equation (6.11) gives the equilibrium condition on the market of foreign bonds. Once again, we will use this equation in two different ways, depending on the exchange rate regime to be investigated.[3]

In order for the accounting of the model to be correct, we have to integrate in its equations ten of the eleven accounting identities issued from the transcription of the FSAM. In this extension of the MFT model, the missing identity will be equation (6.7) which will be replaced by the following equation:

$$s\dot{F}^d_{p1} \equiv pS_p - pI - \dot{B}^d - s\dot{F}^d_{p2} \tag{6.12}$$

With this equation we distinguish the change in households' holdings of foreign bonds implied by their savings decision $s\dot{F}^d_{p1}$ from the one issued from their portfolio decision $s\dot{F}^d_{p2}$.[4] The latter will be defined through Tobinian behavioural equations and will give rise to significant international capital flows in interaction with the behaviour of foreign asset holders. In this extension of the MFT model savings and portfolio rearrangements will be formulated – in contrast to the original model – in terms of flows, while the cash management decision of households (between money and fixed-price domestic bonds) will still be modelled by way of an LM curve which is mirrored by an equivalent stock condition on the market for domestic bonds.

Real disposable income and wealth

By using the Hicksian definition of private disposable income, we will derive a law of motion for real aggregate wealth of the government sector, besides the one we have already determined for the total wealth of the economy. These two laws describe the evolution of surpluses or deficits for both the government sector and the economy as a whole. Therefore they enable to deal with the issue of twin deficits in an open economy with a government sector.

The government sector

The following calculations concern the sources of income and consider that the Hicksian disposable income is the income that, when consumed, preserves the current level of wealth of the considered sector. The resulting definitions of Y_g^H (the government's disposable income) and W_g^a (the government's real wealth position) are the same as in the previous chapter (see p. 100):

$$Y_g^H = T + i\frac{M}{p} + \xi\frac{(M+B)}{p} + r^* W_g^a, \xi = i^* + \hat{s} - i \tag{6.13}$$

with

$$W_g^a := \frac{-(M+B) + sF_c}{p} = -\frac{(M+B)}{p} + \frac{sF_c}{p} = W_g + W_c$$

This implies

$$\begin{aligned}
\dot{W}_g^a &= \frac{-(\dot{M}+\dot{B}) + \dot{s}F_c + s\dot{F}_c}{p} - \frac{\dot{p}}{p}\frac{-(M+B)+sF_c}{p} \\
&= \frac{-(pG + iB - pT - i^* sF_c) + \hat{s}sF_c}{p} - \hat{p}\frac{-(M+B)+sF_c}{p} \\
&= T - i\frac{B}{p} + \hat{p}\frac{M+B}{p} + (i^* + \hat{s} - \hat{p})\frac{sF_c}{p} - G
\end{aligned}$$

which gives

$$\dot{W}_g^a = Y_g^H - G \quad = r^* W_g^a + i\frac{M}{p} + \xi\frac{M+B}{p} + T - G \tag{6.14}$$

The dynamics of total domestic wealth and internationally held domestic bonds

Since this debt position is not assumed as constant, we re-use the equations for the evolution of total wealth W of the economy and consider once again private Hicksian disposable income Y_p^H and private wealth W_p in their interaction with the evolution of aggregate government debt.

$$\begin{aligned}
W &= \frac{sF}{p} = W_p + W_g + W_c + W^* \\
W_p &= \frac{M + B_p + sF_p}{p} \quad \text{(see also below)}
\end{aligned}$$

$$\begin{aligned}
W_g &= \frac{-M-B}{p}, W_c = \frac{sF_c}{p}, W^* = \frac{B^*}{p} \\
\hat{W} &= \hat{s} + \hat{F} - \hat{p} \\
\dot{W} &= \hat{s}W + \frac{s\dot{F}_p}{p} - \hat{p}W \\
&= \hat{s}W + \frac{p(Y-C-G-I) + si^*F - iB^* + \dot{B}^*}{p} - \hat{p}W \\
&= (\hat{s}-\hat{p})W + i^*\frac{sF}{p} + Y - C - G - I - iW^* + \frac{\dot{B}^*}{p} \\
&= (i^* + \hat{s} - \hat{p})W + Y - C - G - I - iW^* + \frac{\dot{B}^*}{p} \\
\dot{W} &= r^*W + Y - C - G - I - iW^* + \frac{\dot{B}^*}{p} \\
\dot{W}^* &= \frac{\dot{B}^*}{p} - \hat{p}W^* \qquad (6.15)
\end{aligned}$$

Private wealth and income

We have for the definition of private wealth and disposable income:

$$W_p = \frac{M + B_p + sF_p}{p} = W - W_g^a - W^* \qquad (6.16)$$

$$\begin{aligned}
Y_p^H &= Y - T + (i^* + \hat{s} - \hat{p})\frac{sF_p}{p} + (i - \hat{p})\frac{B}{p} - \hat{p}\frac{M}{p} \\
&= Y - T + (i^* + \hat{s} - \hat{p})W_p - (i^* + \hat{s} - \hat{p})\frac{M+B}{p} + (i - \hat{p})\frac{B}{p} - \hat{p}\frac{M}{p} \\
&= Y - T + r^*W_p - (i^* + \hat{s} - i)\frac{M+B}{p} - i\frac{M}{p} \\
&= Y - T + r^*(W - W_g^a - W^*) - \xi\frac{M+B}{p} - i\frac{M}{p} \qquad (6.17)
\end{aligned}$$

From the expressions of the disposable income of households and the government, we get:

$$Y_p^H = Y - Y_g^H + r^*(W - W^*) \quad \text{or} \quad Y_p^H + Y_g^H = Y + r^*(W - W^*)$$

The four laws of motion of MFT economies with international capital flows

Foreign inflation is now set equal to zero and we assume fixed policy parameters M, T, G:

$$\dot{W} = r^*W + Y - C(\cdot) - I(\cdot) - G - iW^* + \dot{B}^*/p \qquad (6.18)$$

$$\dot{W}_g^a = r^*W_g^a + \xi\frac{M+B}{p} + i\frac{M}{p} + T - G \qquad (6.19)$$

$$\dot{W}^* = \dot{B}^*/p - \hat{p}W^* \qquad (6.20)$$

that are coupled with the law of motion for the price level p:

$$\hat{p} = \hat{w} = \beta_w(Y - \overline{Y})/(1-\gamma) + \hat{s} + \pi^*$$
$$[\hat{w} = \beta_w(Y - \overline{Y}) + \gamma\hat{p} + (1-\gamma)\widehat{sp^*}] \qquad (6.21)$$

This law of motion represents the reduced form of a standard open economy Phillips curve, with myopic perfect foresight on both the domestic price level and the expected growth rate of the exchange rate (γ the weight of the domestic price level in the domestic consumer price index, see Rødseth (2000, ch.6) for details).[5] Let us note that these laws of motion still assume myopic perfect foresight with respect to the exchange rate and inflation dynamics and thus do not yet distinguish between expected rates of return and actual ones. Such a distinction between actual and perceived rates of return will become important when we will later consider exchange rate dynamics. Let us note also that we have slightly the consumption and investment function of Rødseth (2000, ch.6). In particular we included the real exchange rate into the consumption function (because we will distinguish between the consumption of the domestic and the foreign commodity).

The dynamics of the private sector

Consumption and investment behaviour are determined as before. Consumption depends on real disposable income, domestic and foreign real rates of interest, real wealth and the real exchange rate σ. Investment is determined by capacity utilization and domestic and foreign real rates of interest. The partial derivatives with respect to these variables are assumed to exhibit the usual (Keynesian) signs in a small open economy. Finally, we keep our previous assumption according to which taxes are determined endogenously so that government debt as measured by W_g^a stays constant in time. In this case, the above dynamical system is reduced to the following simpler form:

$$\begin{aligned} \dot{W} &= r^*W + Y - C(Y_p, W_p, r, r^{*e}, \sigma) \\ &\quad - I(Y, r, r^{*e}) - G - iW^* + \dot{B}^*/p \qquad (6.22) \\ \dot{W}^* &= \dot{B}^*/p - \hat{p}W^* \qquad (6.23) \\ \hat{p} &= \beta_w(Y - \overline{Y})/(1-\gamma) + \varepsilon(s) + \pi^* \qquad (6.24) \end{aligned}$$

based on the following definitions and relationships:

$$\begin{aligned} r &= i - \hat{p} \qquad (6.25) \\ r^* &= i^* + \hat{s} - \hat{p} \quad [\text{expected rate } r^{*e} = i^* + \varepsilon(s) - \hat{p}] \qquad (6.26) \\ Y_p &= Y + r^{*e}(W - W^*) - G \qquad (6.27) \\ W_p &= W - W_g^a - W^* \qquad (6.28) \\ \sigma &= s/p \quad [p^* = 1] \qquad (6.29) \end{aligned}$$

This dynamical system is to be supplemented by the temporary equilibrium relationships for goods, money and the foreign exchange market:

$$\begin{aligned} Y &= C_1(Y_p^H, W_p, r, r^{*e}, \sigma) + I(Y, r, r^{*e}) + G + X(Y^*, \sigma) \qquad (6.30) \\ M/p &= m^d(Y, i), \; [m^d = kY\exp(\alpha(i^* - i)) \text{ for example}] \qquad (6.31) \\ s\dot{F}_{p2}/p &= f^d(\xi^e, W_p) = -f^{d*}(\xi^{*e}, W^*) = \dot{B}^*/p \qquad (6.32) \end{aligned}$$

with $\xi^e = i^* + \varepsilon(s) - i, \xi^{*e} = i^* + \varepsilon^*(s) - i$. As far as the goods market equilibrium is concerned, we have suppressed imports and thus consider only domestic goods (goods type 1). We assume that only consumption goods (goods type 2) are imported so that we replace $C(Y_p, W_p, r, r^{*e}, \sigma)$ by $C_1(Y_p, W_p, r, r^{*e}, \sigma)$ and reduce net exports NX to exports X. Therefore the market for imported goods behaves in a passive fashion (whereby consumption demand of imported commodities is always served and thus not a restriction for the working of the domestic economy).

The new relationship is the equation describing exchange equilibrium on the international capital market of domestic against foreign bonds:

$$f^d(\bar{i}^* + \varepsilon(s) - i, W - W_g^a - W^*) = -f^{d*}(\bar{i}^* + \varepsilon^*(s) - i, W^*)$$

On the left-hand side we have the flow demand of domestic residents for foreign bonds (if positive, otherwise the supply of such bonds) measured in terms of domestic goods. On the right hand side, the expression $f^{d*}(i^* + \varepsilon^*(s) - i)$ provides the demand of foreigners for domestic bonds (or alternatively the supply of such bonds) also measured in terms of domestic goods.[6] This equilibrium equation describes the capital flows of the capital account that are not caused by the savings decisions within the domestic economy. In the case of uniform expectations of de- or appreciation in the world economy, i.e., when $f^{d*}(\bar{i}^* + \varepsilon(s) - i, \cdot) = f^d(\bar{i}^* + \varepsilon(s) - i, \cdot)$ holds (when therefore domestic and foreign asset holders have the same demand schedule), we assume that this implies $f^{d*} = f^d = 0$ since both parties are then expecting the same risk premium and should therefore be buyers or sellers of foreign bonds, causing a reaction of the exchange rate that reduces the resulting excess demand (or supply) to zero.

Steady state determination

Let us note that the regressive expectations mechanisms must fulfill some consistency requirement in order to allow for a meaningful steady state consideration, namely $\varepsilon(s_o) = \varepsilon^*(s_o) = 0$ for the steady state value of the exchange rate. Furthermore we make use of the law of motion for the capital stock in the following steady state consideration and assume:

$$\hat{K} = I/K = I(Y/K, r, r^{*e})/K = 0$$

as side condition for these considerations $I = 0$. From the Phillips curve, we get $\hat{p} = 0, Y_o = \overline{Y}$ and thus $r_o^* = r_o^{*e} = i^*$, $r_o = i_o$ and $\xi_o = i^* - i = \xi_o^*$.

Next, the conditions $\dot{W}^*$, $\dot{B}^* = 0$ imply $f^{d*}(\xi^*, W^*) = 0$. We assume, as a simplified form for the function $f^{d*}(\xi^*, W^*) = f^{d*}(\xi^*)W^*$, a multiplicative expression with $f^{d*}(0, W^*) = 0$. The disappearance of international capital flows in the steady state implies that $i_o = i^*$ at the steady state. From the LM curve we get, in the case of the regime of a given money supply, $p_o = M/m^d(\overline{Y}, i^*)$.

International capital market equilibrium $f^d(0, W - W^* - W_g^a) = -f^{d*} = 0$ implies a steady state value for $W - W^*$ which, when inserted into the IS curve (together with the other steady state values already determined), implies a steady state value for the real exchange rate $\sigma = s/p$ and thus also a steady state value for the nominal exchange rate s.

Since we already had $\dot{B}^* = 0$, we finally get from the established equation for total savings that $\dot{F}_p$ must be zero as well. In other words, $\dot{W} = 0$ will be automatically guaranteed. This however means that there is zero root hysteresis in the levels of W and W^* since only their difference is uniquely determined in the steady state. The steady state value of the capital stock K is finally uniquely determined through the condition $0 = I(\overline{Y}/K, i^*, i^*)$.

A summing up

In the above considered MFT model extension we assumed that cash management comes first and is always characterized by the partial stock money market equilibrium condition $M/p = m^d(Y, i)$ $[B/p = B^d/p]$. Domestic agents then plan to reallocate their interest-bearing assets according to their behavioural relationships $f^d(\xi^e, W_p)$ $[f^d(\xi^{*e}, W^*)]$. The flow of savings (with $\dot{M} = 0$ by assumption) is then added to these portfolio changes as far as financial assets are concerned (with resulting additional flows of foreign bonds being determined by $s\dot{F}_{p1} = pNX + si^*F_p$). This stylized ordering of stock and flow conditions is intended to avoid any confusion between international capital flows and the allocation of savings. In the model, goods, money and the international capital market are of course considered simultaneously and – for example – used to determine the variables Y, i, s (in the case of flexible exchange rates and a given money supply in the economy).

The money market is of traditional LM-curve type and can thus be represented graphically in the usual way. A graphical representation of the international bond markets is provided in Figure 6.1. In this figure we consider a regime of flexible exchange rates that are then to be determined from the interaction of demand and supply on the international capital markets.

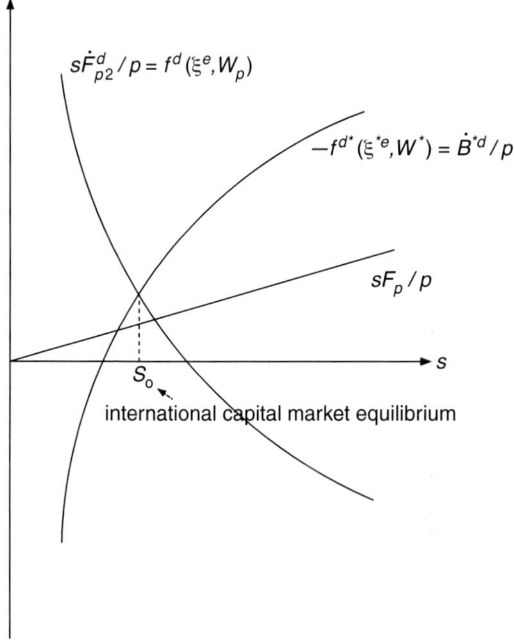

Figure 6.1 Exchange rate determination on the international capital market

This figure shows the level of the exchange rate s_o at the intersection of the domestic demand curve for foreign bonds (the supply curve for domestic bonds) and the foreign demand curve for domestic bonds (the supply curve for foreign bonds) and where therefore capital flow equilibrium is established. The equilibrium exchange rate depends on foreign characteristics, in contrast to the case considered in Chiarella, Flaschel, Franke and Semmler (2009) where domestic bonds are considered as non-traded goods and where therefore the supply of such bonds (in the case of a flexible exchange rate regime) is simply given by the bonds held domestically, F_p. In this case the equilibrium in the domestic market for foreign bonds would be determined by the intersection of the f^d curve with the straight line shown in the above figure and would thus be independent from foreign asset demands, definitely a situation that is too simple to characterize today's international financial system. Let us note that the $-f^{d*}$ curve is a supply curve of foreign bonds (while in the form f^{d*} it would represent a demand curve for foreign bonds). In the case where it is identical to the f^d curve, the intersection of the f^d, f^{d*} must lie on the horizontal axis (i.e. there is no international capital flow).

We will see later that the model remains similar to the original MFT approach with respect to its comparative static results (since the formal properties of the equilibrium condition for the market for foreign bonds have remained the same). However, the evolution of foreign bonds held domestically as well as abroad can now change radically in the course of time and is no longer a simple reflection of the savings decision in the domestic economy.

International finance: some basic results

Inflation dynamics and international capital flows under interest and exchange rate pegs

In the following, we base our considerations on the same assumptions as in Chapter 5, which are briefly repeated here for sake of convenience:

- $i = i^*$: An interest rate peg by the central bank (via an accommodating monetary policy).
- $s = 1$: A fixed exchange rate via an endogenous supply of dollar denominated bonds by the central bank.
- Given $Y^*, p^*(i^*)$: The small country assumption.
- W_g^a: A tax policy of the government that keeps the aggregate wealth of the government fixed.
- $G_2, I_2 = 0$: Only consumption goods are import commodities which are never rationed.
- $\overline{\omega}$: The real wage is fixed by a conventional type of markup pricing.
- $\overline{r}_f^n$: The normal (capacity utilization) rate of return of firms is fixed (since the real wage is a given magnitude) and set equal to i^* for simplicity.
- $Y^p = \overline{y}^p K, N^d = Y/x$: Fixed proportions in production.
- $\overline{K}$: The capacity effect of investment is ignored. Potential output $\overline{Y}^p = 1$ is therefore a given magnitude.
- $\overline{Y} = x\overline{N} = 1$: A given level of the full employment output.

On the basis of the above assumptions, the real rates of interest are equalized for the domestic economy: $r^* = i^* - \hat{p} = i - \hat{p} = r$.

Furthermore, the risk premium ξ is zero. Finally, due to the assumed tax policy, the disposable income of the household sector is $Y_p = Y + r^*(W - W^*) - G$. and private wealth W_p is given by $W - W^* - W_g^a$.

The real portfolio stock demand for money and the excess flow demand for foreign bonds of the private sector (including foreigners) are now:

$$M^d = pm^d(Y, i) \tag{6.33}$$

$$-\dot{F}_c/p = f^d(0, W - W_g^a - W^*) + f^{d*}(0, W^*) \tag{6.34}$$

They must be satisfied by an accommodating monetary policy and out of the stocks of foreign bonds held by the central bank. They are therefore not important for the dynamics of the model under normal circumstances (non-exhausted reserves). The second equation distinguishes the present model from our analysis in Chapter 5. It is of crucial importance when the stability of the fixed exchange rate system is in question.

The real exchange rate $\sigma = (sp^*)/p$, i.e. the amount of domestic goods that are exchanged per unit of foreign good is reduced to $1/p$ due to the above normalization assumptions. Households buy investment goods for firms and use the normal rate of profit in order to estimate their performance, which is constant. We consider only one real rate, r, in the following formulation of the consumption decisions (for domestic and foreign goods) and the investment decisions of the household sector (which again coincide with those in Chapter 5):

$$C_1 = C_1(Y_p^H, W_p, r, \sigma): \text{ consumption demand for the domestic good}$$

$$C_2 = C_2(Y_p^H, W_p, r, \sigma): \text{ consumption demand for the foreign good}$$

$$C = C_1(Y_p^H, W_p, r, \sigma) + C_2(Y_p, W_p, r, \sigma)/\sigma: \text{ total consumption}$$

$$I = I(Y, r): \text{ investment demand, for domestic goods solely}$$

The goods market equilibrium is again given by:

$$Y = C_1(Y + r(W - W^*) - G, W - W^* - W_g^a, r, \sigma) + I(Y, r) + G + X(Y^*, \sigma)$$

The dynamic equations of the model are now the following ones (the growth of the capital stock is neglected by assumption):

$$\hat{p} = \hat{w} = \beta_w(Y - \overline{Y}) + \gamma\hat{p} + (1-\gamma)\widehat{sp}^* \tag{6.35}$$

$$\dot{W} = rW + Y - C(Y + r(W - W^*) - G, W - W^* - W_g^a, r, 1/p) - I(Y,r) - G - i^*W^* + \dot{B}^*/p \tag{6.36}$$

$$\dot{W}^* = \dot{B}^*/p - \hat{p}W^* \tag{6.37}$$

The second and third laws of motion are our new representation of the balance of payments in real terms, while the first one is once again the standard money wage Phillips curve. On the basis of a constant markup pricing, this equation can be again reformulated as follows:

$$\hat{p} = \frac{1}{1-\gamma}\beta_w(Y - \overline{Y}) \tag{6.38}$$

$$d(W - W^*)/dt = r(W - W^*) + Y - C(Y + r(W - W^*) - G, W - W^* - W_g^a, r, 1/p) - I(Y,r) - G \tag{6.39}$$

We use reduced expressions for the second and the third law of motion. The first law has to be inserted within them in order to get a system of differential equations that depends on p, $W - W^*$ and the statically endogenous variable $Y(\cdot)$. The position of the IS curve only depends on the difference $W - W^*$ between real domestic holding of foreign bonds and foreign holdings of domestic bonds, since the temporary equilibrium output Y depends only on the two state variables p, $W - W^*$ through the following goods market equilibrium condition ($\sigma = 1/p$):

$$Y = C_1\left(Y + \left(i^* - \frac{1}{1-\gamma}\beta_w(Y - \overline{Y})\right)(W - W^*) - G, W - W^* - W_g^a, i^* - \frac{1}{1-\gamma}\beta_w(Y - \overline{Y}), 1/p\right) + I\left(Y, i^* - \frac{1}{1-\gamma}\beta_w(Y - \overline{Y})\right) + G + X(Y^*, 1/p) \tag{6.40}$$

The core dynamics

We assume for the moment that the parameters of this equilibrium condition are such that the conventional dependency of IS-equilibrium output on the price level results in $\partial Y/\partial p < 0$. It is obvious that $\partial Y/\partial(W - W^*) > 0$. The resulting dynamical system in the state variables $p, \Omega = W - W^*$ is by and large of the same type as the one considered in Chiarella, Flaschel, Franke and Semmler (2006, ch.12) and can be treated in the same way.

For reasons of simplicity, we maintain the assumption that aggregate government wealth (basically the government deficit) stays constant in time and investigate now the steady state solution and the dynamics surrounding it:

$$\hat{p} = \frac{1}{1-\gamma}\beta_w(Y(\Omega, p) - \overline{Y})$$

$$\dot{\Omega} = r\Omega + X(Y^*, 1/p) - \sigma C_2(Y + r\Omega - G, \Omega - W_g^a, r, 1/p)$$

where the properties of the IS-equilibrium are characterized by the standard partial derivatives just discussed. Since the system is formally equivalent to the one in Chapter 5, p. 118 (with Ω replacing W), we get the same results. It seems that the introduction of bilateral international capital flows does not lead to any changes within the concrete framework considered here.

Given the above dynamical system, we can recover the dynamics of the two wealth variables W, W^* in the following way:

$$\dot{W}^* = f^{d*}(0, W^*) - \hat{p}(Y(p, \Omega)W^*$$

$$W = \Omega + W^*$$

which completes the picture. In comparison to Chiarella, Flaschel, Franke and Semmler (2009, ch.12) we have to consider two variables W, W^* in place of W alone. Moreover, the central bank behaviour is now impacted by what foreigners are doing on the market for foreign exchange and is thus now much more vulnerable with respect to its foreign reserve holdings, even if the adjustment process of interacting W, W^*, p dynamics is stable. The next steps, in order to fully analyse the situation of an interest and exchange rate peg would be to take into account the dynamics of the Government Borrowing Restriction and the possible instability scenarios.

The case of flexible exchange rates

As in Chapter 5, we now consider the case of perfectly flexible exchange rates and flexible interest rates. In this case the money supply is given and the central bank allows international capital markets to determine the exchange rate through the supply (demand) and demand (supply) of foreign (domestic) bonds. The IS-, LM-, FF-schedules determine now simultaneously the output Y, the domestic rate of interest i and the exchange rate s. We simplify this equilibrium portion of the model by assuming that money demand depends on normal output $\overline{Y}$ instead of actual output. This implies that the rate of interest i depends on the state variable p of the dynamics.

In the case of the Cagan money demand function $m^d = kY \exp(\alpha(i^* - i))$, we get:

$$i = i^* + \frac{\ln p - \ln M + \ln k + \ln \overline{Y}}{\alpha} = i(p)$$

Furthermore, to insert this function into the equilibrium condition of the international capital market implies a dependency of the exchange rate s on the state variable of the dynamics that is independent of the characteristics of goods market equilibrium. This equilibrium condition can subsequently be solved for the output Y in order to obtain the comparative statics of the IS curve with respect to the three state variables p, W, W^*. Once again, we assume that the central bank may use open market operations in domestic bonds and change the composition of the household's portfolio, but it does not issue money otherwise. We also assume that taxes are determined endogenously so that the real debt of the government W_g^a remains constant.

Temporary equilibrium

In order to get the full asset markets equilibrium, as characterized by the LMFX curve, we need to consider the international flow market for bonds (with $s\dot{F}_{p2}/p = \dot{B}^*/p$):

$$f^d(i^* + \varepsilon(s) - i(p, M), W - W^* - W_g^a) \overset{LMFX}{=} -f^{d*}(i^* + \varepsilon^*(s) - i, W^*) \quad (6.41)$$

It is easy to see that a decrease in i shifts both curves of Figure 6.1 to the right, which implies that the exchange rate will increase in such a case (the opposite will occur in the case of an increasing foreign interest rate i^*). An increase in the foreign wealth of domestic residents W will increase the exchange rate, while an increase in the domestic bond holding W^* of foreigners will have ambiguous effects. Finally, an increase in money supply must increase the current exchange rate beyond this level and therefore leads to overshooting exchange rate reactions.[7]

Let us consider, on the basis of the given capital market schedule $s = s(W, W^*, p)$ the IS-equilibrium curve of the presently considered situation:

$$\begin{aligned} Y \overset{IS}{=} & \; C_1(Y + (i^* + \varepsilon(s) - \hat{p}(Y))(W - W^*) - G, W - W^* - W_g^a, i^* \\ & + \varepsilon(s) - \hat{p}(Y), i(p) - \hat{p}(Y), s/p) + I(Y, i^* + \varepsilon(s) - \hat{p}(Y), i(p) - \hat{p}(Y)) \\ & + G + X(Y^*, s/p) \qquad (6.42) \end{aligned}$$

We assume for the time being that the parameters of this equilibrium condition are such that $\partial Y/\partial p < 0$. (the conventional dependency of IS-equilibrium output on the price level). With respect to the wealth terms W, W^*, it is obvious that $\partial Y/\partial(W) > 0$ and $\partial Y/\partial(W^*) < 0$. In order to derive conclusions on how the equilibrium output level depends on the price level p and on W, W^*, one needs to use: our regressive expectations regime; the dependence of the nominal rate of interest and the real exchange rate on the price level; and the functional dependence of the nominal exchange rate on p, W, W^* derived above. The outcome is ambiguous, but points to a certain degree to a (conventional) negative overall dependence of Y on p. We shall assume that this is indeed the case in our discussion of overshooting exchange rates, since the opposite case would imply a destabilizing feedback of the price level on its rate of change via the Phillips curve mechanism. We thus have a schedule $Y = Y(p, W, W^*)$ that characterizes the goods market equilibrium on the basis of full asset markets equilibrium. Shocks to the exchange rate s will give rise to shocks in the variables W, W^*. The situation after such shocks is determined by a smooth evolution according to the laws of motion discussed below.

Laws of motion

We have by now determined the statically endogenous variables of the considered MFT regime (i, s, Y) through the three equilibrium relationships that characterize the model. The state variables of the model are

p, W, W^* (while the movement of the capital stock is still neglected). The laws of motion for these variables are given by:

$$\dot{W} = r^*(W - W^*) + Y - C(Y_p, W - W^* - W_g^a, r, r^{*e}, \sigma) - I(Y, r, r^{*e}) - G + \dot{W}^* \tag{6.43}$$

$$\dot{W}^* = \dot{B}^*/p - \hat{p}(Y)W^* = f^{d*}(\xi^{*e}, W^*) - \hat{p}(Y)W^* \tag{6.44}$$

$$\hat{p} = \beta_w(Y - \overline{Y})/(1 - \gamma) + \varepsilon(s) + \pi^*,\ \pi^* = 0 \tag{6.45}$$

based on the following definitions and relationships:

$$r = i(p) - \hat{p}(Y) \tag{6.46}$$

$$r^* = i^* + \hat{s} - \hat{p}(Y) \quad [\text{expected rate} \quad r^{*e} = i^* + \varepsilon(s) - \hat{p}(Y)] \tag{6.47}$$

$$\xi^* = i^* + \hat{s} - i(p) \quad [\text{expected rate} \quad \xi^{*e} = i^* + \varepsilon(s) - i(p)] \tag{6.48}$$

$$Y_p = Y + r^{*e}(W - W^*) - G \tag{6.49}$$

$$\sigma = s/p \quad [p^* = 1] \tag{6.50}$$

and the equilibrium schedules $Y(W, W^*, p)$, $s(W, W^*, p)$.

The law of motion for W is complex since the static relationships $s(W, W^*, p)$, $Y(W, W^*, p)$ have to be inserted within it in various places. A full treatment of the model is thus almost impossible so one must have recourse to simplifications like the one considered in Chapter 5 (see p. 113). Further modifications of the above approach could, however, include a direct modelling of the exchange rate dynamics in order to avoid these difficulties and allow for a better comparison between the case of bilateral international capital flows and the case of non-tradable domestic bonds. However, even models of this kind can include many scenarios where the steady state of the economy is surrounded by repelling forces in place of attracting ones.

Capital flight and currency crises

In this section, we briefly consider situations where new forces may lead to the breakdown of a fixed exchange rate system, or to bad equilibria in a flexible exchange rate system, if a capital flight away from the domestic bonds occurs on a scale that is sufficiently large. Indeed, while the high degree of the actual international capital mobility has enabled the economies to have easy and cheap access to foreign funding, it has also made them more vulnerable to speculative attacks and sudden capital outflows. When an important fraction of the liabilities of a country is denominated in a foreign currency, the occurrence of a speculative attack and the subsequent sharp nominal depreciation of the currency is likely to cause a breakdown in investment and aggregate demand, due to the activation of credit constraints.

We sketch here how the MFT approach can be extended to cover international capital markets.

Regime I: interest and exchange rate peg

As a start, let us consider a scenario where the nominal exchange rate is pegged at a constant level (determined by the domestic monetary authorities) and the central bank sets the level of the domestic interest rate. In such a case, the domestic monetary authorities are disposed to accommodate any demand for domestic and foreign bonds (and also for domestic money) of both domestic and foreign agents, and therefore to remove any disequilibrium in the domestic and the foreign exchange markets.

In such a situation, foreigners (and domestic residents) may be able to sell domestic bonds against foreign ones on a larger scale and may thereby rapidly exhaust the amount of foreign bonds held by the domestic central bank. Such a one-sided process would thus lead to the following law of motion for central bank reserves in a fixed exchange rate system (assuming, as mentioned, an interest rate peg):

$$-s\dot{F}_c/p = f^d(0, W - W_g^a - W^*, f_p) + f^{d*}(0, W^*) > 0, \quad f_p = sF_p/p$$

that is based on the following portfolio reallocation situation:

$$\frac{s\dot{F}^d_{p2}}{p} = \delta(f^d(0, W_p) - f_p), \quad \frac{s\dot{B}^d_{p2}}{p} = \delta\left(\left[W_p - \frac{M}{p} - f^d(0, W_p)\right] - \frac{B_p}{p}\right)$$

If this occurs repeatedly and on a large scale (with capital gains expectations based on a breakdown of the fixed exchange rate system and an expected depreciation of the domestic currency) the fixed exchange rate regime will indeed break down at some point.

The international capital market for domestic bonds is than determined by a regime of flexible exchange rates, as follows:

$$s\dot{F}_{p2}/p = f^d(i^* - \varepsilon(s) - i, W - W^* - W_g^a, f_p) = -f^{d*}(i^* - \varepsilon^*(s) - i, W^*) = \dot{B}^*/p$$

Such a situation may lead to a depreciation of the domestic currency[8] and thus confirm what has been expected by international speculators. This may possibly also be accompanied by a leaning-against-the-wind interest rate policy by the central bank that would increase the domestic rate i above the international one in order to attract capital inflows.

If the defence of the currency peg by the domestic monetary authorities is not successful and the resulting depreciation of domestic currency is of a significant magnitude, a balance sheet crisis and a large output loss à la Krugman might occur.[9] The situation might be even if there are global players that can use leverage to buy large amounts of domestic bonds, exchange them at the given currency peg into foreign bonds, and then contribute to occurrence of an exchange rate crisis.

Regime II: flexible exchange rates and given money supply

We now consider a second scenario with perfectly flexible exchange rates and a domestic money supply kept fixed by the domestic monetary authorities. In this case, global players can also attempt to make capital gains from the occurrence of speculative attacks, by borrowing with only small capital investment a large amount of domestic bonds, and then triggering the occurrence of a large devaluation of the currency through the establishment of a bad equilibrium in a multiple equilibrium situation.

In such a situation of ongoing capital flight, the equilibrium condition on the international market for foreign bonds implies:

$$f^d(i^* - \varepsilon(s) - i, W - W^* - W_g^a, f_p) + f^{d*}(i^* - \varepsilon^*(s) - i, W^*) = 0 \quad (6.51)$$

The incorporation of international actors and global players might give rise to the occurrence of repeated currency devaluations, and in the worst case, of a depreciation spiral, if demand functions of both domestic and foreign agents $f^d(\cdot) + f^{d*}(\cdot)$ shift to higher foreign bond demand levels.[10]

A two-country Mundell–Fleming–Tobin world

The next step is to extend the previous approach to a two-country model which means that the mutual influence of the home and the foreign country on each other has explicitly to be taken into account. In comparison with the model of the last section this requires the following changes:

- In order to treat both countries in the same way, we will now define W^*, the foreign country's real (gross) wealth position, analogously to the corresponding magnitude of the home country. Thus, we will redefine W^* as $W^* = \frac{s^*B^*}{p^*}$, which coincides with the previous definition ($W^* = \frac{B^*}{p}$) only in the case of purchasing power parity, that is not fulfilled in the current framework.
- In addition to this topic a really symmetric treatment of both countries has important consequences for the flows of government bonds between them, especially with regard to that part of the flows which comes about in a passive way via the savings equation. In this regard equations (6.15) and (6.18) imply the following equation for $s\dot{F}_p$:

$$s\dot{F}_{p1} = p(Y - C - I - G) + si^*F - i\underbrace{(B - B_p)}_{\equiv B^*} \tag{6.52}$$

- Thus, if the sum of the home country's net exports and net interest payments from abroad is positive, this leads to a first (and up to a certain degree unintended) inflow of additional foreign bonds. This means that the foreign country pays with bonds of its government.

If, however, it is the home country that has to make such payments, it does so by means of its foreign bonds, i.e. $s\dot{F}_{p1}$ is now negative. Thus, the foreign country receives the same type of payments in the form of its own bonds (sold in earlier times to the home country).

In order to overcome this asymmetric behaviour of the two countries it is recommendable to assume that – e.g., in the case of a negative right hand side of equation (6.52) – 50 per cent of the sum to be transferred to the other country is paid in form of domestic bonds and the other 50 per cent is paid in form of foreign bonds (provided that the country under consideration has accumulated enough of them in the past which will be assumed in the following). Formally, from the home country's point of view this gives rise to the following equations:

$$s\dot{F}_{p1} = \frac{1}{2}[p(Y - C - I - G) + si^*F - iB^*] \tag{6.53}$$

$$\dot{B}_{p1} = \frac{1}{2}[p(Y - C - I - G) + si^*F - iB^*] \tag{6.54}$$

with $\dot{B}_{p1}$ denoting the part of payments which is done via domestic bonds. For the entire change in the home country's stock of foreign bonds $s\dot{F}$ ($=s\dot{F}_p$ due to the absence of a systematic intervention by the central bank), this means:

$$s\dot{F}_p \equiv s(\dot{F}_{p1} + \dot{F}_{p2}) = \frac{1}{2}[p(Y - C - I - G) + si^*F - iB^*] + pf^d(\cdot) \tag{6.55}$$

where $s\dot{F}_{p2}$ denotes as before the desired change in sF in conjunction with the private agents' portfolio decision and is given via the function f^d.

1. For the dynamics of W, this has now the following consequences:

$$\begin{aligned}\dot{W} &= \hat{s}W + \frac{s\dot{F}}{p} - \hat{p}W \\ &= (\hat{s} - \hat{p})W + \frac{\frac{1}{2}[p(Y - C - I - G) + si^*F - iB^*] + pf^d(\cdot)}{p} \\ &= (\hat{s} - \hat{p})W + \frac{1}{2}(Y - C - I - G) + \frac{1}{2}i^*W \\ &\quad - \frac{1}{2}i\frac{sp^*}{p}W^* + f^d(\cdot)\end{aligned} \tag{6.56}$$

2. Clearly, the corresponding equation for $\dot{W}^*$ is now of a similar type (explicitly mentioned below).
3. The equilibrium condition for the international flow market for bonds now:

$$\begin{aligned}\dot{F}_{p2} &= pf^d\left(i^* + \varepsilon(s) - i, W - \frac{p^*}{s^*p}W^* - \overline{W}_g^a\right) \\ &= sp^*b^{d*}\left(i + \varepsilon^*(s^*) - i^*, W^* - \frac{p}{sp^*}W - \overline{W}_g^a\right) = s\dot{B}^*_{p2}\end{aligned} \tag{6.57}$$

4. with b^{d*} denoting the real demand for new domestic bonds by foreign investors. In the case of a fixed exchange rate (to be

considered below) this equation has of course to be replaced by a corresponding function describing the central banks' intervention.

5. Second, the foreign country's rate of inflation ($\hat{p}^*$), which was given exogenously so far, has now to be determined analogously to $\hat{p}$:

$$\hat{p}^* = \frac{\beta_w^*}{1-\gamma^*}(Y^* - \overline{Y}^*) + \varepsilon^*(s^*) + \hat{p} \tag{6.58}$$

6. Note, however, that in the case of perfect foresight in both countries with regard to the other country's rate of inflation, the right-hand side of this equation can be inserted for $\hat{p}^*$ in equation (6.24) which determines $\hat{p}$. Thus, the latter variable cancels out on both sides so that the rate of change of the price level is no longer defined (a problem that also occurs in conjunction with perfect foresight in other models). In order to avoid this difficulty, it is advisable here to replace the assumption of perfect foresight by another type of expectation formation, for example, by regressive expectations similar to the corresponding assumption in conjunction with the exchange rate. For our subsequent considerations, however, we will simply assume that the inhabitants of the home country always expect a rate of inflation in the foreign country equal to zero, which can be justified by insufficient information of the home country's agents about what is going abroad. Clearly, the same assumption is made for the other country.
7. Furthermore, we now also need the foreign country's IS–LM-block in order to determine the statically endogenous variables Y^* and i^*.

In the following, we will shed some light on the resulting system, first in the case of a flexible exchange rate and thereafter in the case of a fixed one.

Flexible exchange rates

The entire dynamical system has now the following structure:

$$\begin{aligned}\dot{W} = (\hat{s} - \hat{p})W + \frac{1}{2}i^*W + \frac{1}{2}\Big[Y - C\Big(Y_p, W_p, i - \hat{p}, i^* + \varepsilon(s) - \hat{p}, \frac{sp^*}{p}\Big) \\ - I(Y, i - \hat{p}, i^* + \varepsilon(s) - \hat{p}) - G\Big] \\ - i\frac{sp^*}{p}W^* + f^d(i^* + \varepsilon(s) - i, W_p)\end{aligned} \tag{6.59}$$

$$\begin{aligned}
\dot{W}^* &= (s^* - \hat{p}^*)W^* + \frac{1}{2}iW^* \\
&\quad + \frac{1}{2}\Bigg[Y^* - C^*\left(Y_p^*, W_p^*, i^* - \hat{p}^*, i + \varepsilon^*(s^*) - \hat{p}^*, \frac{s^*p}{p^*}\right) \\
&\qquad - I^*(Y^*, i^* - \hat{p}^*, i + \varepsilon^*(s^*) - \hat{p}^*) - G^*\Bigg] \\
&\quad - i^*\frac{s^*p}{p^*}W + b^{d*}(i + \varepsilon^*(s^*) - i^*, W_p^*) && (6.60) \\
\hat{p} &= \frac{\beta_w}{1-\gamma}(Y - \overline{Y}) + \varepsilon(s) + \hat{p}^* && (6.61) \\
\hat{p}^* &= \frac{\beta_w^*}{1-\gamma^*}(Y^* - \overline{Y}^*) + \varepsilon^*(s^*) + \hat{p} && (6.62)
\end{aligned}$$

with

$$\begin{aligned}
W_p &= W - \frac{p^*}{s^*p}W^* - \overline{W}_g^a \text{ (as before)}, \; W_p^* = W^* - \frac{p}{sp^*}W - \overline{W}_g^a, \\
Y_p &= Y + (i^* + \varepsilon(s) - \hat{p})\left(W - \frac{p^*}{s^*p}W^*\right) - G \text{ and} \\
Y_p^* &= Y^* + (i + \varepsilon^*(s^*) - \hat{p}^*)\left(W^* - \frac{p}{sp^*}W\right) - G^*
\end{aligned}$$

In addition to this, we have the IS–LM block for both countries for the determination of Y, Y^*, i and i^*:

$$\begin{aligned}
Y &= C_1\left(Y_p, W_p, i - \hat{p}, i^* + \varepsilon(s) - \hat{p}, \frac{sp^*}{p}\right) + I(Y, i - \hat{p}, i^* + \varepsilon(s) - \hat{p}) \\
&\quad + G + X\left(Y^*, \frac{sp^*}{p}\right) \quad (IS) && (6.63) \\
Y^* &= C_1^*\left(Y_p^*, W_p^*, i^* - \hat{p}^*, i + \varepsilon^*(s^*) - \hat{p}^*, \frac{s^*p}{p^*}\right) \\
&\quad + I^*(Y^*, i^* - \hat{p}^*, i + \varepsilon^*(s^*) - \hat{p}^*) + G^* + X^*\left(Y, \frac{s^*p}{p^*}\right) \quad (IS^*) && (6.64) \\
\frac{\overline{M}}{p} &= m^d(\overline{Y}, i, i^*) \quad (LM) && (6.65) \\
\frac{\overline{M}^*}{p^*} &= m^{d*}(\overline{Y}^*, i^*, i) \quad (LM^*) && (6.66)
\end{aligned}$$

In order to simplify the determination of the temporary equilibrium, we again made use of the assumption that money demand in both countries depends on the steady state values $\overline{Y}$, or $\overline{Y}^*$, respectively, instead of current income. Furthermore, we also maintain the assumption of a fixed level of aggregate government wealth in both countries ($\overline{W}_g^a$ and $\overline{W}_g^{a*}$), ensured by a suitable tax policy.

Finally, the exchange rate s (which is, of course, equal to $\frac{1}{s^*}$) has to adjust in order to clear the international flow market for bonds according to equation (6.57) mentioned above.

The first step in the computation of the temporary equilibrium consists in the determination of the two rates of interest, i and i^*, from the two LM-equations. Apart from the parameters $\overline{Y}, \overline{Y}^*$, $\overline{M}$ and $\overline{M}^*$, they depend only on the current values of p and p^*: $i = i(p, p^*)$ and $i^* = i^*(p, p^*)$. These values are then inserted into equation (6.57) so that the exchange rate s can be determined on the basis of the current values of W and W^*, leading to $s = s(W, W^*, p, p^*)$ (where the dependence on p and p^* is a direct and an indirect one, the latter stemming from i and i^*). This value (together with s^*, $\varepsilon(s)$ and $\varepsilon^*(s^*)$ immediately resulting from it) is now inserted into the two IS-equations, together with the expressions for $\hat{p}$ and $\hat{p}^*$ obtained from the corresponding dynamic equations (6.61) and (6.62). From the two IS-equations one then gets the current values for Y and Y^*. Let us note however, that for the resulting dynamics for W and W^* we also have to determine the growth rate of s and s^* from the above functional form for s, which leads to two implicit differential equations (a difficulty already mentioned in Chapter 5). Thus, an analysis of the original dynamical system will be quite cumbersome, so that simplifications in the spirit of the earlier sections will be unavoidable.

The steady state, however, can be determined without a major problem if one observes the correspondence between the home country's exports and the foreign country's imports (and vice versa), as usual in two-county-models. The first step, however, is again to ensure that no capital flows take place any more in the steady state. In analogy to the reasoning above, this requires the interest rate in both countries to coincide, i.e. $i_0 = i_0^*$. Note however, that the corresponding value is still unknown at the current stage. Nevertheless we can use it to determine the steady state values of the two price levels, p_0 and p_0^* from the two LM-equations. We thus get $p_0 = p_0(i_0 = i_0^*)$ and $p_0^* = p_0^*(i_0 = i_0^*)$ as functions of the interest rate(s), the concrete value of which is to be determined later.

Furthermore, we can use directly the steady state values $\overline{Y}$ and $\overline{Y}^*$ for domestic and foreign income, which follow immediately from the price dynamics. Thus, there are only the steady state levels of $i_0 = i_0^*$, $s_0 \equiv \frac{1}{s_0^*}$, W_0 and W_0^* to be determined and there are four equations left: the '$\dot{W} = 0$'- and the '$\dot{W}^* = 0$'-equation as well as the two IS-equations. Note, however, that in analogy to the previous section in this chapter, the two wealth expressions W and W^* enter all equations jointly (in form of the difference $W - \frac{p^*}{s^* p} W^*$), so that, once again, only the steady state value of their difference (i.e. the net value of foreign claims or foreign indebtedness) can be determined. This, however, means that one of the equations mentioned must be redundant. As we will see, this is indeed the case.

The first step is to rewrite the two IS-equations in the following way, now explicitly containing imports and the consumption of foreign goods (which are equal to one another according to our previous assumption that imports are only used for private consumption):

$$Y = \underbrace{C_1(\cdot) + \frac{sp^*}{p} C_2(\cdot)}_{\equiv C} + I(\cdot) + G + X(\cdot) - \frac{sp^*}{p} J(\cdot) \tag{6.67}$$

$$Y^* = \underbrace{C_1^*(\cdot) + \frac{s^* p}{p^* C_2^*(\cdot)}}_{\equiv C^*} + I^*(\cdot) + G^* + X^*(\cdot) - \frac{s^* p}{p^*} J^*(\cdot) \tag{6.68}$$

If one now takes into account that the home country's exports are the foreign country's imports, i.e. $X(\cdot) = J^*(\cdot)$ (and $X^*(\cdot) = J(\cdot)$ for the foreign country), one can rewrite the above two equations in the following way:

$$Y - C(\cdot) - I(\cdot) - G = X(\cdot) - \frac{sp^*}{p} J(\cdot) \equiv X(\cdot) - \frac{sp^*}{p} X^*(\cdot) \tag{6.69}$$

$$Y^* - C^*(\cdot) - I^*(\cdot) - G^* = X^*(\cdot) - \frac{s^* p}{p^*} J^*(\cdot) \equiv X^*(\cdot) - \frac{s^* p}{p^*} X(\cdot) \tag{6.70}$$

The expressions on the left hand sides are also present in equation (6.59) and (6.60), respectively, so that the latter (in their steady state formulations $\dot{W} = 0$ and $\dot{W}^* = 0$) can also be expressed as:

$$\dot{W} = i_0^* \left(W - \frac{p^*}{s^* p} W^* \right) = \frac{sp^*}{p} X^*(\cdot) - X(\cdot) \tag{6.71}$$

$$\dot{W}^* = i_0 \left(W^* - \frac{p}{sp^*} W \right) = \frac{s^* p}{p^*} X(\cdot) - X^*(\cdot) \tag{6.72}$$

Multiplication of the second equation by $-\frac{sp^*}{p}$ then immediately yields the first equation, so that only one of them can be used for the determination of the steady state values of the remaining variables. Note, that the above two equations are also intuitively appealing since, for the country with positive net wealth, the corresponding foreign interest income is – completely – used to finance the country's imports whereas the indebted country must have positive net exports to finance the interest payments to the other country.

Thus, there are now three equations left (6.67) and (6.68) and (6.71) or (6.72)) which jointly determine the steady-state-values of $s, i = i^*$ and of the difference $(W - \frac{p^*}{s^* p} W^*)$.

Fixed exchange rates

The formal setup for the case of fixed exchange rates is basically the same as before, with only three exceptions:

- First, all expressions $\hat{s}, \hat{s}^*, \varepsilon(s)$ and $\varepsilon^*(s^*)$ cancel out for obvious reasons. (Note, however, that principally expectations concerning a change of the exchange rate might remain if there is a certain probability of a change in the parity; although this might be an interesting extension of the current approach, it is not considered here.)
- Second, the market clearing condition (6.57) has to be replaced by an intervention function of one of the central banks (or both):

$$\bar{s}\dot{F}_c = (-\theta)\left[pf^d\left(i^* - i, W - \frac{\bar{s}p^*}{p}W^* - \overline{W}_g^a\right) - \bar{s}p^*b^{d*}\left(i - i^*, W^* - \frac{\bar{s}^*p}{p^*}W - \overline{W}_g^a\right)\right] \quad (6.73)$$

$$\dot{B}_c = (1-\theta)\left[pf^d\left(i^* - i, W - \frac{\bar{s}p^*}{p}W^* - \overline{W}_g^a\right) - \bar{s}p^*b^{d*}\left(i - i^*, W^* - \frac{\bar{s}^*p}{p^*}W - \overline{W}_g^a\right)\right] \quad (6.74)$$

- The desired scenario can now be steered by an appropriate choice of the parameter θ which measures the fraction of the prevailing excess demand for (or supply of) foreign bonds that is served by an intervention of the home country's central bank.
- In conjunction with the last topic it has to be mentioned that the actual change in the home country's foreign assets now strongly depends on the concrete value of θ. If, e.g., the home country's central bank is the one to intervene whereas there is no action on the part of the foreign monetary authority (i.e. $\theta = 1$) and if $pf^d > \bar{s}p^*b^{d*}$ holds true, the actual change in F is determined by the second expression, since the domestic excess demand for foreign bonds is served by the domestic central bank. Thus, the excess demand only leads to a redistribution of foreign bonds between the central bank and the private sector in the home country. If, on the other hand, $pf^d < \bar{s}p^*b^{d*}$ holds true, it is again the expression $\bar{s}p^*b^{d*}$ which determines $\dot{F}_2$ since now the excess supply of foreign bonds is absorbed by the domestic central bank. Note, however, that the exact opposite conclusions are valid for the other country, i.e. the change of B^* is determined by the country's own demand for foreign bonds. One way to enforce symmetry here is to postulate that $\theta = \frac{1}{2}$ due to an assumed obligation for both central banks (similar to that of the former EMS) to intervene by the same amount in the case of disequilibrium.

Another way to avoid the difficulties just mentioned is to assume (similar to the corresponding earlier proceeding) that a coordinated monetary policy takes place between the two countries and ensures $i = i^*$, so that – according to our previous assumptions in the preceding subsection – no financial flows between the two countries and thus also no interventions on the part of the central banks take place any more.

The determination of the steady state is then very similar to the proceeding in the previous subsection. The only difference is that instead of s (which is an exogenously given parameter in the present context), it is now the price ratio $\frac{p_0}{p_0^*}$ which is determined (together with $(W - \frac{p^*}{s^*p}W^*)_0$ and $i_0 = i_0^*$) by the equations (6.67), (6.68) and (6.71). This in turn implies – again via the two LM-equations – a corresponding ratio between the two money supplies, $\frac{M}{M^*}$, which must hold in the steady state.

Conclusion

The main contribution of this chapter was the introduction of bilateral international capital flows in the MFT model. Although a thorough reconsideration of the budget constraints was necessary, the resulting dynamics turned out not to differ significantly from the previous case (where domestic bonds were non-tradables). It should be mentioned, however, that a relaxation of certain simplifying assumptions (common for both scenarios considered) might alter these findings, so that there is still a promising field for future research.

On the other hand, it should be noted that the present setup reveals a considerable degree of complexity, especially with regard to the rich set of feedback channels present in the model: Hicksian disposable income effects, Pigou price level effects, Keynes price level effects, the Mundell–Tobin effect of inflationary expectations in both the consumption and the investment function, Dornbusch exchange rate effects, portfolio effects, and the stated stock-flow interactions. The interaction of these effects allowed for a variety of (in-)stability results, too numerous to allow their investigation here. We therefore focused on a regime with pegged interest rate as well as exchange rate and contrasted this situation with a regime where the exchange rate is perfectly flexible and the money supply a given magnitude under the control of the central bank of the domestic economy. The (in-)stability results that were obtained suggested that this type of approach is rich in implications, but unfortunately poor in providing simple and unambiguous answers for those who prefer simple economic conclusions.

7
Fiscal and Monetary Policy, Stocks and the Term Structure of Interest Rates

In this final chapter we will use the insights obtained in the two previous ones, namely that financial markets must be modelled by flow adjustment rules when balance of payments effects are to be discussed. In view of this, we now also employ disequilibrium adjustment rules for the financial markets in the case of a closed economy, though these rules remain based on a Tobinian portfolio (desired stocks) approach to financial markets. Moreover – in order to keep the model simple compared to the KMG approach – we now make use of a dynamic multiplier approach to goods markets behaviour in place of the full Metzlerian expected sales/unintended inventory changes approach, in order to overcome the extreme limit case of continual IS-equilibrium in the simplest way possible (the latter can lead to implausible comparative static results compared to its disequilibrium formulation in the case when income distribution matters on the market for goods).

In short, we are therefore now considering a dynamic general disequilibrium modelling approach which is intended to prepare the grounds for, so to speak, a Keynesian DSGD(isequilibrium) alternative to the now fashionable new Keynesian DSGE(quilibrium) models that dominate the mainstream literature.

Introduction

The financial crisis that spread world wide as a great recession put in evidence the need to understand better the fragility and potentially destabilizing feedbacks of advanced macroeconomies, in particular through a Keynesian disequilibrium model.

As the history of macroeconomic dynamics and business cycles has taught us, fragilities and destabilizing feedbacks are known to be potential features of all markets – the product markets, the labour market, and the financial markets. In this chapter we focus on the financial market. We use a Tobin-like macroeconomic portfolio approach, coupled with the interaction of heterogeneous agents on the financial markets.

The study of financial instability has been undertaken in many partial models but we consider it here within a framework with interconnectedness of the goods and the financial markets. Furthermore, we try to find out which kind of potential fiscal and monetary policies could help, in Minsky's (1986) words, stabilizing an unstable economy. We will see that a counter-cyclical monetary policy (indeed a typical Minskian policy) that focuses on the market for stocks could for instance be an option.

We also see that the private sector of the economy is likely to be a source of instability (another Minskian result), since its steady state is generally surrounded by centrifugal forces. These forces thus have to be tamed by appropriate fiscal and monetary policy measures. We show in this respect that a Tobin-type tax on capital gains or an open market policy that trades in long-term bonds are also capable of stabilizing the steady state of the economy.

In the next section we comment on and investigate the asset market structure considered in our model type by contrasting it with the traditional Keynesian approach of Turnovsky (1995). The model that is based on this structure of the financial markets is presented in the following section. We then investigate the stability of the real-financial market interaction of the model. Following on from this, we use this analysis to investigate what policy measures can improve the working of the private sector of the economy.

Financial markets and the effectiveness of monetary policy

We start from (and extend) the modelling framework of Asada *et al.* (2010b) which considers the following set of financial assets: money M (issued by the central bank), fixed-price bonds B (issued by the government, with $p_b = 1$) and equities E (issued by firms at price p_e). This representation has the advantage that money and bonds can be aggregated without any price interference. Moreover there is only one risky asset (equities) for which capital gains and capital gain expectations have to be taken into account. Sargent (1987, p.12) notes with respect to the variable B that it

> is a variable-coupon bond that is issued by the government. The bond is essentially a savings deposit, changes in the interest rate altering the coupon, but leaving the dollar value of bonds outstanding unchanged.

This characterization implies that the supplies of money and bonds $\overline{M} + \overline{B}$ can be characterized as providing the money supply $M2$ from the various definitions of such money supplies.

But should we really use as baseline financial structure for a model of the real-financial market interaction a scenario where government can issue money (perfectly liquid – and thus riskless – fixed price interest bearing bonds)? There of course exist some financial assets, issued by the government, which exhibit a high degree of liquidity (due to their short-term maturity horizon), but the bulk of government expenditures is not financed in this way, and in particular not at a constant price for the new issue, since this not only interferes with the objectives of the central bank, but would also be an ideal objective for rising liquidity preference (hoarding), due to the positive yield this asset provides – especially when it is considered as perfect substitute for equities as in Sargent (1987). Moreover, we have shown in a Tobinian portfolio choice framework, under mild assumptions on the employed portfolio demand functions for such a range of financial assets, that monetary policy is then completely ineffective, since, in this case, it only influences the cash management process between money and bonds, but does not reach the equity market and thus the financing structure of firms (see Asada *et al.*, 2010a).[1]

Turnovsky (1995, Part I) also uses a dynamic portfolio balance macroeconomic model where he considers the following representation of the financial part of his portfolio model:[2]

$$M^d = f_m(Y, r, \rho)(M + B + p_k K) \tag{7.1}$$

$$B^d = f_b(Y, r, \rho)(M + B + p_k K) \tag{7.2}$$

$$p_k K^d = f_k(Y, r, \rho)(M + B + p_k K) \tag{7.3}$$

with

$f_{m2}(Y, r, \rho) + f_{b2}(Y, r, \rho) + f_{k2}(Y, r, \rho) \equiv 0, f_{m3}(Y, r, \rho) + f_{b3}(Y, r, \rho) + f_{k3}(Y, r, \rho) \equiv 0$ and $M^d + B^d + p_k K^d = M + B + p_k K$ and with the gross substitution assumption being made. This representation of the asset market structure of the economy is similar in scope to the one considered above, since the variable ρ is defined as the (statically expected) rate of return on holding capital at the market value $p_k K$. In the following we however prefer to represent the capital market by means of equities E and their price p_e in an explicit manner and therefore define Tobin's average q in the usual way. We also will use heterogeneous and partly forward-looking expectations in our model (in place of static ones) and will add long-term bonds as a further risky asset to the portfolio structure to be investigated.

We concentrate in this section on the financial markets and therefore treat output Y as a parameter and consider the three asset markets in equilibrium with the corresponding supplies. Due to *Walras' law of stocks*, we need to consider only two of these equilibrium conditions and use them to determine the two endogenous variables r, the rate of interest and ρ, the rate of profit.

This is a very simple representation of financial markets where expectations play no role at all, since there are no capital gains, and where the rate of profit is determined through a resale market for physical capital, an assumption usually not made in Keynesian approaches to macrodynamics.[3] In this model, monetary policy can influence the rate of profit ρ of the economy directly through the financial market structure of the economy, which is moreover here independent of the conflict about income distribution between capital and labour.

We view the above structure as not being adequate for building a Keynesian portfolio model of the real-financial market interaction, in particular when the current situation on the actual financial markets is taken into account. As Keynes wrote in 1936:

> Speculators may do no harm as bubbles on a steady stream of enterprise. But the position is serious when enterprise becomes the bubble on a whirl-pool of speculation. When the capital development of a country becomes a by-product of the activities of a casino, the job is likely to be ill-done. The measure of success attained by Wall Street, regarded as an institution of which the proper social purpose is to direct new investment into the most profitable channels in terms of future yield, cannot be claimed as

> one of the outstanding triumphs of laissez-faire capitalism – which is not surprising, if I am right in thinking that the best brains of Wall Street have been in fact directed towards a different object. (Keynes, 1936, p. 159)

It is in our view impossible to make sense out of this quotation on the basis of the above portfolio approach. As in Asada *et al.* (2010a), we therefore employ now – as baseline modification of the asset demand structure of the Turnovsky approach – equities E and share prices p_e in place of the value of the physical capital stock. We assume for analytical simplicity that all profits are paid out as dividends to equity owners. This chapter will moreover extend its asset market structure towards a treatment of the term structure of interest rates and will show in this regard that, on the one hand, the insights gained in Chapters 3 and 4, concerning safe and risky assets, can be preserved and meaningfully extended while, on the other hand, the role of monetary policy can be reformulated now in significant ways so that the effectiveness of an interest rate policy rule will now be given. The enhancement of the financial markets of the economy by one further risky asset does not restructure their working in a fundamental way but the working of monetary policy can be redesigned in a way that appears to be capable of overcoming certain problematic features of its past improper working in the given world of unleashed financialization.

Since macroeconomics has to economize on the use of financial instruments in order to remain tractable we will use the theoretically seen polar case to fixed-price bonds, namely perpetuities in place of the short-term bonds for the financing the government deficit. This is the other typical bond configuration that is used in macroeconomics.[4] However, to replace B by long-term bonds B^l with a variable price p_b with the rate of interest augmented by capital gains, $1/p_b + \hat{p}_b$, raises the question of how the short-term interest rate is now provided, since there is no longer a market for it.

We therefore assume that the central bank issues short-term bonds B in place of money M and is therefore paying interest on its money supply B. Our new structure of financial markets is therefore as follows: money B, with rate of interest r, issued by the central bank, perpetuities B^l with an expected rate of return $\frac{1}{p_b} + \pi^e_b$, issued by the government, and equities E, issued by firms, with an expected rate of return $\frac{pY - wL^d}{p_e E} + \pi^e_e$, with profits $pY - wL^d$ as the dividend payments of firms.

We use, as in Asada *et al.* (2010b), an explicit stock demand (portfolio) approach to financial markets, but no longer with three equilibrium conditions, for short-term and long-term bonds and equities. We now integrate, in addition, the hypothesis that there are no full stock adjustments at each moment in time. Instead we assume that only a portion of actual stock excess demand is impacting the asset market, so that there is now imperfect stock adjustment occurring (due to adjustment costs and other considerations of asset holders in their articulation of flow asset demands at the asset market).

Since the central bank has full control over the short-term rate of interest we assume in the following either an interest rate peg or an interest rate policy rule as the monetary policy of the central bank. Note that the central bank can set the short-term rate of interest here without any open market operation (through simple announcement), since it pays this interest on the money it has issued. The money supply is therefore under the full control of the central bank even in the case of an interest rate peg.

This is by and large the modelling framework we will use in this chapter and it will be augmented again by a simple dynamic multiplier process as far as the real markets are concerned. The chapter then investigates the stability of the formulated real-financial market interaction. On this basis it shows (if the stability of the private sector is not given) what monetary (and fiscal) policy can do in order to stabilize such an unstable economy.

Keynesian asset price dynamics and the multiplier

In this section we simplify the real part of the Turnovsky (1995) model by ignoring inflation and growth altogether and by representing the quantity adjustment process by a simple dynamic multiplier approach. This simplifies the Metzlerian inventory accelerator mechanism of the KMG model of Chiarella and Flaschel (2000a) (and thus suppresses it as a source of instability besides the wage–price spiral). It turns the real part of the economy into a stable one (from this partial perspective) if the propensity to spend is less than one. We only take the stock-market effect on investment (and consumption) behaviour here into account, through the impact of Tobin's q on these goods demand functions, since we conceive the share prices as measuring the state of confidence in the economy and thus use it as argument in the investment (and consumption) function in place of the commonly used short-term rate of interest.

This gives as representation of the real side, the following law of motion:[5]

$$\hat{Y} = \beta_y[(Y^d - Y)/Y] = \beta_y[(a_y Y + a_q(q - q^o) + \overline{A} - Y)/Y] \qquad (7.4)$$

where $a_y \in (0, 1), a_q > 0$ and where $\overline{A}$ summarizes autonomous expenditures (fiscal policy and more). This is a standard textbook dynamic multiplier process, with a change in the employed aggregate demand function where Tobin's average q, in its deviation from its steady state value q^o, is now used in place of the short-term interest rates. Since prices, the capital stock and the stock of equities are considered as given in this section, we assume $\frac{E}{pK}$ to be equal to one for simplicity so that Tobin's average $q = \frac{p_e E}{pK}$ is equal to the share price p_e in the following.

We save complexity on the real side of the economy, but add complexity on its financial side by assuming that the financial assets B, B^l, E are imperfect substitutes and that capital gain expectations are also imperfect and working in a portfolio structure as the one in Tobin (1982). We assume that the stocks of the financial assets B, B^l, E are exogenously given in the following Tobinian representation of the asset markets, despite a given interest rate peg:[6]

$$\overline{B} = B^d = f_b(r, r_e^e, r_b^e)W_p^n, \quad f_b(r, r_e^e, r_b^e) + f_{b^l}(r, r_e^e, r_b^e) + f_e(r, r_e^e, r_b^e) \equiv 1 \qquad (7.5)$$

$$p_e\overline{E} = p_e E^d = f_e(r, r_e^e, r_b^e)W_p^n, r_e^e = \frac{pY - wL^d}{p_e\overline{E}} + \overline{\pi}_e^e = \rho/q + \overline{\pi}_e^e \qquad (7.6)$$

$$p_b\overline{B}^l = p_b B^{ld} = f_{b^l}(r, r_e^e, r_b^e)W_p^n, r_b^e = 1/p_b + \pi_b^e,$$

$$W_p^n = \overline{B} + p_b\overline{B}^l + p_e\overline{E} \qquad (7.7)$$

As for the rate of profit, we have:

$$\rho = \frac{pY - wL^d}{pK} = \frac{Y}{K}(1 - \omega/z), \quad \omega = w/p < z = Y/L^d = \text{const.}$$

where we assume a constant value for the labour productivity coefficient $z > w/p$ that has to exceed the real wage $\omega = w/p$ of course.

Only two of these equations are independent from each other and can be used to determine the variables p_b, p_e. Note that the expression r_e^e defines the rate of return on equities (the sum of the dividend rate of return ρ/q and expected capital gains on equities π_e^e), since all profits are assumed to be paid out as dividends. We moreover assume that the central bank is fixing the rate of interest r on its outstanding bonds at each moment in time and changes the number of interest bearing bonds B (if desired) through open market operations of the type $dB = p_b dB^l$. We assume finally that the demands for financial assets exhibit the gross substitute property and therefore depend positively on their own rate on return and negatively on the rates of return of the other assets, i.e. in particular, money demand B^d depends positively on the rate of interest and negatively on the rates of return on equities and long-term bonds. Note that – in contrast to Asada *et al.* (2010b) – there is no longer a hierarchy present in this setup of financial assets and the portfolio choice of asset holders.

We are now considering adjustment processes for bond prices as well as equity prices based on the following stock disequilibria:

$$\hat{p}_e = \beta_e[\alpha_e(f_e(r, r_e^e, r_b^e)W_p^n - p_e\overline{E})], \quad \alpha_e \in (0, 1) \tag{7.8}$$

$$\hat{p}_b = \beta_b[\alpha_b(f_{b^l}(r, r_e^e, r_b^e)W_p^n - p_b\overline{B}^l)], \quad \alpha_b \in (0, 1) \tag{7.9}$$

We are assuming that only a fraction α_b of current stock disequilibria, $f_{b^l}(r, r_e^e, r_b^e)W_p^n - p_b\overline{B}^l$ in the case of bonds, is entering the asset markets as demand or supply (based on adjustment costs arguments), i.e., $1/\alpha_e$ for example represents the delay with which the stock imbalance $f_e(r, r_e^e, r_b^e)W_p^n - p_e\overline{E}$ is supposed to be balanced. Such an approach was seen to be necessary in an open economy, where flows but not stock imbalances enter the capital account of the balance of payments. It is a plausible modelling procedure in a continuous time set-up in the case of closed economies. The flow processes on the asset markets are then translated into asset price changes by using speed parameters β in the front of these expressions.

We now show the existence of an overall equilibrium for the above equations and demonstrate thereafter that this equilibrium is stable under the above adjustment of asset prices in a neighbourhood of the steady state position. In the steady state we have (since expected capital gains are zero then):

$$\begin{aligned}\overline{B} &= f_b(r, \rho/q, 1/p_b)(\overline{B} + p_b\overline{B}^l + p_e\overline{E}), \quad r \text{ given}\\ p_e\overline{E} &= f_e(r, \rho/q, 1/p_b)(\overline{B} + p_b\overline{B}^l + p_e\overline{E})\\ p_b\overline{B}^l &= f_{b^l}(r, \rho/q, 1/p_b)(\overline{B} + p_b\overline{B}^l + p_e\overline{E})\end{aligned}$$

We use the first and the third equation in order to determine the steady state. The first equation defines in a general way a negative relationship between the prices p_e, p_b, due to the implicit function theorem, the slope of which is given by:

$$\frac{\partial p_b}{\partial q} = -\frac{f_{b2}(\cdot)(-\rho/q^2)W_p^n + f_b E}{f_{b3}(\cdot)(-1/p_b^2)W_p^n + f_b B^l} < 0$$

As for the slope of the function that is implicitly defined by the third equilibrium condition, we get in a similar way:

$$\frac{\partial p_b}{\partial q} = -\frac{f_{b^l 2}(\cdot)(-\rho/q^2)W_p^n + f_{b^l} E}{f_{b^l 3}(\cdot)(-1/p_b^2)W_p^n + (f_{b^l} - 1)B^l} > 0$$

This time, the slope of the curve defined by the implicit function theorem is positive, since $f_{b^l 2}(\cdot) < 0, f_{b^l 3}(\cdot) > 0$ and $f_{b^l} \in (0, 1)$. We note that these two features also hold for all other capital gain expectations as long as these expectations are given (are static).

Therefore the stationary state q, p_b on the financial markets is uniquely determined and assume that the parameters behind the functions f_b, f_{b^l} are such that it exists everywhere in the neighbourhood of the steady state q^o, p_b^o of the full dynamical system (where $Y^o = \frac{\overline{A}}{1-a_y}$ holds in addition).

Stable real-financial market interactions?

We get from the above the following proposition for the stability of the asset markets when capital gain expectations are static.

Proposition 1: stable financial markets interaction

Assume that capital gain expectations are static. Then, the dynamics

$$\hat{q} = \beta_e[\alpha_e(f_e(r, r_e^e, r_b^e)W_p^n - q\overline{E})], \quad \alpha_e \in (0,1) \tag{7.10}$$

$$\hat{p}_b = \beta_b[\alpha_b(f_{b^l}(r, r_e^e, r_b^e)W_p^n - p_b\overline{B}^l)], \quad \alpha_b \in (0,1) \tag{7.11}$$

converges to the current stationary state of the asset markets for all adjustment speeds of asset prices p_e, p_b.

Proof

The matrix of partial derivatives of the considered two laws of motion is given by:

$$J = \begin{pmatrix} \beta_e\alpha_e[f_{e2}(\cdot)(-\rho/q^2)W_p^n + (f_e - 1)\overline{E}] & \beta_e\alpha_e[f_{e3}(\cdot)(-1/p_b^2)W_p^n + f_e\overline{B}^l] \\ \beta_b\alpha_b[f_{b^l2}(\cdot)(-\rho/q^2)W_p^n + f_{b^l}\overline{E}] & \beta_b\alpha_b[f_{b^l3}(\cdot)(-1/p_b^2)W_p^n \\ & + (f_{b^l} - 1)\overline{B}^l] \end{pmatrix}$$

The trace of this matrix is obviously negative, while, for the determinant, we obtain the expression:

$$J = \beta_e\alpha_e\beta_b\alpha_b \begin{vmatrix} -f_{e2}(\cdot)\rho/q^2W_p^n + (f_e - 1)\overline{E} & -f_{e3}(\cdot)/p_b^2W_p^n + f_e\overline{B}^l \\ -f_{b^l2}(\cdot)\rho/q^2W_p^n + f_{b^l}\overline{E} & -f_{b^l3}(\cdot)/p_b^2W_p^n + (f_{b^l} - 1)\overline{B}^l \end{vmatrix}$$

We have

$$-(f_{e2} + f_{b^l2})(\cdot)\rho/q^2W_p^n + (f_e + f_{b^l} - 1)\overline{E} = f_{b2}(\cdot)\rho/q^2W_p^n - f_b\overline{E} < 0$$

and

$$-(f_{e3} + f_{b^l3})(\cdot)/p_b^2W_p^n + (f_e + f_{b^l} - 1)\overline{B}^l = f_{b3}(\cdot)/p_b^2W_p^n - f_b\overline{B}^l < 0$$

and thus get that the negative entries in the diagonal dominate the positive entries in the off-diagonal. This implies that the determinant of J must be positive and thus proves the validity of the Routh–Hurwitz stability conditions for such a planar dynamical system.

Therefore the real and the financial markets are, when considered in isolation (and with sufficiently tranquil capital gain expectations), both stable. The next step is therefore to investigate what happens when they are interacting as a full 3D dynamical system. According to the above, the Jacobian of the full 3D system at the steady state is given by:

$$J = \begin{pmatrix} \beta_y(a_y - 1) & \beta_y a_q & 0 \\ \beta_e\alpha_e f_{e2}\rho'/qW_p^n & \beta_e\alpha_e[-f_{e2}\rho/q^2W_p^n + (f_e - 1)\overline{E}] & \beta_e\alpha_e[-f_{e3}/p_b^2W_p^n + f_e\overline{B}^l] \\ \beta_b\alpha_b f_{b^l 2}\rho'/qW_p^n & \beta_b\alpha_b[-f_{b^l 2}\rho/q^2W_p^n + f_{b^l}\overline{E}] & \beta_b\alpha_b[-f_{b^l 3}/p_b^2W_p^n + (f_{b^l} - 1)\overline{B}^l] \end{pmatrix}$$

$$= \begin{pmatrix} - & + & 0 \\ + & - & + \\ - & + & - \end{pmatrix}$$

The trace of J is obviously negative and the principal minor of order 2:

$$J_1 = \begin{vmatrix} \beta_e\alpha_e[-f_{e2}\rho/q^2W_p^n + (f_e - 1)\overline{E}] & \beta_e\alpha_e[-f_{e3}/p_b^2W_p^n + f_e\overline{B}^l] \\ \beta_b\alpha_b[-f_{b^l 2}\rho/q^2W_p^n + f_{b^l}\overline{E}] & \beta_b\alpha_b[-f_{b^l 3}/p_b^2W_p^n + (f_{b^l} - 1)\overline{B}^l] \end{vmatrix}$$

is positive according to the above proposition as is the principal minor J_2. And for the remaining principal minor of order 2 we get:

$$J_3 = \begin{vmatrix} \beta_y(a_y - 1) & \beta_y a_q \\ \beta_e\alpha_e f_{e2}\rho'/qW_p^n & \beta_e\alpha_e[-f_{e2}\rho/q^2W_p^n + (f_e - 1)\overline{E}] \end{vmatrix}$$

$$= \beta_y\beta_e\alpha_e f_{e2}/qW_p^n \begin{vmatrix} a_y - 1 & a_q \\ \rho' & -\rho/q \end{vmatrix} + \beta_y(a_y - 1)(f_e - 1)\overline{E}$$

which is positive if the speed parameter β_e is chosen sufficiently small. Note however that the Routh–Hurwitz conditions only require the sum of principal minors of order 2 to be positive, which is a much weaker condition.

For the determinant of the Jacobian J, one gets from the above:

$$|J| = \beta_y \beta_e \alpha_e \beta_b \alpha_b \begin{vmatrix} a_y - 1 & a_q & 0 \\ f_{e2}\rho'/qW_p^n & -f_{e2}\rho/q^2 W_p^n + (f_e - 1)\overline{E} & -f_{e3}/p_b^2 W_p^n + f_e \overline{B}^l \\ f_{b^l 2}\rho'/qW_p^n & -f_{b^l 2}\rho/q^2 W_p^n + f_{b^l}\overline{E} & -f_{b^l 3}/p_b^2 W_p^n + (f_{b^l} - 1)\overline{B}^l \end{vmatrix}$$

$$= J_3 J_{33} + \beta_y \beta_e \alpha_e \beta_b \alpha_b (f_{e3}/p_b^2 W_p^n - f_e \overline{B}^l) \begin{vmatrix} a_y - 1 & a_q \\ f_{b^l 2}\rho'/qW_p^n & -f_{b^l 2}\rho/q^2 W_p^n + f_{b^l}\overline{E} \end{vmatrix}$$

In order to get a negative determinant, we therefore have to show that the determinant

$$\begin{vmatrix} a_y - 1 & a_q \\ f_{b^l 2}\rho'/qW_p^n & -f_{b^l 2}\rho/q^2 W_p^n + f_{b^l}\overline{E} \end{vmatrix}$$

is positive – in addition to the already assumed positivity of the minor J_3. The last expression here shows that this *for example* holds if the marginal propensity to purchase goods $a_y \in (0, 1)$ is sufficiently close to 1.

The condition $(-trJ)(J_1 + J_2 + J_3) - |J| > 0$ can be fulfilled by choosing the adjustment speed of the dynamic multiplier process sufficiently large, since it enters the product term with power 2 and the determinant only in a linear form. Summing up, we thus have the following in the case of static chartist capital expectations ($\beta_{\pi_{ec}} = \beta_{\pi_{bc}} = 0$).

Proposition 2: stable 3D real-financial markets interaction

Let us assume that the parameter $\beta_y$is sufficiently large and the parameter β_e sufficiently small. Let us assume moreover that the parameter a_y is sufficiently close to one (but smaller than one). Then, the dynamics

$$\dot{Y} = \beta_y[(a_y - 1)Y + a_q(q - q^o) + \overline{A}] \tag{7.12}$$

$$\hat{q} = \beta_e[\alpha_e(f_e(r, r_e^e, r_b^e)W_p^n - q\overline{E})] \tag{7.13}$$

$$\hat{p}_b = \beta_b[\alpha_b(f_{b^l}(r, r_e^e, r_b^e)W_p^n - p_b\overline{B}^l)] \tag{7.14}$$

is locally asymptotically stable around its steady state position.

This proposition and its proof show however that the coupling of two stable, but partial processes does not need to provide a stable interaction of the two partial processes.

We now extend the model by endogenizing capital gain expectations. We distinguish between fundamentalists f and chartists c and assume for the former that they expect capital gains to converge back with speeds $\beta_{\pi_{ef}}, \beta_{\pi_{bf}}$ to their steady state position (which is zero). Chartists, by contrast (for analytical simplicity), make use of a simple adaptive mechanism to forecast the evolution of capital gains in the equity market and the market for long-term bonds. Market expectations are then an average of fundamentalist and chartist expectations with weight γ. We stress here that these simple expectations formation mechanisms are chosen to make the dynamics analytically tractable. They can of course be replaced by much more refined forward and backward looking expectation rules when the model is treated numerically. We do not expect that this changes the results in a significant way if these learning mechanisms are built in the spirit of the ones we introduce and employ below:

$$\dot{\pi}^e_{ef} = \beta_{\pi_{ef}}(0 - \pi^e_{ef}) \tag{7.15}$$

$$\dot{\pi}^e_{ec} = \beta_{\pi_{ec}}(\hat{q} - \pi^e_{ec}) \tag{7.16}$$

$$\dot{\pi}^e_{bf} = \beta_{\pi_{bf}}(0 - \pi^e_{bf}) \tag{7.17}$$

$$\dot{\pi}^e_{bc} = \beta_{\pi_{bc}}(\hat{p}_b - \pi^e_{bc}) \tag{7.18}$$

$$\pi^e_e = \gamma_e \pi^e_{ef} + (1 - \gamma_e)\pi^e_{ec} \tag{7.19}$$

$$\pi^e_b = \gamma_c \pi^e_{bf} + (1 - \gamma_b)\pi^e_{bc} \tag{7.20}$$

On the basis of the 3D stability proposition one then easily gets:

Corollary 1: stable 5D real-financial markets interaction

Assume that the conditions of the preceding proposition are met and that the speed parameters for chartists are sufficiently small (or the parameter γ_e, γ_b sufficiently close to 1). Then, the dynamics

$$\dot{Y} = \beta_y[(a_y - 1)Y + a_q(q - q^o) + \overline{A}]$$

$$\hat{q} = \beta_e[\alpha_e(f_e(r, \rho/q + \overline{\pi}^e_e, 1/p_b + \pi^e_b)W^n_p - q\overline{E})]$$

$$\hat{p}_b = \beta_b[\alpha_b(f_{b^l}(r, \rho/q + \overline{\pi}^e_e, 1/p_b + \pi^e_b)W^n_p - p_b\overline{B}^l)]$$

augmented by the above adjustment rules for capital gain expectations, is locally asymptotically stable around its steady state position.

The proof of this corollary is straightforward, since the absence of chartists implies a 5D Jacobian matrix given by the investigated 3D one and the negative entries $J_{44} = \beta_{\pi_{ef}} \gamma_e, J_{55} = \beta_{\pi_{bf}} \gamma_b$. Fundamentalists – if sufficiently dominant – may therefore calm down the situation that chartists may create. By contrast if there are only chartists present, we get positive entries in the entries J_{44}, J_{55} in the trace of J, if the parameters β_e, β_b are sufficiently large. These entries will outperform the other entries in the trace of J if the parameters $\beta_{\pi_{ec}}, \beta_{\pi_{bc}}$ are chosen sufficiently large. Depending on the choice of other parameters the behaviour of chartists may however be neutralized to a larger degree if all the other stability conditions apply.

If the determinant of the considered three dimensional dynamics is made negative (by an appropriate choice of the parameter a_y), we get by appropriate row manipulations in the full 5D Jacobian that its determinant must be negative as well. Increasing adjustment speeds can then imply loss of stability only by way of so-called Hopf bifurcations, i.e. in general, by way of the death of a stable corridor around the steady state position of the economy or the birth of a stable persistent fluctuation around it. The dynamical system of this chapter can therefore provide a theory of business fluctuations caused through the interaction of the real with the financial markets.

Let us note that the positive feedback loop (for example in the case of the stock market) between

$$\begin{aligned} \hat{q} &= \beta_e[\alpha_e(f_e(\cdot, \ldots + \overline{\pi}^e_e, \cdot)W^n_p - q\bar{E})] \\ \dot{\pi}^e_{ec} &= \beta_{\pi_{ec}}(\hat{q} - \pi^e_{ec}) \end{aligned}$$

is of no importance (if present in the minors of order higher than 1), since the implied rows in the Jacobian matrix J can be simplified as indicated by the following reduced form laws of motion:

$$\begin{aligned} \hat{q} &= \beta_e[\alpha_e(f_e(\cdot, \ldots + 0, \cdot)W^n_p - q\bar{E})] \\ \dot{\pi}^e_{ec} &= \beta_{\pi_{ec}}(0 - \pi^e_{ec}) \end{aligned}$$

Depending on the value of its parameters, the economy can be either robust or vulnerable to chartists' centrifugal behaviour.

The above row reduction methods show that the upper 4D minor must be positive and the determinant of the full 5D Jacobian negative if the latter also holds for the upper 3D minor. As already indicated, stability through excessive chartist behaviour can therefore only get lost by way of Hopf bifurcations, i.e., in a cyclical fashion, by the birth of a stable persistent oscillation or by the death of a stability basin around the steady state (or in exceptional cases by passing through a centre-type dynamics).

We briefly contrast the above analysis with the case where neoclassical perfection is given. This perfection assumes that there holds $\beta_e, \beta_b = \infty, \alpha_e, \alpha_b = 1$, assumes perfect asset substitution, and assumes myopic perfect foresight with respect to capital gains ($\beta_{\pi bc}\beta_{\pi ec} = \infty$). These assumptions taken together imply that there always holds:

$$r = \rho/q + \hat{q} = 1/p_b + \hat{p}_b$$

The dynamical system is in its core dynamics then reduced to

$$\dot{Y} = \beta_y[(a_y - 1)Y + a_q(q - q^o) + \overline{A}] \tag{7.21}$$

$$\hat{q} = r - \rho(Y)/q \tag{7.22}$$

which is of the usual saddlepoint type if the 2D determinant in the former expression J_3 is positive and thus stabilizing for all considered adjustment speeds. Yet the perfect limit case is then unstable, but it exhibits a stable submanifold that – when the economy is on it – leads it back to the stationary state (see Blanchard, 1981). Since Sargent and Wallace (1973), the neoclassical procedure was to assume that the economy always jumps to this stable submanifold and is thus made stable by assumption (in the case of anticipated shocks via a bubble in the old dynamics until the shock actually occurs). The jump variable technique of the rational expectations school therefore simply excludes the possibility of an unstable economy by assumption. The reader is referred to Chiarella, Flaschel, Franke and Semmler (2009) for detailed evaluations of this methodology, its attractiveness and its various anomalies:

> I have called this book *The General Theory of Employment, Interest and Money*, placing the emphasis on the prefix general. The object of

> such a title is to contrast the character of my arguments and conclusions with those of the classical theory of the subject, upon which I was brought up and which dominates the economic thought, both practical and theoretical, of the governing and academic classes of this generation, as it has for a hundred years past. I shall argue that the postulates of the classical theory are applicable to a special case only and not to the general case, the situation which it assumes being a limiting point of the possible positions of equilibrium. Moreover, the characteristics of the special case assumed by the classical theory happen not to be those of the economic society in which we actually live, with the result that its teaching is misleading and disastrous if we attempt to apply it to the facts of experience. (Keynes, 1936, p.3)

In the following section we therefore return to the case of imperfect asset substitution and imperfect capital gain expectations and will investigate, for this case, what fiscal and monetary policy can do in order to (further) stabilize the economy, in particular in cases where the private sector is generating a repelling steady state. We conclude this section with the observation that the model provides an example of a proper Keynesian representation of the real- financial market interaction, in contrast to both the expectations-free Turnovsky (1995) representation of the financial markets at the one extreme and the super-performance of rational expectations agents at the other one.

Stabilizing an unstable economy: Tobin-type taxes, interest rate rules and open market policies

> As we approach the last decade of the twentieth century, our economic world is in apparent disarray. After two secure decades of tranquil progress following World War II, in the late 1960s the order of the day became turbulence — both domestic and international. Bursts of accelerating inflation, higher chronic and higher cyclical unemployment, bankruptcies, crunching interest rates, and crises in energy, transportation, food supply, welfare, the cities, and banking were mixed with periods of troubled expansions. The economic and social policy synthesis that served us so well after World War II broke down in the mid-1960s. What is needed now is

> a new approach, a policy synthesis fundamentally different from the mix that results when today's accepted theory is applied to today's economic system. (Minsky, 1982, p.3)

The present section suggests that the feedback structure of the economy must be taken into account in order to find the proper measures or rules for monetary policy. Moreover, significant institutional change may be needed for the implementation of the simple theoretical rules proposed below. Though simple in its theoretical structure, this section nevertheless breaks new grounds for monetary policy making, concerning the role of money and the interest rate policy of the central bank.

In view of the considered 5D extension of our model where expectations are no longer static and impacting the asset market in significant ways, the most obvious thing to do seems to raise taxes on capital gains in order to reduce the casino-component in the market for equities and for long-term bonds. This is necessary since these markets have the function to channel savings into investment in an efficient way, and not be shaped through the gambling activities of asset holders. This was already clearly stressed in Keynes (1936, p.159) and was an important subject in the works of Hyman Minsky (1982, 1986).

We therefore apply **Tobin-type tax rates** $\tau_e, \tau_b \in (0, 1)$ to the capital gains achieved by chartists and get on this basis, as a reformulation of their expectations formation process, the following net capital gains expectation rules:[7]

$$\begin{aligned}\dot{\pi}_e^e &= \gamma_e \dot{\pi}_{ef}^e + (1-\gamma_e)\dot{\pi}_{ec}^e = \gamma_e \beta_{\pi_{ef}}(0 - \pi_{ef}^e) \\ &\quad + (1-\gamma_e)\beta_{\pi_{ec}}(\tau_e \hat{q} - \pi_{ec}^e) \qquad (7.23)\end{aligned}$$

$$\begin{aligned}\dot{\pi}_b^e &= \gamma_b \dot{\pi}_{bf}^e + (1-\gamma_b)\dot{\pi}_{bc}^e = \gamma_b \beta_{\pi_{bf}}(0 - \pi_{bf}^e) \\ &\quad + (1-\gamma_b)\beta_{\pi_{bc}}(\tau_b \hat{p}_b - \pi_{bc}^e) \qquad (7.24)\end{aligned}$$

In view of the 5D stability analysis of the preceding section, we immediately get the proposition that *Tobin tax rates that are chosen sufficiently high will eliminate all instability caused through the expectations formation* of the model. It therefore then suffices to concentrate on the 3D core dynamics of the model and to investigate what policy options are conceivable in these subdynamics that allow the increase of the range of parameter choices where the private sector of the economy is subject to converging dynamics.

We consider first a **conventional type of Taylor rule**, based on the output gap solely, since there is no inflation gap in this model. This gives the following simple interest rate policy rule. We stress again that this rule can be applied without any need for open market operations by the central bank in our model:

$$r = r^o + \beta_r(Y - Y^o), \quad \beta_r > 0$$

The considered 3D Jacobian of the private sector of the model

$$J = \begin{pmatrix} - & + & 0 \\ + & - & + \\ - & + & - \end{pmatrix}$$

is then augmented by a matrix of the qualitative form

$$J^+ = \begin{pmatrix} 0 & + & 0 \\ - & - & + \\ - & + & - \end{pmatrix} \quad \text{with} \quad \begin{vmatrix} 0 & + & 0 \\ - & - & + \\ - & + & - \end{vmatrix} < 0$$

The original determinant is thereby made a smaller one and thus more likely to be negative as compared to the situation without a Taylor rule. Choosing β_r large enough will in particular make any initially given determinant negative.

The only further change in the minors of the original J happens in the principal minor J_3 which is augmented by

$$J_3^+ = \begin{pmatrix} 0 & + \\ - & - \end{pmatrix} \quad \text{with} \quad \begin{vmatrix} 0 & + \\ - & - \end{vmatrix} > 0$$

We thus get the further proposition that the *stability condition* we have imposed on the matrix J_3 is thereby *relaxed*, and this to a significant degree, if the parameter β_r is sufficiently increased. All other minors of the original matrix J are the same as before. The change in the Routh–Hurwitz condition

$$(-trJ)(J_1 + J_1 + J_3 + J_3^+) + (|J| + |J^+|)$$

is however ambiguous and must eventually be improved by the choice of a higher adjustment speed in the employed dynamic multiplier process. This condition should however not be of a really significant nature.

One may also consider, at least from a theoretical perspective, the following **Tobin's q-based extension of the Taylor rule**:

$$r = r^o + \beta_{ry}(Y - Y^o) + \beta_{rq}(q - q^o), \quad \beta_{ry}, \beta_{rq} > 0$$

This rule now raises the interest rate further if the stock market is strong and vice versa and thus takes the stock market index as some further expression for the state of confidence in the economy. Note that this rule is here superior to a rule that concentrates on long-term bond prices in place of share prices, since aggregate demand does not depend on the long-term rate of interest here.

The 3D Jacobian $J + J^+$ is thereby augmented by a matrix of the qualitative form:

$$J^{++} = \begin{pmatrix} - & 0 & 0 \\ + & - & + \\ - & - & - \end{pmatrix} \quad \text{with} \quad \begin{vmatrix} - & 0 & 0 \\ - & - & + \\ - & - & - \end{vmatrix} < 0$$

The original determinant is thereby made even smaller and thus more likely to be negative as compared to the situation without a Taylor rule. In this situation, all minors of order 2 are also improved in their stability implications as well as the trace of J. Moreover the addition to the 3D determinant is now of the qualitative type $J_{11}J_1$ and thus does not question the positivity of the final Routh–Hurwitz condition:

$$(-trJ)(J_1 + J_1 + J_3) + |J|$$

We thus get the proposition that an *interest rate policy which takes the state of the equity market into account* and tries to make it less volatile *is unambiguously successful*. This result is not so obvious when the central bank uses the gap $p_b - p_b^o$ in place of the stock market gap (which moreover is not considered with so much public interest and emphasis as the market for shares) as far as the state of confidence for the considered macroeconomy is concerned.[8]

Concerning long-term bonds, the central bank might however use open market operations and thus for example the following static

open market policy rule which changes the supply of short-term against long-term bonds according to the rule:

$$\overline{B}(p_b) = -p_b\overline{B}^l(p_b), \quad d\overline{B}(p_b)/dp_b < 0$$

This rule is assumed to impact supply conditions solely, while demand is still articulated on the basis of the original wealth position of the asset holders. In this case, the 3D Jacobian J is augmented by a matrix of the qualitative form:

$$J^{+++} = \begin{pmatrix} - & + & 0 \\ + & - & 0 \\ - & + & - \end{pmatrix}$$

with similar properties as in the case of equities just considered (if the upper principal minor of order 2 is positive). We thus finally get the proposition that *trading in long-term bonds* in the above way therefore *provides additional stability* to the considered dynamics of the private sector. In other words, monetary policy can do a lot in this still simple framework in order to improve the working of the economy through its impact on the financial sector of the model.

Conclusions and outlook

We have reached, in this chapter, a stage where the structure of financial markets (with the exception of credit relationships) can be considered from the macroeconomic perspective as being modelled in a basically complete – and nevertheless basic – way where, therefore, all fundamental financial instruments (except credit) are present regarding the financing decisions of firms (if the assumed long-term bonds are also considered as corporate bonds besides government bonds).

We have considered in such a framework the stability properties of the private sector of the economy and – in the case of its instability – the policy measures that are capable of overcoming the centrifugal forces around the steady state of the economy. These policy measures were given by a Tobin-type tax on capital gains for long-term bonds as well as equities, certain interest rate policy rules concerning equities (and long-term bonds), as well as open market operations of the central bank in the market for long-term bonds.

In future investigations of macroeconomic interaction between the real and the financial markets, one must however reintroduce the advanced treatment of the real markets considered and analysed in Chapters 3 and 4 of this book. The present chapter only indicates the direction into which these chapters have to be developed further, including their treatment of Metzler–Harrod type accelerator mechanisms in the market for goods, the wage–price spiral, the interaction of growth with income distribution and the stock-flow consistency that is provided by an explicit treatment of the budget equations of the private households, firms and the government, as well as the stock-flow interaction this implies.

These central topics remain however to be reconsidered for future research from the perspective of the financial market structure we have designed in this chapter:

> So here's what I think economists have to do. First, they have to face up to the inconvenient reality that financial markets fall far short of perfection, that they are subject to extraordinary delusions and the madness of crowds. Second, they have to admit – and this will be very hard for the people who giggled and whispered over Keynes – that Keynesian economics remains the best framework we have for making sense of recessions and depressions. Third, they'll have to do their best to incorporate the realities of finance into macroeconomics. Many economists will find these changes deeply disturbing. (Paul Krugman, *New York Times*, 6 September, 2009)

Mathematical Appendices and Notation

Appendix I.1 The law of motion for real wages

The growth rate of real wages is the growth rate of nominal wages minus price inflation:

$$\hat{\omega} = \left(\frac{d\frac{w}{p}}{dt}\right) / \left(\frac{w}{p}\right) = \left(\frac{\frac{dw}{dt}p - w\frac{dp}{dt}}{p^2}\right)\frac{p}{w} = \frac{dw}{dt}/w - \frac{dp}{dt}/p = \hat{w} - \hat{p}$$

Plugging in the laws of motion for nominal wages and prices given in equations (3.42) and (3.43) we obtain:

$$\begin{aligned}
\hat{p} &= \beta_p(u - \overline{u}) + \kappa_p\hat{w} + (1 - \kappa_p)\pi \\
&= \beta_p(u - \overline{u}) + \kappa_p(\beta_w(e - \overline{e}) + \kappa_w\hat{p} + (1 - \kappa_w)\pi) + (1 - \kappa_p)\pi \\
&= \beta_p(u - \overline{u}) + \kappa_p\beta_w(e - \overline{e}) + \kappa_p\kappa_w\hat{p} + \kappa_p(1 - \kappa_w)\pi + (1 - \kappa_p)\pi \\
&= \frac{\beta_p(u - \overline{u}) + \kappa_p\beta_w(e - \overline{e}) + (1 - \kappa_w\kappa_p)\pi}{1 - \kappa_w\kappa_p} \\
&= \kappa(\beta_p(u - \overline{u}) + \kappa_p\beta_w(e - \overline{e})) + \pi \\
\text{and } \hat{w} &= \kappa(\beta_w(e - \overline{e}) + \kappa_w\beta_p(u - \overline{u})) + \pi
\end{aligned}$$

with $\kappa = (1 - \kappa_w\kappa_p)^{-1}$.

Appendix I.2 Computation of expected capital gains

Expectations play an important role in the capital markets because they are a central component of the expected rate of return on equities. As we have seen in equation (3.18) the actual overall expectation of equity price inflation is the weighted average of expectations held by fundamentalists and chartists. From the law of motion in equation (3.17) and knowing the initial value of π_{ef} denoted by $\pi_{ef}(t_0)$ we can derive the definite solution:

$$\pi_{ef}(t) = (\pi_{ef}(t_0) - \overline{\eta})e^{-\beta_{\pi_{ef}} t} + \overline{\eta}$$

Now we give the definite solution for the expected equity price inflation held by chartists. From (3.16) we can derive the general solution:

$$\pi_{ec}(t) = \beta_{\pi_{ec}} \int_{t_0}^{t} \hat{p}_e(s)e^{-\beta_{\pi_{ec}}(t-s)} ds$$

Note that this representation is equivalent to the exponential lag distribution if $t_0 = -\infty$. For this see Gandolfo (1996, ch.12.4). From the general solution one can easily derive the definite solution:

$$\pi_{ec}(t) = \pi_{ec}(t_0)e^{-\beta_{\pi_{ec}}(t-t_0)} + \beta_{\pi_{ec}} \int_{t_0}^{t} \hat{p}_e(s)e^{-\beta_{\pi_{ec}}(t-s)} ds$$

where $\pi_{ec}(t_0)$ is the initial value of the expectations about growth the rate in equity prices performed by the chartists. Building up the weighted sum of the definite solutions according to equation (3.18) we obtain equation (4.10).

Appendix II Comparative statics

Defining F to be the difference between the money market clearing interest rate and the bond market clearing interest rate depending on q and other variables we get from (4.28) and (4.29):

$$F(\rho^e, q, \pi_e, m, b) = \frac{\alpha_{m0} - \alpha_{m2}(\rho^e/q + \pi_e) - m/(m+b+q)}{\alpha_{m1}} - \frac{-\alpha_{b0} + \alpha_{b2}(\rho^e/q + \pi_e) + b/(m+b+q)}{\alpha_{b1}}$$

We know that the steady state values of ρ^e, π_e, m, and b are positive and thus are also positive in a neighbourhood around the steady state. The equilibrium condition is $F(\ldots)=0$. Applying the implicit function theorem we can derive qualitative dependencies of q on changes of other variables. Therefore, we can compute the partial derivative of $F(\ldots)$ with respect to Tobin's q.

$$\partial F/\partial q = \left[\frac{\alpha_{m2}\rho^e}{\alpha_{m1}q^2} + \frac{m}{\alpha_{m1}(m+b+q)^2} + \frac{\alpha_{b2}\rho^e}{\alpha_{b1}q^2} + \frac{b}{\alpha_{b1}(m+b+q)^2}\right]$$

One can easily check that this term is positive.

The influence of expected rate of return on capital on q

The partial derivative of Tobin's q with respect to ρ^e is given by the following computation:

$$\begin{aligned}\frac{\partial q}{\partial \rho^e} &= -\frac{\partial F/\partial \rho^e}{\partial F/\partial q} \\ &= \left(\frac{\alpha_{m2}}{\alpha_{m1}q} + \frac{\alpha_{b2}}{\alpha_{b1}q}\right) / \frac{\partial F}{\partial q}\end{aligned}$$

Both, numerator and denominator are positive. Hence $\partial q/\partial \rho^e > 0$ holds or in words: Tobin's q depends positively on the expected rate of return on capital.

The influence of expected equity price inflation on q

We compute:

$$\begin{aligned}\frac{\partial q}{\partial \pi_e} &= -\frac{\partial F/\partial \pi_e}{\partial F/\partial q} \\ &= \left(\frac{\alpha_{m2}}{\alpha_{m1}} + \frac{\alpha_{b2}}{\alpha_{b1}}\right) / \frac{\partial F}{\partial q}\end{aligned}$$

Again the numerator is positive and $\partial q/\partial \pi_e > 0$. Rising inflationary expectations with respect to equity prices leads to a rising q.

The influence of the cash balance on q

$$\begin{aligned}\frac{\partial q}{\partial m} &= -\frac{\partial F/\partial m}{\partial F/\partial q} \\ &= -\left[\frac{1}{\alpha_{m1}}\left(-\frac{m+b+q-m}{(m+b+q)^2}\right) + \frac{1}{\alpha_{b1}}\left(-\frac{-b}{(m+b+q)^2}\right)\right] / \frac{\partial F}{\partial q} \\ &= \left[1/\alpha_{m1}\frac{b+q}{(m+b+q)^2} - 1/\alpha_{b1}\frac{b}{(m+b+q)^2}\right] / \frac{\partial F}{\partial q}\end{aligned}$$

Making use of the gross substitution property $\alpha_{m1} < \alpha_{b1}$ the last expression is positive and we get $\partial q/\partial m > 0$. An increase in cash balances leads to an increase in q.

The influence of the stock of bonds on q

$$
\begin{aligned}
\frac{\partial q}{\partial b} &= -\frac{\partial F/\partial b}{\partial F/\partial q} \\
&= -\left[\frac{1}{\alpha_{m1}}\left(-\frac{-m}{(m+b+q)^2}\right) + \frac{1}{\alpha_{b1}}\left(-\frac{m+b+q-b}{(m+b+q)^2}\right)\right] \Big/ \frac{\partial F}{\partial q} \\
&= \left[1/\alpha_{m1}\frac{-m}{(m+b+q)^2} + 1/\alpha_{b1}\frac{m+q}{(m+b+q)^2}\right] \Big/ \frac{\partial F}{\partial q}
\end{aligned}
$$

which is positive if

$$
\frac{m}{\alpha_{m1}} < \frac{m+q}{\alpha_{b1}} \quad \text{or equivalently} \quad q > m\left(\frac{\alpha_{b1}}{\alpha_{m1}} - 1\right)
$$

holds. Here we obtain the ambiguity in (4.32). Because of the adding up constraint in (3.47) can be written by $-\alpha_{m1} + \alpha_{b1} - \alpha_{e1} = 0$ a necessary condition for $\frac{\partial q}{\partial b} > 0$ is that α_{e1} is sufficiently small.

Appendix III Proofs of the stability propositions

Proof of proposition 4

The Jacobian of the system (4.34) is:

$$
J = \begin{pmatrix}
-mi_1\frac{\partial q}{\partial m} & -mi_1\frac{\partial q}{\partial b} & -m\frac{\partial i}{\partial y^e} \\
-\bar{\mu} - bi_1\frac{\partial q}{\partial m} & -\bar{\mu} - bi_1\frac{\partial q}{\partial b} & -\tau_w\omega\frac{1}{x}\frac{\partial y}{\partial y^e} - b\frac{\partial i}{\partial y^e} \\
(\beta_{y^e} + y^e)i_1\frac{\partial q}{\partial m} & (\beta_{y^e} + y^e)i_1\frac{\partial q}{\partial b} & \beta_{y^e}\left(\frac{\partial c}{\partial y^e} + \frac{\partial i}{\partial y^e} - 1\right) + y^e\frac{\partial i}{\partial y^e}
\end{pmatrix}
$$

Note that all other variables possessing a dynamic law are set to their steady state values.

The Routh–Hurwitz conditions for a 3×3–system are given by:

$$\det J < 0 \tag{A1}$$

$$\operatorname{tr} J < 0 \tag{A2}$$

$$J_1 + J_2 + J_3 > 0 \tag{A3}$$

$$(-\operatorname{tr} J)(J_1 + J_2 + J_3) + \det J > 0 \tag{A4}$$

where the J_i are the second order principal minors of J.

Beginning with condition (A2) we have to calculate the trace:

$$\begin{aligned}\operatorname{tr} J = &-mi_1 \frac{\partial q}{\partial m} - \overline{\mu} - bi_1 \frac{\partial q}{\partial b} + (\beta_{y^e} + y^e)\left(i_1 \frac{\partial q}{\partial y^e} + i_2 \frac{1}{y^p}\frac{\partial y}{\partial y^e}\right) \\ &+ \beta_{y^e}\left(\frac{\partial c}{\partial y^e} - 1\right)\end{aligned}$$

The conditions for the trace to be negative are derived now by first showing that $-mi_1 \frac{\partial q}{\partial m} - bi_1 \frac{\partial q}{\partial b}$ and $\frac{\partial c}{\partial y^e} - 1$ are negative. Second we show that $(\beta_{y^e} + y^e)\left(i_1 \frac{\partial q}{\partial y^e} + i_2 \frac{1}{y^p}\frac{\partial y}{\partial y^e}\right)$ is positive:

$$\begin{aligned}&-mi_1 \frac{\partial q}{\partial m} - bi_1 \frac{\partial q}{\partial b} \\ &= i_1\left(\det \frac{\partial(F_1, F_2)}{\partial(r, q)}\right)^{-1} m(\alpha_{b1} b - \alpha_{m1} b + \alpha_{b1} q) + b(\alpha_{m1} m + \alpha_{m1} q - \alpha_{b1} m) \\ &= i_1\left(\det \frac{\partial(F_1, F_2)}{\partial(r, q)}\right)^{-1} (\alpha_{b1} mq + \alpha_{m1} bq)\end{aligned}$$

Remember that the determinant was negative, hence the whole term is negative. Now we show that the term $\frac{\partial c}{\partial y^e} - 1$ is negative:

$$\begin{aligned}&\frac{\partial c}{\partial y^e} - 1 \\ &= (1 - \tau_w)\omega \frac{1}{x}\frac{\partial y}{\partial y^e} + (1 - s_c)\left(1 - \omega \frac{1}{x}\frac{\partial y}{\partial y^e}\right) - 1 \\ &= (s_c - \tau_w)\omega \frac{1}{x}\frac{\partial y}{\partial y^e} - s_c\end{aligned}$$

which is in the rest point by means of the steady state value of ω:

$$\frac{-n - \overline{g} - s_c\delta + (1 - s_c)\overline{t}^n}{y^e}$$

Knowing that in steady state the government runs a deficit, the only positively entering term $(1-s_c)\overline{t}^n$ must be smaller than $\overline{g}$, hence $\frac{\partial c}{\partial y^e} - 1$ must be negative.

The term $(\beta_{y^e} + y^e)\left(i_1\frac{\partial q}{\partial y^e} + i_2\frac{1}{y^p}\frac{\partial y}{\partial y^e}\right)$ can be rewritten by:

$$\begin{aligned}&(\beta_{y^e} + y^e)\left(i_1\frac{\partial q}{\partial \rho^e}\frac{\partial \rho^e}{\partial y^e} + i_2\frac{1}{y^p}\frac{\partial y}{\partial y^e}\right)\\ &= (\beta_{y^e} + y^e)\left(i_1\frac{\partial q}{\partial \rho^e}\frac{\partial \rho^e}{\partial y^e} + i_2\frac{1}{y^p}(1 + n\beta_{n^d})\right)\end{aligned}$$

In Chapter 4 (p. 74) we have shown that $\frac{\partial q}{\partial \rho^e}$ is positive such that the whole term consists of positive entries. The term can be bounded to be sufficiently small by first, assuming a sufficiently small i_2, which makes the second part of the term in brackets small. Second, we assume sufficiently small values of $\left|\frac{\partial fm}{\partial r}\right| = \alpha_{m1}$ and $\left|\frac{\partial fm}{\partial r_e^e}\right| = \alpha_{m2}$ at the steady state, which let the first part of the sum in the brackets small enough as we will show now.

According to this we can write:

$$\frac{\partial q}{\partial \rho^e} = \frac{\frac{1}{q}(\alpha_{m1}\alpha_{b2} + \alpha_{b1}\alpha_{m2})(m + b + q)^2}{\frac{\rho^e}{q^2}(\alpha_{m1}\alpha_{b2} + \alpha_{b1}\alpha_{m2})(m + b + q)^2 + \alpha_{m1}b + \alpha_{b1}m}$$

From the right hand side one can easily see, that it could take sufficiently small values down to zero, when α_{m1} and α_{m2} are chosen small enough. In the following we will assume that the α_{m1}, α_{m2}, and i_2 are sufficiently small, such that:

$$\frac{\partial c}{\partial y^e} + \frac{\partial i}{\partial y^e} - 1 < 0$$

In addition with a sufficiently large β_{y^e} this assumption ensures a negative trace.

With respect to the Routh–Hurwitz condition (A3) a sufficient condition for the sum of the principal minors to be positive is that all principal minors are positive:

$$J_3 = \begin{vmatrix} -mi_1 \dfrac{\partial q}{\partial m} & -mi_1 \dfrac{\partial q}{\partial b} \\ -\overline{\mu} - bi_1 \frac{\partial q}{\partial m} & -\overline{\mu} - bi_1 \dfrac{\partial q}{\partial b} \end{vmatrix} = \overline{\mu} mi_1 \left(\frac{\partial q}{\partial m} - \frac{\partial q}{\partial b} \right)$$

According to proposition 3 we know that this expression is positive:

$$J_2 = \begin{vmatrix} -mi_1 \dfrac{\partial q}{\partial m} & -m \dfrac{\partial i}{\partial y^e} \\ (\beta_{y^e} + y^e) i_1 \dfrac{\partial q}{\partial m} & \beta_{y^e} \left(\dfrac{\partial c}{\partial y^e} + \dfrac{\partial i}{\partial y^e} - 1 \right) + y^e \dfrac{\partial i}{\partial y^e} \end{vmatrix}$$

$$= \begin{vmatrix} -mi_1 \dfrac{\partial q}{\partial m} & -m \dfrac{\partial i}{\partial y^e} \\ 0 & \beta_{y^e} \left(\dfrac{\partial c}{\partial y^e} - 1 \right) \end{vmatrix} > 0$$

J_2 must be positive, because of the assumptions made in the proposition ensure that $(\partial c)/(\partial y^e) + (\partial i)/(\partial y^e) - 1 < 0$ holds:

$$J_1 = \begin{vmatrix} -\overline{\mu} - bi_1 \dfrac{\partial q}{\partial b} & -\tau_w \omega \dfrac{1}{x} \dfrac{\partial y}{\partial y^e} - b \dfrac{\partial i}{\partial y^e} \\ (\beta_{y^e} + y^e) i_1 \dfrac{\partial q}{\partial b} & \beta_{y^e} \left(\dfrac{\partial c}{\partial y^e} + \dfrac{\partial i}{\partial y^e} - 1 \right) + y^e \dfrac{\partial i}{\partial y^e} \end{vmatrix} > 0$$

This last statement is true, because the assumption $|(\partial f_e)/(\partial r)|$ small enough implies that $(\partial q)/(\partial b) > 0$ holds, as we have found in Appendix II.

Now we prove the Routh–Hurwitz condition (A1): the determinant of J must be negative:

$$|J| = \begin{vmatrix} -mi_1\dfrac{\partial q}{\partial m} & -mi_1\dfrac{\partial q}{\partial b} & -m\dfrac{\partial i}{\partial y^e} \\ -\overline{\mu} - bi_1\dfrac{\partial q}{\partial m} & -\overline{\mu} - bi_1\dfrac{\partial q}{\partial b} & -\tau_w\omega\dfrac{1}{x}\dfrac{\partial y}{\partial y^e} - b\dfrac{\partial i}{\partial y^e} \\ (\beta_{y^e} + y^e)i_1\dfrac{\partial q}{\partial m} & (\beta_{y^e} + y^e)i_1\dfrac{\partial q}{\partial b} & \beta_{y^e}\left(\dfrac{\partial c}{\partial y^e} - 1\right) + (\beta_{y^e} + y^e)\dfrac{\partial i}{\partial y^e} \end{vmatrix}$$

$$= \begin{vmatrix} -mi_1\dfrac{\partial q}{\partial m} & -mi_1\dfrac{\partial q}{\partial b} & -m\dfrac{\partial i}{\partial y^e} \\ -\overline{\mu} & -\overline{\mu} & -\tau_w\omega\dfrac{1}{x}\dfrac{\partial y}{\partial y^e} \\ 0 & 0 & \beta_{y^e}\left(\dfrac{\partial c}{\partial y^e} - 1\right) \end{vmatrix}$$

which is negative due to $\beta_{y^e}\left(\frac{\partial c}{\partial y^e} - 1\right) < 0$. The last Routh–Hurwitz condition $(-\mathrm{tr}\,J)(J_1 + J_2 + J_3) + \det J > 0$ finally can be fulfilled by letting β_{y^e} to be large enough, because rising adjustment speeds lead to a decreasing trace and rising sum of principal minors and to decreasing determinant. But β_{y^e} enters $(-\mathrm{tr}\,J)(J_1 + J_2 + J_3)$ quadratic and the determinant only linear. Hence, for sufficiently large adjustment speed the last Routh–Hurwitz condition is also fulfilled.

Thus all Routh–Hurwitz conditions are fulfilled when i_2, α_{m1}, α_{m2} are sufficiently small and β_{y^e} sufficiently large.

Proof of proposition 5

The Jacobian of the system (4.35) is given by:

$$J^* = \begin{pmatrix} J_{1,1} & J_{1,2} & J_{1,3} - m\kappa\beta_p\dfrac{1}{y^p}\dfrac{\partial y}{\partial y^e} & -mi_1\dfrac{\partial q}{\partial \omega} \\ J_{2,1} & J_{2,2} & J_{2,3} - b\kappa\beta_p\dfrac{1}{y^p}\dfrac{\partial y}{\partial y^e} & -\tau_w\dfrac{y}{x} - bi_1\dfrac{\partial q}{\partial \omega} \\ J_{3,1} & J_{3,2} & J_{3,3} & \beta_{y^e}(s_c - \tau_w)\dfrac{y}{x} + (\beta_{y^e} + y^e)i_1\dfrac{\partial q}{\partial \omega} \\ 0 & 0 & \omega\kappa(\kappa_w - 1)\beta_p\dfrac{1}{y^p}\dfrac{\partial y}{\partial y^e} & 0 \end{pmatrix}$$

with $\beta_p = 0$ we know that the system possesses three eigenvalues with negative real part and one eigenvalue of zero, the negative real part eigenvalues being identical to the eigenvalues of the Jacobian J^* of system (4.34). Let now β_p become positive, but small enough. Employing the fact that the eigenvalues are continuous in the entries of the Jacobian (see, for example, Sontag, 1990), we know that with sufficiently small perturbations of the entries of the Jacobian (small β_p) the negative real parts will stay negative. With three eigenvalues with negative real parts we can make use of the property that the product of the eigenvalues of a matrix equals the determinant of the matrix. There follows that the fourth eigenvalue must be negative if the determinant of the Jacobian is positive. Hence for proving proposition 5 it is equivalent to showing that the determinant of J^* shown below is positive:

$$|J^*| = -\omega\kappa(\kappa_w - 1)\beta_p \frac{1}{y^p}\frac{\partial y}{\partial y^e} \begin{vmatrix} J_{1,1} & J_{1,2} & -mi_1 \dfrac{\partial q}{\partial \omega} \\ J_{2,1} & J_{2,2} & -\tau_w \dfrac{y}{x} - bi_1 \dfrac{\partial q}{\partial \omega} \\ J_{3,1} & J_{3,2} & \beta_{y^e}(s_c - \tau_w)\dfrac{y}{x} + (\beta_{y^e} + y^e)i_1 \dfrac{\partial q}{\partial \omega} \end{vmatrix}$$

The term $-\omega\kappa(\kappa_w - 1)\beta_p \frac{1}{y^p}\frac{\partial y}{\partial y^e}$ is positive, because κ_w can only take values in the interval $[0, 1]$. All other terms are positive. This means that $|J^*|$ will be positive if and only if the second component of the product, the determinant of the following 3×3 system is positive too:

$$\begin{vmatrix} -mi_1 \dfrac{\partial q}{\partial m} & -mi_1 \dfrac{\partial q}{\partial b} & -mi_1 \dfrac{\partial q}{\partial \omega} \\ -\overline{\mu} - bi_1 \dfrac{\partial q}{\partial m} & -\overline{\mu} - bi_1 \dfrac{\partial q}{\partial b} & -\tau_w \dfrac{y}{x} - bi_1 \dfrac{\partial q}{\partial \omega} \\ (\beta_{y^e} + y^e)i_1 \dfrac{\partial q}{\partial m} & (\beta_{y^e} + y^e)i_1 \dfrac{\partial q}{\partial b} & \beta_{y^e}(s_c - \tau_w)\dfrac{y}{x} + (\beta_{y^e} + y^e)i_1 \dfrac{\partial q}{\partial \omega} \end{vmatrix} > 0$$

Multiplying the first row by $(\beta_{y^e} + y^e)/m$ and adding this to the third row of the matrix and multiplying the first row by $-b/m$ and adding this to the second row we do not change the determinant and we can obtain thereby the expression:

$$\begin{vmatrix} -mi_1\dfrac{\partial q}{\partial m} & -mi_1\dfrac{\partial q}{\partial b} & -mi_1\dfrac{\partial q}{\partial \omega} \\ -\overline{\mu} & -\overline{\mu} & -\tau_w\dfrac{y}{x} \\ 0 & 0 & \beta_{y^e}(s_c-\tau_w)\dfrac{y}{x} \end{vmatrix} > 0$$

$$\beta_{y^e}(s_c-\tau_w)\frac{y}{x}\overline{\mu}mi_1\left(\frac{\partial q}{\partial m}-\frac{\partial q}{\partial b}\right) > 0$$

From lemma 1 we know that this inequality must hold true.

Proof of proposition 6

The Jacobian of the 5×5 system in proposition 6 can be written by:

$$J^{**} = \begin{pmatrix} J^\star_{1,1} & J^\star_{1,2} & J^\star_{1,3} - m\kappa\kappa_p\dfrac{\beta_w}{xl}\dfrac{\partial y}{\partial y^e} & J^\star_{1,4} & m\kappa\kappa_p\beta_w\dfrac{y}{xl^2} \\ J^\star_{2,1} & J^\star_{2,2} & J^\star_{2,3} - b\kappa\kappa_p\dfrac{\beta_w}{xl}\dfrac{\partial y}{\partial y^e} & J^\star_{2,4} & b\kappa\kappa_p\beta_w\dfrac{y}{xl^2} \\ J^\star_{3,1} & J^\star_{3,2} & J^\star_{3,3} & J^\star_{3,4} & 0 \\ J^\star_{4,1} & J^\star_{4,2} & J^\star_{4,3} + \dfrac{\omega\kappa(1-\kappa_p)\beta_w}{xl}\dfrac{\partial y}{\partial y^e} & J^\star_{4,4} & -\dfrac{\omega\kappa(1-\kappa_p)\beta_w y}{xl^2} \\ -li_1\dfrac{\partial q}{\partial m} & -li_1\dfrac{\partial q}{\partial b} & -l\dfrac{\partial i}{\partial y^e} & -li_1\dfrac{\partial q}{\partial \omega} & 0 \end{pmatrix}$$

where $J^\star_{i,j}$ are the entries of the Jacobian of the system (4.35). We follow the same idea as in the preceding proof. Hence, it is sufficient to show that $|J^{**}| < 0$ holds, if the parameter β_w is sufficiently small. In a first step we do some row operations within the matrix which do not change its determinant: $-b/m$ times the first row and added to the second row gives the new second row, $(\beta_{y^e} + y^e)/l$ times the fifth row and added to the third row gives the new third row, $-l/m$ times the first row and added to the fifth row gives the new fifth row.

The determinant is therefore equal to:

$$|J^{**}| = \begin{vmatrix} J^{**}_{1,1} & J^{**}_{1,2} & J^{**}_{1,3} & J^{**}_{1,4} & J^{**}_{1,5} \\ -\overline{\mu} & -\overline{\mu} & -\frac{\tau_w}{x}\frac{\partial y}{\partial y^e} & -\tau_w \frac{y}{x} & 0 \\ 0 & 0 & \beta_{y^e}\left[-\tau_w \frac{\omega}{x}\frac{\partial y}{\partial y^e} - s_c\left(1 - \frac{\omega}{x}\frac{\partial y}{\partial y^e}\right)\right] & \beta_{y^e}(s_c - \tau_w) & 0 \\ 0 & 0 & \omega\kappa\left[(1-\kappa_p)\frac{\beta_w}{xl}\frac{\partial y}{\partial y^e} + (\kappa_w - 1)\frac{\beta_p}{y^p}\frac{\partial y}{\partial y^e}\right] & 0 & -\omega\kappa(1-\kappa_p)\beta_w \frac{y}{xl^2} \\ 0 & 0 & l\kappa\left[\frac{\beta_p}{y^p}\frac{\partial y}{\partial y^e} + \kappa_p \frac{\beta_w}{xl}\frac{\partial y}{\partial y^e}\right] & 0 & -l\kappa\kappa_p\beta_w \frac{y}{xl^2} \end{vmatrix} < 0$$

We know that the upper left 2×2 submatrix has a positive determinant, thus in order to have a negative determinant of the full matrix, we need that the lower right 3×3 submatrix has a negative determinant. This submatrix is denoted by h_1 and we have to show that $|h_1| < 0$:

$$|h_1| = -\beta_{y^e}(s_c - \tau_w) \times \begin{vmatrix} \omega\kappa\left[(1-\kappa_p)\frac{\beta_w}{xl}\frac{\partial y}{\partial y^e} + (\kappa_w - 1)\frac{\beta_p}{y^p}\frac{\partial y}{\partial y^e}\right] & -\omega\kappa(1-\kappa_p)\beta_w \frac{y}{xl^2} \\ l\kappa\left[\frac{\beta_p}{y^p}\frac{\partial y}{\partial y^e} + \kappa_p \frac{\beta_w}{xl}\frac{\partial y}{\partial y^e}\right] & -l\kappa\kappa_p\beta_w \frac{y}{xl^2} \end{vmatrix}$$

In case of $0 < \kappa_p \leq 1$ the latter equals:

$$|h_1| = -\beta_{y^e}(s_c - \tau_w) \begin{vmatrix} \omega\kappa\left[(\kappa_w - 1) - \frac{1-\kappa_p}{\kappa_p}\right]\frac{\beta_p}{y^p}\frac{\partial y}{\partial y^e} & 0 \\ l\kappa\left[\frac{\beta_p}{y^p}\frac{\partial y}{\partial y^e} + \kappa_p \frac{\beta_w}{xl}\frac{\partial y}{\partial y^e}\right] & -l\kappa\kappa_p\beta_w \frac{y}{xl^2} \end{vmatrix}$$

which is negative, because $s_c > \tau_w$ and κ_p is in (0,1).
In the case $\kappa = 0$ we get:

$$|h_1| = -\beta_{y^e}(s_c - \tau_w) \times \begin{vmatrix} \omega\left[\frac{\beta_w}{xl}\frac{\partial y}{\partial y^e} + (\kappa_w - 1)\frac{\beta_p}{y^p}\frac{\partial y}{\partial y^e}\right] & -\omega\beta_w\frac{y}{xl^2} \\ l\frac{\beta_p}{y^p}\frac{\partial y}{\partial y^e} & 0 \end{vmatrix}$$

which is negative too.

Proof of proposition 7

The Jacobian of system (4.37) is:

$$J^{***} = \begin{pmatrix} J^{**}_{1,1} & J^{**}_{1,2} & J^{**}_{1,3} & J^{**}_{1,4} & J^{**}_{1,5} & -m\kappa\left(\beta_p\frac{-\beta_n}{y^p} + \kappa_p\beta_w\frac{-\beta_n}{xl}\right) - m\frac{\partial i}{\partial v} \\ J^{**}_{2,1} & J^{**}_{2,2} & J^{**}_{2,3} & J^{**}_{2,4} & J^{**}_{2,5} & J^{***}_{2,6} \\ J^{**}_{3,1} & J^{**}_{3,2} & J^{**}_{3,3} & J^{**}_{3,4} & J^{**}_{3,5} & J^{***}_{3,6} \\ J^{**}_{4,1} & J^{**}_{4,2} & J^{**}_{4,3} & J^{**}_{4,4} & J^{**}_{4,5} & J^{***}_{4,6} \\ J^{**}_{5,1} & J^{**}_{5,2} & J^{**}_{5,3} & J^{**}_{5,4} & J^{**}_{5,5} & 0 \\ J^{***}_{6,1} & J^{***}_{6,2} & J^{***}_{6,3} & J^{***}_{6,4} & 0 & J^{***}_{6,6} \end{pmatrix}$$

where

$$J^{***}_{2,6} = \tau_w\omega\frac{\beta_n}{x} - b\kappa\left(\beta_p\frac{-\beta_n}{y^p} + \kappa_p\beta_w\frac{-\beta_n}{xl}\right) - b\frac{\partial i}{\partial v}$$

$$J^{***}_{3,6} = \beta_{y^e}(\tau_w - s_c)\omega\frac{\beta_n}{x} + (\beta_{y^e} + y^e)\frac{\partial i}{\partial v}$$

$$J^{***}_{4,6} = \omega\kappa\left[(1 - \kappa_p)\beta_w\frac{-\beta_n}{xl} + (\kappa_w - 1)\beta_p\frac{-\beta_n}{y^p}\right]$$

$$J^{***}_{6,1} = -(v+1)i_1\frac{\partial q}{\partial m}$$

$$J^{***}_{6,2} = -(v+1)i_1\frac{\partial q}{\partial b}$$

$$J^{***}_{6,3} = \frac{\partial y}{\partial y^e} - \frac{\partial c}{\partial y^e} - (v+1)\frac{\partial i}{\partial y^e}$$

$$J^{***}_{6,4} = (\tau_w - s_c)\frac{y}{x} - (v+1)i_1\frac{\partial q}{\partial \omega}$$

$$J^{***}_{6,6} = -\beta_n - n - \left[(\tau_w - s_c)\omega\frac{\beta_n}{x}\right] - (v+1)\frac{\partial i}{\partial v}$$

If β_n is zero we obtain:

$$|J^{***}| = -n|J^{**}|$$

because the last column would only consist of zeros, except of the entry $J^{***}_{6,6} = -n$. Thus one eigenvalue is $-n$. The other five eigenvalues are those of the upper left 5×5 matrix, which are negative as we have shown in the proof of proposition 6. Letting β_n become positive but sufficiently small, the negativity of the eigenvalues will be preserved.

Proof of proposition 8

The Jacobian of the dynamic system (4.38) is given by:

$$J^{****} = \begin{pmatrix} J^{***}_{1,1} & J^{***}_{1,2} & J^{***}_{1,3} & J^{***}_{1,4} & J^{***}_{1,5} & J^{***}_{1,6} & -m \\ J^{***}_{2,1} & J^{***}_{2,2} & J^{***}_{2,3} & J^{***}_{2,4} & J^{***}_{2,5} & J^{***}_{2,6} & -b \\ J^{***}_{3,1} & J^{***}_{3,2} & J^{***}_{3,3} & J^{***}_{3,4} & J^{***}_{3,5} & J^{***}_{3,6} & 0 \\ J^{***}_{4,1} & J^{***}_{4,2} & J^{***}_{4,3} & J^{***}_{4,4} & J^{***}_{4,5} & J^{***}_{4,6} & 0 \\ J^{***}_{5,1} & J^{***}_{5,2} & J^{***}_{5,3} & J^{***}_{5,4} & J^{***}_{5,5} & J^{***}_{5,6} & 0 \\ J^{***}_{6,1} & J^{***}_{6,2} & J^{***}_{6,3} & J^{***}_{6,4} & J^{***}_{6,5} & J^{***}_{6,6} & 0 \\ 0 & 0 & J^{****}_{7,3} & 0 & J^{****}_{7,5} & J^{****}_{7,6} & -(1-\alpha)\beta_\pi \end{pmatrix}$$

where

$$\begin{aligned} J^{****}_{7,3} &= \alpha\beta_\pi\kappa\left(\frac{\beta_p}{y^p} + \frac{\kappa_p\beta_w}{xl}\right)\frac{\partial y}{\partial y^e} \\ J^{****}_{7,5} &= -\alpha\beta_\pi\kappa\kappa_p\beta_w\frac{y}{xl^2} \\ J^{****}_{7,6} &= \alpha\beta_\pi\kappa\left(\beta_p\frac{-\beta_n}{y^p} + \kappa_p\beta_w\frac{-\beta_n}{xl}\right) \end{aligned}$$

Again we only have to show that the determinant is negative. Multiplying the first row by $\alpha\beta_\pi/m$ and adding this to the seventh row and adding to this new seventh row $-\alpha\beta_\pi/l$ times the fifth row we get a seventh row with zeros with the exception of the last element which is $-\beta_\pi$. We know that the determinant is the determinant of the upper left 6×6 matrix times $-\beta_\pi$ yielding a negative determinant, because we know from the proof of proposition 7 that the upper left 6×6 matrix has a positive determinant.

Appendix IV Proof of the policy theorem

Sketch of proof for theorem 7

Under the conditions assumed to hold on the asset markets we can solve for Tobin's q explicitly and get:[1]

$$q = \frac{f_e(r_e^e)}{1 - f_e(r_e^e)}(m+b) = q(r_e^e, m+b), \ \ i.e., \ \ \frac{\partial q}{\partial r_e^e} = \frac{f'_e(r_e^e)}{(1 - f_e(r_e^e))^2}(m+b) > 0$$

The Jacobian matrix of the given extension of the original model is augmented through the stock market policy by an additional matrix to be obtained from:

$$\begin{aligned}
\dot{m} &= -\beta_{mq}(q - q^o)m \\
\dot{b} &= g - t_c - \tau_w \omega \frac{y}{x} - \mu m - b(\pi^c + i(\cdot)) \\
\dot{y}^e &= \beta_{y^e}[c + i(\cdot) + \delta + g - y^e] + y^e(i(\cdot) - n)
\end{aligned}$$

which only differs from the original one in its first row. This row can be used to eliminate the $i_q(\cdot)$ in the $i(\cdot)$ function when calculating the principal minors of the here appended Jacobian. From this one can easily get that the Routh–Hurwitz conditions of the expanded dynamics all exceed the originally given ones, while the final Routh–Hurwitz condition is fulfilled, since the determinant of the above laws of motion is a simple composition of one principal minor of order 2 and the third element in the trace of this matrix.

Appendix V Notation

Statically or dynamically endogenous variables

B, B^d	Bonds, bond demand
C_c	Consumption of asset holders
C_w	Consumption of workers
E, E^d	Equities, equity demand
G	Government expenditure
I	Fixed business investment
K	Capital stock
L	Labour supply
L^d	Level of employment
M, M^d	Money supply, money demand

M_f, M_c	Cash balance of firms and asset holders
N	Stock of inventories
N^d	Desired stock of inventories
$S = S_p + S_f + S_g$	Total savings
S_f, S_f^n	Savings of firms, nominal savings of firms
S_g, S_g^n	Government savings, nominal government savings
S_p, S_p^n	Private savings, nominal private savings
T	Total real taxes
$u = Y/Y^p$	Rate of capacity utilization
$e = L^d/L$	Rate of employment
s	Nominal exchange rate *(sigma* the real rate)
W	Real wealth
Y	Output
Y^d	Aggregate demand $C + I + \delta K + G$
Y^e	Expected aggregate demand
Y^p	Potential output
$v = N/K$	Inventory–capital ratio
$\omega = w/p$	Real wage ($u = \omega/x$ the wage share)
π	Expected rate of inflation (medium-run)
ρ, ρ^e	Rate of return on capital, expected rate of return on capital
p	Price level
p_e	Price of equities
r	Nominal rate of interest ($= i$ in chs 5,6, price of bonds $p_b = 1, r$ real rate of interest)
r_e^e	Rate of return on equities
w	Nominal wages
IN	Desired inventory investment
IN_m	Firms' desired cash balance adjustment

Parameters

$\overline{e}$	NAIRU-type normal utilization rate concept (of labour)
$\overline{u}$	NAIRU-type normal utilization rate concept (of capital)
δ	Depreciation rate
$\overline{\mu}$	Growth rate of the money supply
$\overline{g}$	Intensive government purchases (const.)

$\overline{\eta}$	Fundamentalists long run expectations equity price inflation
n	Natural growth rate
$i_1, i_2 > 0$	Investment parameters
$\beta_w \geq 0$	Wage adjustment parameter
$\beta_p \geq 0$	Price adjustment parameter
$\beta_\pi \geq 0$	Inflationary expectations adjustment parameter
$\alpha \in [0, 1]$	Weight of actual inflation on expected inflation
$\alpha_{ec} \in [0, 1]$	Ratio of chartists to chartists and fundamentalists
$\alpha_\rho \in [0, 1]$	Share of retained earnings on profits
$\beta_n^d > 0$	Desired inventory – expected sales ratio
$\beta_n > 0$	Inventory adjustment parameter
$\beta_m^d > 0$	Desired cash balance – expected sales ratio
$\beta_m > 0$	Cash balance adjustment parameter
$\beta_y^e > 0$	Demand expectations adjustment parameter
$\kappa_w \in [0, 1], \kappa_p \in [0.1]$	Weights for short- and medium-run inflation
κ	$=(1-\kappa_w\kappa_p)^{-1}$
$y^p > 0$	Potential output–capital ratio
$y > 0$	Actual output-capital ratio
x or $z > 0$	Output–labour ratio
$t(t^n\ c = t - rb)$	Taxes (net of interest) per capital
$s_c \in [0, 1]$	Savings ratio (out of profits and interest)

Mathematical notation

$\dot{x}$	Time derivative of a variable x
$\widehat{x}$	Growth rate of x
l', l_w	Total and partial derivatives
$\breve{x}$	Steady state value of X
$y_w = y'(l)l_w$	Composite derivatives
r_o, *etc.*	Steady state values
$y = Y/K$, *etc.*	Real variables in intensive form
$m = M/(pK)$, *etc.*	Nominal variables in intensive form

Notes

1 General Introduction

1. However the models presented here are still based on linear behavioural or technological relationships. This allows us to focus on the implications of unavoidable 'natural' nonlinearities.
2. The classical handbook on linear dynamical tools for economists is Lorenz (1993).
3. Such a metaphor is of course inspired by Goodwin's (1967) nonlinear model of 'class struggle' which is based on the 'predator–prey' equations proposed by Lotka and Volterra for the description of the dynamics of biological systems.
4. Barro's criticism can be applied to AS–AD growth models developed in the 1970s. However the charge of inconsistency between the AD and AS curves cannot be sustained in the case of many presentations of the AS–AD model, either because they do not explicitly discuss the derivation of the AD curve in terms of fixed-price IS–LM models or they do not explicitly introduce price-taking behaviour in deriving the AS curve (Dutt, 2002).
5. 'Rational' expectations are assumed to incorporate all the relevant information available and to be correct on average.
6. Chiarella *et al.* (2005).
7. The two Phillips curves of the KMG model rely on an 'inflation climate' variable π which is itself a weighted average of *adaptive* and *regressive* expectations (see definitions below). The KMG model avoids the expression 'expected rate of inflation' for this variable since π is conceived, in an uncertain environment, as some average inflation over a longer time in the past and asymptotically rational expectations over the future.

2 Advances in AS–AD Model Building: Real Disequilibria and Portfolio Choice

1. Flaschel and Krolzig (2006), Flaschel, Kauermann and Semmler (2007) and Chen and Flaschel (2006).
2. In intensive form expressions the following gives rise to $u = y/y^p$ with $y^p = f((f')^{-1}(\omega))$. Note that we use lower case letters as representation of level magnitudes that are measured relative to the capital stock K.
3. See Asada, Chiarella, Flaschel and Franke (2010, ch.3) for details.
4. Asada, Chiarella, Flaschel and Franke (2010) provide details of such an approach and its empirical and numerical investigation.
5. See Asada, Chiarella, Flaschel and Franke (2010) for a detailed treatment of this model type.

6. This will be shown in detail in Chapter 3 of the book.
7. Note that the above considers – as before – bonds to be of the fixed price variety (with price 1) so that $\overline{M}+\overline{B}$ is a meaningful expression in this framework. Sargent (1987, p.12) notes with respect to the variable B that it 'is a variable-coupon bond that is issued by the government. The bond is essentially a savings deposit, changes in the interest rate altering the coupon, but leaving the dollar value of bonds outstanding unchanged.'
8. The obtained dynamics are considered in detail in Chiarella, Flaschel, Franke and Semmler (2009).
9. See the mathematical appendix.
10. The price level is a given magnitude in this section.

3 Tobinian Stock-Flow Interactions in the KMG Framework

1. The 'interest rate' on bonds used in the original KMG model was a bit puzzling since it was solely associated with the money market. Here it will be determined, more logically, on the bonds market in its interaction with the other asset markets.
2. The term 'social' in 'social accounting matrix' means 'for the economy as a whole'. In other words, 'social accounting' means exactly the same thing as 'national accounting'. See Vanoli (2005, pp.169–71) for a historical analysis of the origins of the 'SAM' terminology.
3. The Cambridge Growth Project was a large econometric research project set up at the Department of Applied Economics of the University of Cambridge in 1960 and ending in 1987. Its major academic contribution was the Cambridge Multisectoral Dynamic Model of the British economy which was used to forecast economic growth.
4. Godley and Lavoie (2007, p.13).
5. We will use standard SAMs in Chapters 5 and 6.
6. In the table, bold lines in columns differentiate between the sector accounts and in rows between the intersectorial flows. The different kind of intersectorial flows are expenditure flows (consumption, investment...), distributive income flows (wages, interest payments...), financial flows (transactions on financial assets and liabilities) and others (depreciation of capital).
7. Firms' net investment is equals to their gross investment $pI+p\delta K$ minus the depreciation of capital $p\delta K$.
8. What we call a tautological row is a row containing only one item (with both a positive and a negative sign) which therefore induces an obvious identity. For instance this is the case in the second row and its associated accounting identity: $pG \equiv pG$. In contrast the first row is not tautological since it contains three different items. Thus its associated accounting identity should appear in the model : $pC \equiv pC_w + pC_c$.
9. In other words, we do not allow for regime switches as they are discussed in ch.5 of Chiarella, Flaschel, Groh and Semmler (2000).

10. See Chiarella, Flaschel, Groh and Semmler (2000) for the inclusion of workers' savings into a KMG framework.
11. We explain in an appendix that money holdings for transaction purposes are only considered with respect to firms. This is the opposite assumption of what is usually considered in the macroeconomic literature.
12. See Chiarella, Flaschel, Groh and Semmler (2000) for the treatment of neoclassical smooth factor substitution.
13. See Sargent (1987) for another application of this assumption.
14. See in particular the model of Keynesian macrodynamics of Sargent (1987).
15. These flow demands appeared in equation (3.9).
16. See for example Bernanke and Parkinson (1991), and Diallo *et al.* (2010) for different type of evidence on this stylized fact.
17. See again Diallo *et al.* (2010) for details.
18. Such a statement does however not mean that such policies are easy to implement in the real world.
19. See Chiarella and Flaschel (2000a) and Chiarella, Flaschel, Groh and Semmler (2000).
20. We refer the reader to Asada, Chiarella, Flaschel and Franke (2010) for more detailed numerical studies of the implications of kinked money wage Phillips Curves.
21. The reference models of the subsequent SFC literature are those of Taylor (2004), Zezza and Dos Santos (2004) and Godley and Lavoie (2007).
22. These applied models were mainly used to analyse the balance of payments problems of the United Kingdom.
23. This point was first stressed by Taylor (2008) in his review of Godley's work.
24. The rate of capacity utilization does not appear in their modelling of inflation although the authors note in the introduction of their book that high levels of capacity utilization generate inflationary pressures (Godley and Lavoie, 2007, p18).
25. In one of their models, Godley and Lavoie (2007, p.387) suggest refining the relation linking the wage inflation rate and the rate of employment by assuming that there is no additional inflationary pressure when the latter increases but remains within a certain range. With such a mechanism their model exhibits a post-Keynesian Phillips Curve with a horizontal segment.
26. In this model, short-term bonds stand for bank loans.
27. See Introduction and Chapter 1.
28. According to this hypothesis the normal functioning of capitalist economies leads inevitably to financial crises. Minsky's theory is based on the idea that a period in which the economy is doing well leads to riskier behaviour, in particular to higher leverage ratio for both financial and non-financial firms.
29. Therefore they are more in line with the Cambridge tradition of applied economics than their SFC and KMG counterparts.

30. Calibration is the method by which CGE model builders test the values given to the parameters of the behavioural equations and other functional forms. For a presentation of this method see Mitra-Kahn (2008).
31. One might claim that Tobin as well was influenced by Leontief who was his professor at Harvard.
32. In his excellent account of Stone's work, Johansen (1985, p.27) noted that 'Stone and his colleagues have carried out the most fundamental and thorough work on this method with respect to input–output analysis and have thus provided support for a means of treating changes in input-output coefficients which have been applied in many countries'.
33. Pyatt was a student of Stone who worked on the Cambridge Growth Project. Together with Thorbecke, he developed *Fixed-Price Multiplier* models. These applied models are based on a SAM and assume that each economic sector behaves according to linear relationships with fixed coefficients calculated from the SAM.
34. For instance L. Taylor (2004, p.2), refers to his Structuralist theoretical models as SFC ones. See Taylor (1990) for a presentation of Structuralist CGE models.
35. However it may be argued that CGE models, even Neoclassical ones, have never been general equilibrium models in the Arrow–Debreu or Walras tradition (Mitra-Kahn, 2008).
36. See Robinson (1991), Adam and Bevan (1998), Thissen (2000), and Thissen and Lensink (2001). Rosensweig and Taylor (1990) and Easterly (1990) propose Structuralist FCGE models which also integrate Tobinian portfolio choices.

4 Analysis and Policy Implications of the KMG–Tobin Model

1. See the law of motion for bonds per unit of capital b.
2. Note with respect to this part of the proposition that the steady state values used in the above assumption are calculated before this assumption is applied to a determination of the steady state value of the nominal rate of interest.
3. See the next section.
4. See Proposition 1.
5. We do not pay attention here to the border case where $\left(\frac{\alpha_{b1}}{\alpha_{m1}} - 1\right)\breve{m} = 1$ holds true. Note here also that the α_{ij} sum to one for $j = 0$ and to zero for $j = 1, 2$ which implies that $\frac{\alpha_{b1}}{\alpha_{m1}} - 1$ is always non-negative.
6. Note that l may vary, but does not feed back into the presently considered sub-dynamics.
7. Which corresponds to a strong Keynes effect in the corresponding working model of ch.6 in Chiarella and Flaschel (2000a).
8. See the proof of Proposition 8.
9. See Chiarella and Flaschel (2000a) in the case of the working KMG model.

10. Note that l may vary, but does not feed back into the presently considered sub-dynamics.
11. This would correspond to a strong Keynes effect in the corresponding working model of ch.6 of Chiarella and Flaschel (2000a).
12. See the section on the comparative statics of the asset markets for indications on the way such an issue must be approached.
13. As Keynes (1936) already noted as a behavioural rule, a fact ignored by those economists who disregard the psychology of workers.
14. Which makes central bank money now endogenous in a pronounced way. Note however that we do not yet consider commercial banks and the endogeneity of the money supply that they are creating.
15. See in particular the definition of Π_c.

5 Tobinian Stock-Flow Interactions in the Mundell–Fleming Model

1. In the next chapter we will introduce bilateral international capital flows.
2. Except, as we will see, in the case of financial flows.
3. For example, in Table 5.1, taxes pT are paid *by* the private sector *to* the government.
4. Here it would be quite hard to interpret the first column of the SAM in terms of 'output costs' since the KMG model does not disaggregate the domestic output into wages and profits.
5. Therefore the government only has to pay interest on the bonds B held by the private sector.
6. Indeed traditional CGE models focused mainly on trade and income distribution issues.
7. With this method the FSAM is no longer a square matrix. Another method is to introduce, for every financial asset, a new column labelled 'increase in assets' *and* a new row representing 'increase in liabilities'. In this case 'like all SAMs, the FSAM is square with each column sum equal to the corresponding row sum' (Robinson, 1991, p.1517). However the disadvantage of the latter method is that it gives rise to larger matrices.
8. Changes in central bank reserves $\dot{F}_c^d$ appear in brackets because, as we will see, they are not relevant in the case of a regime of perfectly flexible exchange rates.
9. As in Asada, Chiarella, Flaschel and Franke (2003), where this condition is considered as a limit case to imperfect substitutability of internationally traded bonds.
10. The component '$\cdot$' in the net export function stands for the variables that determine the domestic absorption in terms of consumption and investment demand.
11. In the case of a flexible exchange rate regime and a given money supply we will for example get jumps in the variables s, σ, W, W_g^a when there is a shock in money supply occurring.
12. See Rødseth (2000, ch.6) for its motivation.

13. Such an approach is further justified through the observation that the dynamics of the nominal stock magnitude B is involved in the above considered real dynamics as long as $\xi \neq 0$ holds true which shows that the real dynamics is then in fact a hybrid as far as the distinction between real and nominal variables is concerned.
14. Note that this procedure is only one possibility. More generally, if i_o is not fixed at the level i^* in advance, the steady state can be determined without any requirements for T and G as postulated below. The steady state value of i will then usually differ from i^*, which is, however, no problem because the uncovered interest parity need not to be fulfilled in this model.
15. The same difficulty applies to the use of the risk premium ξ in the law of motion for W_g^a unless $M+B$ is assumed as zero (which is not a reasonable assumption). Note here again that such magnitudes are replaced by expected ones as far as definitions of disposable income and related magnitudes are concerned.
16. It is not difficult to show by means of the implicit functions theorem that the equilibrium exchange rate on the foreign exchange market is still a relatively simple function $s=s(W, W_g^a, p)$ in the special case where output in the LM curve is frozen at its steady state level, i.e., where the theory of the nominal interest rate is independent of what happens on the goods market. In this case, we get: $\dot{s}=s_W\dot{W}+s_{W_g^a}\dot{W}_g^a+s_p\dot{p}$. Such an expression must be used to substitute the $\hat{s}$ component in the variables r^*, ξ giving rise to an implicit differential equation system that is very difficult to handle.
17. This result comes from equations (5.6), (5.9) and (5.12) with $\dot{F}_c^d=0$.
18. And consider of course all foreign variables as given for the small open economy.
19. Note that – due to the assumed goods market equilibrium – $Y-C-I-G$ can always be replaced by NX if this is convenient for certain calculations of the model's implications.
20. As in the previous section, this procedure is only chosen to ensure $i_o=i^*$. In the more general case where i_o is allowed to differ from this value, no assumption has to be made concerning the level of G.
21. Note that – due to the assumed goods market equilibrium – $Y-C-I-G$ can always be replaced by $NX(Y, Y^*, s)$ if this is convenient for certain calculations of the model's implications.
22. See Asada, Chiarella, Flaschel and Franke (2003, ch.5) for a detailed presentation of the Dornbusch model and its various extensions.
23. Again no assumptions concerning G are required once deviations of i_o from i^* are allowed for. Recall in this regard that, according to the Tobinian portfolio approach used here, domestic and foreign bonds are only imperfect substitutes so that the uncovered interest parity normally does not hold.
24. In principle, the government here enforces two things in the steady state, namely that the domestic interest rate must be at the international level

and that the level of exports is such that goods market equilibrium is then assured, with a zero level of net investment by the assumption on the investment function. The real exchange rate is then a consequence of the level of $\overline{X}$ needed for goods market equilibrium.

25. and also $\overline{W}^a_g, \sigma_0 F_c$.
26. The argument must be more detailed if the short run reaction in the value of W is taken into account, but would then of course demand a thorough discussion of the conditions under which dynamics drives this variable back to its steady state level.

6 International Capital Flows: Two Extensions of the MFTobin Model

1. The only difference is that the SAM now includes interest payments iB^* by the government to the rest of the world. Therefore the savings of the government and the foreign sector are now slightly modified.
2. With regards to households' holdings of foreign bonds we will later separate the savings decision of households from their portfolio decision.
3. See Chapter 5, p. 95.
4. In other words the missing accounting identity is actually the following one: $s\dot{F}^d_{p2} \equiv s\dot{F}_p - s\dot{F}^d_{p1}$.
5. In the case of regressively formed expectations one has to use the scheme $\varepsilon(s), \varepsilon'(s)$ in place of $\hat{s}$.
6. One may argue here that this real foreign bond demand should be measured in foreign goods and thus has to be multiplied by the real exchange rate $\sigma = sp^*/p$ before it can be added to the real foreign bond demand of domestic residents. We leave this alternative approach for future investigations here.
7. We note that the comparative statics is easier here than in the stock approach of Chiarella, Flaschel, Franke and Semmler (2009), since more partial in nature and since the real exchange rate does not matter here, due to our assumption that foreign real demand on the international capital markets is expressed in terms of the domestic commodity and not in terms of the foreign one. We leave again the discussion of this latter case for future reconsiderations of the MFT model with international capital markets.
8. As derived in details in Flaschel and Semmler (2006) and Proaño, Flaschel and Semmler (2005).
9. Note that the strength of the Krugman balance sheet effect (according to which investment depends negatively on the nominal exchange rate s) depends on the degree of exchange risk exposure of the domestic firms: The higher the degree of hedging of the firms' foreign currency debt positions, the lower aggregate investment is likely to be affected by changes in the nominal exchange rate, see Röthig, Semmler and Flaschel (2007).

10. This type of extension of the MFT approach employed in Flaschel and Semmler (2006) and in Proaño, Flaschel and Semmler (2005), where only domestic markets for domestic and \$-denominated bonds were present, that would represent an important step forward in the modelling of currency crises and consideration of large output loss situations.

7 Fiscal and Monetary Policy, Stocks and the Term Structure of Interest Rates

1. See Asada *et al.* (2010b) for details.
2. In order to make it comparable to our subsequent modelling of such an approach we ignore here, however, inflation (assume a single price level p instead) and also transfer the Turnovsky model to the notation used in this chapter.
3. See Sargent (1987, ch.III) for details of this 'classical' type of a Keynesian model.
4. See Turnovsky (1995, p.22) for a brief discussion of bonds with a finite maturity date T in a continuous time framework.
5. In contrast to Asada *et al.* (2010b) we now consider the case where no equity price smoothing occurs, i.e., we assume that the parameter β_e used in Asada *et al.* (2010b) equals infinity.
6. See the argument in the preceding section.
7. The Tobin tax was originally formulated as a transactions tax which should have similar stabilization effects, but which acts on the α – parameters of the capital market adjustment rules in a way that would introduce a kink at $\alpha = 0$ and thus a mathematical complexity we try to avoid in this chapter.
8. This may change however if the prices of long-term bonds act on output dynamics in the same way we have assumed for share prices q.

Mathematical Appendices and Notation

1. Note that the rate of change $\dot{p}_e$ can in principle be calculated from such an expression, but will involve a large number of further laws of motion of the dynamics and is therefore not easily predictable in the given model type.

References

Adam, C. and D. Bevan (1998) *Costs and Benefits of Incorporating Asset Markets into CGE Models – Evidence and Design Issues*, Working Paper No. 202, Institute of Economics and Statistics, University of Oxford.

Adelman, I. and S. Robinson (1978) *Income Distribution Policy in Developing Countries: Case Study of Korea*, Oxford: Oxford University Press (for the World Bank).

Agénor, P.-R., Izquierdo, A. and H. Fofack (2003) *IMMPA: A Quantitative Macroeconomic Framework for the Analysis of Poverty Reduction Strategies*, Washington, DC: The World Bank.

Asada, T., Chen, P., Chiarella, C. and P. Flaschel (2006) 'Keynesian Dynamics and the Wage–Price Spiral: A Baseline Disequilibrium Model', *Journal of Macroeconomics*, 28, 90–130.

Asada, T., Chiarella, C., Flaschel, P. and R. Franke (2003) *Open Economy Macrodynamics. An Integrated Disequilibrium Approach*, Heidelberg: Springer.

Asada, T., Chiarella, C., Flaschel, P. and R. Franke (2010) *Monetary Macrodynamics*, London: Routledge.

Asada, T., Chiarella, C., Flaschel, P., Mouakil, T., Proaño, C. and W. Semmler (2010a): 'Stabilizing an Unstable Economy: On the Choice of Proper Policy Measures', *Economics, The Open-Access, Open-Assessment E-journal, 3*, 16 July, 2010: http://www.economics-ejournal.org/economics/journalarticles/2010–21.

Asada, T., Charpe, M., Flaschel, P., Malikane, C., Mouakil, T. and C. Proaño (2010b) 'Output, Stock Markets and Macro-Policy Measures in a Keynesian Portfolio Model', *Intervention*, forthcoming.

Backus, D., Brainard W., Smith G. and J. Tobin (1980) 'A Model of U.S. Financial and Non-financial Economic Behavior', *Journal of Money, Credit, and Banking*, 12, 259–93.

Barro, R. (1994) 'The Aggregate-supply/Aggregate-demand Model', *Eastern Economic Journal*, 20, 1–6.

Bernanke, B. and M. Parkinson (1991) 'Procyclical Labor Productivity and Competing Theories of the Business Cycle: Some Evidence from Interwar U.S. Manufacturing Industries', *Journal of Political Economy*, 99, 439–59.

Blanchard, O.J. (1981) 'Output, the Stock Market, and Interest Rates', *American Economic Review*, 71, 132–43.

Blanchard, O. and X. Katz (1999) 'Wage Dynamics. Reconciling Theory and Evidence', *American Economic Review*, Papers and Proceedings, 69–74.

Bourguignon, F., de Melo J. and A. Suwa (1991) 'Modeling the Effects of Adjustment Programs on Income Distribution', *World Development*, 19 (November), 1527–44.

Breece, J., McLaren, K., Murphy C. and A. Powell (1994) 'Using the Murphy Model to Provide Short-run Macroeconomic Closure for ORANI', *Economic Record*, 70, 292–314.

Charpe, M. (2008) 'Institutions économiques et diversité des formes de fragilité financière. Théorie et applications aux cas japonais et sud-américain', Phd. dissertation, Ecole des Hautes Etudes en Science Sociales, Paris.

Chen, P. and P. Flaschel (2006) 'Measuring the Interaction of Wage and Price Phillips Curves for the U.S. Economy', *Studies in Nonlinear Dynamics and Econometrics*, 10, 1–35.

Chiarella, C. and P. Flaschel (1996) 'An Integrative Approach to Prototype 2D Macromodels of Growth, Price and Inventory Dynamics', *Chaos, Solitons & Fractals*, 7, 2105–33.

Chiarella, C. and P. Flaschel (1998) 'Dynamics of "Natural" Rates of Growth and Employment', *Macroeconomic Dynamics*, 2, 345–68.

Chiarella, C. and P. Flaschel (1999) 'Keynesian Monetary Growth in Open Economies', *Annals of Operations Research*, 89, 35–59.

Chiarella, C. and P. Flaschel (2000a) *The Dynamics of Keynesian Monetary Growth. Macro Foundations*, Cambridge: Cambridge University Press.

Chiarella, C. and P. Flaschel (2000b) '"High Order" Disequilibrium Growth Dynamics: Theoretical Aspects and Numerical Features', *Journal of Economic Dynamics and Control*, 24, 935–63.

Chiarella, C., Flaschel, P. and H. Hung (2011) 'Keynesian Disequilibrium Dynamics: Estimated Convergence, Roads to Instability and the Emergence of Complex Business Fluctuations', AUCO, *Czech Economic Review*, forthcoming.

Chiarella, C., Flaschel P. and R. Franke (2005) *Foundations for a Disequilibrium Theory of the Business Cycle. Quantitative Analysis and Qualitative Assessment*, Cambridge: Cambridge University Press.

Chiarella, C., Flaschel, P., Franke, R. and W. Semmler (2009) *Financial Markets and the Macroeconomy. A Keynesian Perspective*, New York: Routledge.

Chiarella, C., Flaschel, P., Groh, G. and W. Semmler (2000) *Disequilibrium, Growth and Labor Market Dynamics. Macro Perspectives*, Springer: Heidelberg.

Chiarella, C., Flaschel, P., Proaño, C. and W. Semmler (2010) *Portfolio Choice, Asset Accumulation and the Business Cycle. Tobin's Legacy Continued*, Book manuscript, New School University, New York.

Clarida, R., Gali, J. and M. Gertler (1999) 'The Science of Monetary Policy: a New Keynesian Perspective', *Journal of Economic Literature*, 37, 1661–707.

Diallo, B., Flaschel, P. and C. Proaño (2010) 'Reconsidering the dynamic interaction between real wages and the macroeconomy', *Research in World Economy*, forthcoming.

Dornbusch, R. (1976) 'Expectations and Exchange Rate Dynamics', *Journal of Political Economy*, 84, 1161–76.

Dutt, A. K. (2002) 'Aggregate Demand-Aggregate Supply Analysis: A History', *History of Political Economy*, 34, 322–63.

Easterly, W. (1990) 'Portfolio Effects in a CGE Model: Devaluation in a Dollarized Economy', in L. Taylor (ed.) *Socially Relevant Policy Analysis*, Cambridge, MA: MIT Press.

Filardo, A. (1998) 'New Evidence on the Output Cost of Fighting Inflation', *Federal Bank of Kansas City Economic Review*, 33–61.

Flaschel, P. (1993) *Macrodynamics. Income Distribution, Effective Demand and Cyclical Growth*, Bern: Peter Lang (second enlarged edition: Springer, Heidelberg, 2009) .

Flaschel, P. (2006) 'Instability Problems and Policy Issues in Perfectly Open Economies', in T. Asada and T. Ishikawa (eds) *Time and Space in Economics*, Tokyo: Springer.

Flaschel, P., Franke, R. and W. Semmler (1997) *Dynamic Macroeconomics. Instability, Fluctuations and Growth in Monetary Economies*, Cambridge, MA: MIT Press.

Flaschel, P. and F. Hartmann (2011), 'Financial markets, banking and the design of monetary policy. A stable baseline scenario'. CEMM Bielefeld: Working paper.

Flaschel, P., Kauermann, G. and W. Semmler (2007) 'Testing Wage and Price Phillips Curves for the United States', *Metroeconomica*, 58, 550–81.

Flaschel, P. and H.-M. Krolzig (2006) 'Wage–price Phillips Curves and Macroeconomic Stability: Basic Structural Form, Estimation and Analysis', in C. Chiarella, P. Flaschel, R. Franke and W. Semmler (eds) *Quantitative and Empirical Analysis of Nonlinear Dynamic Macromodels. Contributions to Economic Analysis*, Amsterdam: Elsevier.

Flaschel, P. and C. Proaño (2009) 'The J2 Status of "Chaos" in Macroeconomic Period Models', *Studies in Nonlinear Dynamics and Econometrics*, 13, article 2.

Flaschel, P. and W. Semmler (2006) 'Currency Crisis, Financial Crisis and Large Output Loss', in C. Chiarella, P. Flaschel, R. Franke and W. Semmler (eds) *Quantitative and Empirical Analysis of Nonlinear Dynamic Macromodels. Contributions to Economic Analysis* (series editors, B. Baltagi, E. Sadka and D. Wildasin), Amsterdam: Elsevier, 385–414.

Fleming, J. M. (1962) *Domestic Financial Policies under Fixed and under Flexible Exchange Rates*, International Monetary Fund: Staff Papers, 9, 369–79.

Franke, R. (1996) 'A Metzlerian Model of Inventory Growth Cycles', *Structural Change and Economic Dynamics*, 7, 243–62.

Franke, R. and W. Semmler (1999) 'Bond Rate, Loan Rate and Tobin's q in a Temporary Equilibrium Model of the Financial Sector', *Metroeconomica*, 50(3), 351–85.

Gandolfo, G. (1996) *Economic Dynamics*, 3rd edn, Berlin: Springer.

Gantmacher, F. R. (1971) *The Theory of Matrices*, vol. 2, New York: Chelsea Publishing Company.

Godley, W. (1999) 'Money and Credit in a Keynesian Model of Income Determination', *Cambridge Journal of Economics*, 23, 393–411.

Godley, W. and F. Cripps (1983) *Macroeconomics*, London: Fontana.

Godley, W. and M. Lavoie (2007) *Monetary Economics. An Integrated Approach to Credit, Money, Income, Production and Wealth*, Basingstoke and New York: Macmillan.

Goodwin, R. (1967) 'A Growth Cycle', in C.H. Feinstein (ed.) *Socialism, Capitalism and Economic Growth*, Cambridge: Cambridge University Press, 54–8.

Groth, C. (1992) 'Some Unfamiliar Dynamics of a Familiar Macromodel', *Journal of Economics*, 58, 293–305.

Johansen, L. (1960) *A Multi-sectoral Study of Economic Growth*, Amsterdam: North-Holland Publishing Company.

Johansen, L. (1985) 'Richard Stone's Contributions to Economics', *Scandinavian Journal of Economics*, 87, 4–32.

Kaldor, N. (1966) 'Marginal Productivity and the Macro-Economic Theories of Growth and Distribution', *Review of Economic Studies*, 33, 309–19.

Kaldor, N. (1982) *The Scourge of Monetarism*, Oxford: Oxford University Press.

Keynes, J.M. (1936) *The General Theory of Employment, Interest and Money*, Macmillan and Cambridge University Press, for Royal Economic Society.

King, J.E. (2002) *A History of Post Keynesian Economics Since 1936*, Cheltenham: Edward Elgar.

Köper, C. (2003) 'Real-Financial Interaction in Contemporary Models of AS–AD Growth', in C. Chiarella *et al.* (eds) *Dynamic Economic Theory*, 24, Bern: Peter Lang.

Köper, C. and P. Flaschel (2000) *Towards an Advanced Model of the Real-financial Interaction: A KMG Portfolio Approach*, Revised version (2003), Working paper, University of Bielefeld.

Lavoie, M. (2006) 'Endogenous Money: Accomodationist', in Arestis P. and Sawyer M. (eds) *Handbook on Alternative Monetary Economics*, Cheltenham: Edward Elgar, 17–34.

Lavoie, M. and W. Godley (2001–2) 'Kaleckian Models of Growth in a Coherent Stock-flow Monetary Framework: a Kaldorian view', *Journal of Post Keynesian Economics*, 24 (2), 277–311.

Lorenz, H.-W. (1993) *Nonlinear Dynamical Economics and Chaotic Motion*, 2nd edn, Heidelberg: Springer.

Lucas, R. E. (1972) 'Expectations and the Neutrality of Money', *Journal of Economic Theory*, 4, 103–24.

Mankiw, G. (2001) 'The Inexorable and Mysterious Tradeoff between Inflation and Unemployment', *Economic Journal*, C45–C61.

Mas-Colell, A., Whinston, M. D. and J. R. Green (1995) *Microeconomic Theory*, New York: Oxford University Press.

Meade, J. (1982) *Stagflation, Vol. I Wage–Fixing*, London: George Allen & Unwin.

Metzler, L. A. (1941) 'The Nature and Stability of Inventory Cycles', *Review of Economic Statistics*, 23, 113–29.

Minsky, H. (1982) *Can 'It' Happen Again?*, New York: M.E. Sharpe.

Minsky, H. (1986) *Stabilizing an Unstable Economy*, New Haven: Yale University Press.

Mitra-Kahn, B. J. (2008) *Debunking the Myths of Computable General Equilibrium Models*, Schwartz Center for Economic Policy Analysis Working Paper, 2008–1, New York: The New School for Social Research.

Mundell, R. A. (1963) 'Capital Mobility and Stabilization Policy under Fixed and Flexible Exchange Rates', *Canadian Journal of Economics and Political Science*, 29, 472–85.

Powell, A. and C. Murphy (1997) *Inside a Modern Macroeconometric Model. A Guide to the Murphy Model*, Berlin: Springer.

Proaño, C., Flaschel, P. and W. Semmler (2005) 'Currency and Financial Crises in Emerging Market Economies in the Medium-run', *Journal of Economic Asymmetries*, 2, 105–30.

Proaño, C., Flaschel, P. and W. Semmler (2008)' "Currency Crises and Monetary Policy in Economies with Partial Dollarization of Liabilities', *ICFAI Journal of Monetary Economics*, 3, 14–39.

Pyatt, G. (1988) 'A SAM Approach to Modeling', *Journal of Policy Modeling*, 10, 327–52.

Robinson, S. (1991) 'Macroeconomics, Financial Variables, and Computable General Equilibrium Models', *World Development*, 19 (11), 1509–25.

Robinson, S. (2003) *Macro Models and Multipliers: Leontief, Stone, Keynes, and CGE Models*, International Food Policy Research Institute.

Rødseth, A. (2000) *Open Economy Macroeconomics*, Cambridge: Cambridge University Press.

Romer, D.(2000) 'Keynesian Macroeconomics without the LM Curve', *Journal of Economic Perspectives*, 14(2), 149–69.

Rose, H. (1967) 'On the Non-linear Theory of the Employment Cycle', *Review of Economic Studies*, 34, 153–73.

Rose, H. (1990) *Macroeconomic Dynamics: A Marshallian Synthesis*, Cambridge, MA: Blackwell.

Rosensweig, J.A. and L. Taylor (1990) 'Devaluation, Capital Flows, and Crowding-Out: A CGE Model with Portfolio Choice for Thailand', in L. Taylor, (ed.) *Socially Relevant Policy Analysis*, Cambridge, MA: MIT Press.

Röthig, A., Semmler, W. and P. Flaschel (2007) *Hedging, Speculation, and Investment in Balance-Sheet Triggered Currency Crises*, Australian Economic Papers, 224–33.

Sargent, T. (1979) *Macroeconomic Theory*, 2nd edn (1987), New York: Academic Press.

Sargent, T. and N. Wallace (1973) 'The Stability of Models of Money and Growth with Perfect Foresight', *Econometrica*, 41, 1043–8.

Sargent, T. and N. Wallace (1975) 'Rational Expectations, the Optimal Monetary Instrument, and the Optimal Money Supply Rule', *Journal of Political Economy*, 83, 241–54.

Solow, R. (1956) 'A Contribution to the Theory of Economic Growth', *Quarterly Journal of Economics*, 70, 65–94.

Sontag, E. D. (1990) *Mathematical Control Theory: Deterministic Finite Dimensional Systems. Texts in Applied Mathematics*, New York: Springer.

Stone, R. and A. Brown (1962) *A Computable Model for Economic Growth*, Cambridge: Cambridge Growth Project.

Taylor, J.B. (1993) 'Discretion versus Policy Rules in Practice', *Carnegie-Rochester Conference Series on Public Policy*, 39, 195–214.

Taylor L. (1990) 'Structuralist CGE models', in L. Taylor, (ed.) *Socially Relevant Policy Analysis*, Cambridge, MA: MIT Press.

Taylor, L. (2004) *Reconstructing Macroeconomics. Structuralist Proposals and Critiques of the Mainstream*, Cambridge, MA: Harvard University Press.

Taylor, L. (2008) 'A Foxy Hedgehog: Wynne Godley and Macroeconomic Modeling', *Cambridge Journal of Economics*, 32, 639–63.

Taylor, L. and S.L. Black (1974) 'Practical General Equilibrium Estimation of Resource Pulls under Trade Liberalizations', *Journal of International Economics* 4, 37–58.

Thissen, M. (2000) *Building Financial CGE Models: Data, Parameters, and the Role of Expectations*, Working Paper, University of Groningen.

Thissen, M. and R. Lensink (2001) 'Macroeconomic Effects of a Currency Devaluation in Egypt: An Analysis with a Computable General Equilibrium Model with Financial Markets and Forward-Looking Expectations', *Journal of Policy Modeling*, 411–19.

Tobin, J. (1969) 'A General Equilibrium Approach to Monetary Theory', *Journal of Money, Credit, and Banking*, 1, 15–29.

Tobin, J. (1982) 'Money and the Macroeconomic Process', *Journal of Money, Credit and Banking*, 14, 171–204.

Turnovsky, S. (1977) *Macroeconomic Analysis and Stabilization Policy*, Cambridge: Cambridge University Press.

Turnovsky, S. (1995) *Methods of Macroeconomic Dynamics*, Cambridge, MA: MIT Press.

Vanoli, A. (2005) *A History of National Accounting*, Amsterdam: IOS Press. Original in French (2002) *Une histoire de la comptabilité nationale*, Paris: La Découverte.

Zezza, G. and C. Dos Santos (2004) 'The Role of Monetary Policy in Post-Keynesian Stock-Flow Consistent Macroeconomic Growth Models', in Lavoie M. and Seccarecia M. (eds), *Central Banking in the Modern World: Alternative Perspectives*, Cheltenham: Edward Elgar.

Author/Name Index

Key: **bold** = extended discussion; f = figure; t = table; n = note, e.g. n1:5 (endnote 5 to Chapter 1); n3:9 (endnote nine to Chapter 3).

Subject Index

Key: **bold** = extended discussion; f = figure; t = table; n = note, e.g. n1:5 (endnote 5 to Chapter 1); n3:9 (endnote nine to Chapter 3).

Dear John, dear Mette,

Here is the result of my last months of work at CFAP. Have a look and you will understand why I chose to come back to the real world in the end ... :-)

I spent two fabulous years in Cambridge, many thanks again for everything.

Yours,

Tarik

Asset Markets, Portfolio Choice and Macroeconomic Activity